HIKING NEW JERSEY

HELP US KEEP THIS GUIDE UP TO DATE

Every effort has been made by the author and editors to make this guide as accurate and useful as possible. However, many things can change after a guide is published—trails are rerouted, regulations change, facilities come under new management, and so forth.

We would love to hear from you concerning your experiences with this guide and how you feel it could be improved and kept up to date. While we may not be able to respond to all comments and suggestions, we'll take them to heart, and we'll also make certain to share them with the author. Please send your comments and suggestions to the following email address:

falconeditorial@rowman.com

Thanks for your input, and happy trails!

HIKING NEW JERSEY

A GUIDE TO THE STATE'S GREATEST HIKING ADVENTURES

SECOND EDITION

Johnny Molloy

ESSEX, CONNECTICUT

FALCONGUIDES ®

An imprint of Globe Pequot, the trade division of The Rowman & Littlefield Publishing Group, Inc.
4501 Forbes Blvd., Ste. 200
Lanham, MD 20706
www.rowman.com
Falcon and FalconGuides are registered trademarks and Make Adventure Your Story is a
trademark of The Rowman & Littlefield Publishing Group, Inc.

Distributed by NATIONAL BOOK NETWORK

Photos by Johnny Molloy unless otherwise noted
Maps by Melissa Baker and The Rowman & Littlefield Publishing Group, Inc.

British Library Cataloguing in Publication Information available

Library of Congress Cataloging-in-Publication Data

Names: Molloy, Johnny, 1961-author. | DeCoste, Paul E. Hiking New Jersey.
Title: Hiking New Jersey: a guide to the state's greatest hiking adventures / Johnny Molloy.
Description: Second edition. | Essex, Connecticut: FalconGuides, [2023] | Revised edition of:
  Hiking New Jersey: a guide to 50 of the Garden
State's greatest hiking adventures / Paul E. DeCoste, Ronald J. Dupont, Jr. ©2009.
Identifiers: LCCN 2022039853 (print) | LCCN 2022039854 (ebook) | ISBN 9781493043347
  (paperback) | ISBN 9781493043354 (epub)
Subjects: LCSH: Hiking—New Jersey—Guidebooks. | Trails—New Jersey—Guidebooks. | New
  Jersey—Guidebooks.
Classification: LCC GV199.42.N5 M65 2023 (print) | LCC GV199.42.N5 (ebook) | DDC
  796.5109749—dc23/eng/20220922
LC record available at https://lccn.loc.gov/2022039853
LC ebook record available at https://lccn.loc.gov/2022039854

CONTENTS

South Jersey

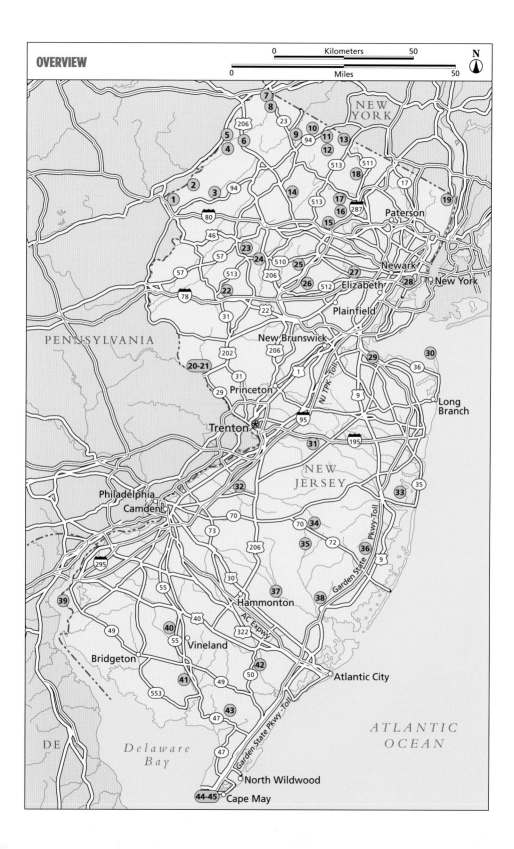

ACKNOWLEDGMENTS

Thanks to the previous authors of *Hiking New Jersey*, Paul E. DeCoste and Ronald J. DuPont Jr., for executing many fine hikes and adding so many great human and natural history vignettes and stories to the well-chosen hikes. Thanks also to Falcon Guides for allowing me to update and revise an already great hiking guide. Finally, thanks to my wife, Keri Anne for her help, and to all the people I met while on the trail.

MEET YOUR GUIDE

Johnny Molloy is one of America's most experienced and prolific outdoor writers. His outdoor passion was ignited on a backpacking trip in Great Smoky Mountains National Park. That first foray unleashed a love of the outdoors that led Johnny to spend over 4,500 nights backpacking, canoe camping, and tent camping throughout the United States and beyond over the past three decades.

Friends enjoyed his outdoor adventure stories; one even suggested he write a book about his adventures. He pursued his friend's idea and soon parlayed his love of the outdoors into an occupation. The results of his efforts are over eighty-five books and guides. His writings include hiking guidebooks, camping guidebooks, paddling guidebooks, comprehensive guidebooks about a specific area, how-to outdoor guides, and true outdoor adventure books covering all or parts of twenty-eight states, including *Hiking the Berkshires*, *Hiking Waterfalls in Pennsylvania*, and *Hiking through History New England*.

Though primarily involved with book publications, Molloy also writes for magazines and websites. He continues writing and traveling extensively throughout the United States, endeavoring in a variety of outdoor pursuits.

A Christian, Johnny is an active member of Christ Community Church of Johnson City and Gideons International. His non-outdoor interests include reading, Christian studies, and University of Tennessee sports. For the latest on Johnny, please visit https://johnnymolloy.com.

The author overlooking Muddy Run on the Parvin Lake Loop

INTRODUCTION

Do I contradict myself?
Very well then I contradict myself,
(I am large, I contain multitudes.)
　　　　　　—Walt Whitman, *Leaves of Grass,* "Song of Myself," 1855

Welcome to the second edition of *Hiking New Jersey*. The first edition—a fine one indeed—has been completely revised and updated, with many new hikes added (all hikes in the original edition included in this edition were rehiked). Few states are as contradictory as New Jersey—it would be hard to find another where gritty urban reality and wild, natural beauty reside in such cheek-by-jowl proximity. Walt Whitman surely appreciated it; he spent the last two decades of his life here.

New Jersey is essentially a sort of peninsula, bounded on the east by the Hudson River, New York Bay, and the Atlantic, and on the south and west by the Delaware Bay and River. Only the New York border on the north is an artificial line. In the northwest, ridges and mountains comprise the Highlands and the Kittatinnies—not big as mountains go, but scenic and surprisingly wild, ruggedly sculpted by the last ice age.

These give way in the center of the state to the rolling hills of the Piedmont—literally foothills—a densely populated corridor running between New York City and Philadelphia. The Piedmont in turn gives way farther south to the broad Coastal Plain, a mixture of pine forests, undulating farmland, wetlands, rivers, and coastline. From Sandy Hook, guarding New York Harbor, south to Cape May, one of America's first seaside resorts, beaches and barrier islands greet the Atlantic Ocean.

It is a varied and lovely topography, but too little known by outsiders. Citizens of surrounding states, seeing only the industrial highway corridor between the Big Apple and the City of Brotherly Love, often miss these delights and mislabel New Jersey a wasteland of factories, marshlands, diesel-fumed truck stops, and, perhaps, the remains of Jimmy Hoffa. No place of significance itself, but merely a route between other places. Many have swallowed, sight unseen, the vision of Sopranos New Jersey, of nightclub-joke New Jersey, of "You live in Jersey? Which exit?" Such is the popular stereotype going back even to Colonial times, when Ben Franklin (apocryphally) said that New Jersey was a barrel tapped at both ends.

This grimy industrial stereotype has some truth in it. Since the 1700s, New Jersey has been at the forefront of American industry, technology, and commerce. Our iron mines, forges, and furnaces made armaments for the American Revolution; our mills spun cotton and silk for export and made sails for clipper ships. We made locomotives, guns, and mortars for the Civil War. The first US oil refinery and port were built here, and we still have one of the largest petroleum storage facilities outside the Middle East. We wove the steel cables for the Brooklyn Bridge and, later, for the Golden Gate Bridge. New Jersey and its citizens gave birth to the lightbulb, the phonograph, the motion picture, the modern submarine, the transistor radio, and the electric guitar.

During World War II, we produced a quarter of all US battleships, along with aircraft and rocket engines (one, in a plane flown by Chuck Yeager, broke the sound barrier). We supplied vast quantities of munitions and explosives for both world wars, and we remain one of America's largest producer of chemicals and pharmaceuticals—and fragrances. When traffic got bad, we invented the cloverleaf intersection.

But we can laugh at the stereotype of New Jersey because we've seen the other New Jersey, too . . . and with this guide so will you. This is the New Jersey of preserved forests and farmland, of streams and waterfalls, of clean beaches and vast wetlands, of endless green mountains. Get this: In the percentage of our land remaining as natural open space, New Jersey outranks twenty-five other US states, including Colorado, Arizona, Wisconsin, Hawaii, and Texas.

Equally astonishing: By area, New Jersey has a higher percentage of parks, forests, and preserved farmland than most other states in America; the Pinelands are the most profoundly and densely wild expanse of land in such proximity to an urban area in the United States; and our wildlife includes not merely white-tailed deer and black bear but also bobcats, bald eagles, and coyotes. In the heart of the Highlands, you could easily imagine yourself in the Adirondacks, while the scrub pine coastal plains are as wild (or wilder) than those found down through the coastal Carolinas and Georgia.

It's supremely satisfying to see the reaction of Appalachian Trail (AT) thru-hikers entering New Jersey (71 miles of America's most famous footpath goes through the state). Some hikers half expect the AT here to be little more than a footpath between housing developments and shopping malls. They are thus astonished at the wonders of the Delaware Water Gap, the grand views from Kittatinny Ridge, and the varied farmlands of the Wallkill Valley. Also by the fact that in the most densely populated state in the nation, they routinely see black bear.

Hikers will be glad to know that New Jersey has more forest today than it did in 1855. The gradual abandonment of old mountain farmsteads and the creation of state parks and forests led to the regrowth of thousands of acres from the late 1800s to the mid-1900s. Mixed hardwoods predominate in the north, while in the south are the famous Pine Barrens (which do, however, include oak and other hardwoods).

This steady increase in forested land after 1900 prompted a return of animal species as well. Farmers in 1910 rarely saw a white-tailed deer, and hunters seeking them went to the Alleghenies or the Adirondacks. Today they are common to the point of being a hazard and a nuisance. Beaver, raccoon, skunk, and fox are all common in rural, suburban, and urban environments. The bald eagle is now present throughout rural areas of New Jersey.

Even through large predators like mountain lion, wolf, and black bear were rendered extinct in New Jersey in the 1800s, the bear has returned aplenty and is a common sight throughout the state. Wolves are still long-gone, but an increasing body of anecdote suggests that the mountain lion is beginning to find its way back to its ancestral prowls, fed in no small part by the abundant deer population.

And there are animal newcomers: possum and coyote, neither original to the state, are both residents now. The yowl-yip-howling of a pack of coyotes in deep woods near sunset will, very definitely, send a chill down your spine and put a spring in your step.

New Jersey boundary monument

Our weather is as diverse as our landscape. Winters, especially in the north, are akin to those in New England, with deep snows and subzero temperatures not uncommon. Winter hiking requires suitable clothing and gear. Elevation change can make a huge difference. A light February rain in the Piedmont can be a blizzard in the Kittatinnies; a pleasant spring day in the Palisades can be bleak winter at High Point.

New Jersey summers can likewise be Southern-style hot, humid, and hazy, with temperatures peaking over 100 degrees at times (don't forget—Cape May does fall south of the Mason-Dixon Line). Sunscreen and water are essentials. Many times of the year are bug-free in New Jersey, but not all. If one Jersey joke has merit, it's the one about the state bird being the mosquito. Watch out for ticks, too. The moral: Wear bug repellent. All times of the year have their glories for the hiker—if you are prepared.

Every level of government in New Jersey has acquired public lands and open space. The federal government owns historic sites (including Morristown National Historical Park), recreational areas (including Delaware Water Gap), seashores (including Sandy Hook), and wildlife refuges (Great Swamp, Edwin B. Forsythe, and Wallkill River, among others).

The State of New Jersey was among the first in the nation to create a state park and forest system, all laced with hiking trails. It is an extensive network of facilities, some of them established over a century ago. These vary from pocket-size parks with densely developed recreational facilities, like Parvin State Park, to vast tracts of wilderness, like Wharton State Forest at over 100,000 acres in area.

The New York–New Jersey region gave birth to a variety of hiking and outing clubs between 1900 and 1920. These groups were mainly composed of folks who wanted to get out of the city and hike in the fresh country air on weekends. They became a force for good, both lobbying for the acquisition and preservation of public lands and volunteering their time to build trails, shelters, and other facilities. In 1920 most of these groups gathered under the aegis of the New York–New Jersey Trail Conference, which since that time has been an important force in promoting conservation and trail building in the region.

The state lands system was given a supercharge in 1961 when voters approved the first Green Acres bond act to acquire open space. Since then over 1.2 million acres have been preserved in New Jersey. Additionally, New Jersey enjoys a superb state park and state forest system, adding to the hike possibilities.

Most county governments also have parks and preserves, often very fine ones, as do some local governments. Essex County was the first in the nation to establish a county park system, beginning with Newark's Branch Brook Park (which has more cherry trees than Washington, DC) in 1895. Some large municipalities, like Newark, own vast tracts of forest as a watershed for their drinking-water reservoirs, and these also provide recreational opportunities. Morris County alone has a park and historic site system that rivals the state's in quality.

Revising and updating this book has been both a challenge and a treat. A challenge because limitations of time and space forced the omission of some wonderful hikes, but also a treat because it led me to explore beautiful places in New Jersey I would've never experienced otherwise: the expansive vistas from High Point, the Delaware River Water Gap, the Pine Barrens, the beaches of Cape May, and other awe-inspiring hiking destinations.

Whether native or visitor, heed well: Don't let your preconceived notions of New Jersey cloud your hiking judgments. Strap on your hiking shoes and see the real New Jersey. They don't call it the Garden State for nothing.

Sunrise over Cheesequake's Crabbing Bridge

WEATHER

The state of New Jersey—from the Highlands in the northwest to the beaches of Cape May—experiences all four seasons in their entirety, and sometimes all at once when you take into account the elevation variation, from sea level along the Atlantic Ocean to 1,803 feet at High Point Monument, as well as the state's north–south geographical range: 160 miles from the northwest corner boundary with Pennsylvania and New York, down to Cape May jutting into Delaware Bay. Summer is fairly mild, especially in the mountains, though the Pine Barrens and south can be downright hot for extended periods. Morning hikers can avoid the common afternoon thunderstorms that arise in summer afternoons. Electronic devices equipped with internet access allow hikers to monitor storms as they come up, though coverage can be spotty in places.

Hikers increase in number when the first northerly fronts of fall sweep cool, clear air across New Jersey. Crisp mornings, great for vigorous treks, give way to warm afternoons, more conducive to family strolls. Winters can be long and will bring frigid subfreezing days and chilling rains and regular snowfalls in the lowlands and even more at the higher elevations. Winter brings far fewer hours of daylight; however, wise hike choices, a brisk hiking pace, and reasonable time management will keep you warm and walking. Each cold month has a few days of mild weather—make the most of them. Spring will be

Higbee Beach offers different experiences in differing kinds of weather.

more variable. A mild day can be followed by a cold one. Extensive rains bring regrowth, but also keep hikers indoors.

A good way to plan your hiking is to check monthly averages of high and low temperatures and average rainfall for each month in Millstone Township, roughly in the

MONTH	AVERAGE HIGH (°F)	AVERAGE LOW (°F)	PRECIPITATION (INCHES)
January	40	23	3.4
February	42	24	3.0
March	50	31	4.1
April	62	41	3.6
May	71	51	3.6
June	80	60	4.4
July	85	66	4.7
August	83	64	4.5
September	77	57	4.2
October	65	46	4.1
November	54	36	3.3
December	44	29	3.3

center of the state. Millstone Township averages 20.1 inches of snow and 51.2 inches of rain per year. The following climate data will give you a good idea of what to expect each month. However, remember temperatures can be cooler and precipitation higher in the adjacent Highlands.

FLORA AND FAUNA

The landscape of New Jersey varies greatly, from the Highlands of the northwest to the central Piedmont to the flat, swampy Pine Barrens, in addition to all the coastal tidal lands along the Atlantic Ocean and Delaware Bay. Despite being the most densely populated state in the union, a surprisingly large amount of forested lands create significant swaths and travel corridors for wildlife to roam. At the top of the food chain stands the black bear. They live in all of New Jersey's inland natural habitats, and there have been bear sightings in all twenty-one counties. You can run into one on almost any trail included in this guide. Although attacks by black bears are very rare, they have happened in New Jersey—a fatal attack occurred in Passaic County back in 2014. State bear population estimates range between 3,000 and 5,000. Seeing a bear is an exciting yet potentially scary experience. If you meet a bear while hiking, stay calm and don't run. Make loud noises to scare off the bear and back away slowly. Remain aware and alert.

Deer will be the land animal you most likely will see hiking New Jersey. They can be found throughout the state. Foxes are common, too, both red and gray species. A quiet hiker may also witness raccoons, or even a coyote. The state turkey population runs around 20,000 and they are reestablishing a presence throughout the state. Expect to see beavers around ponds, especially where their dams are visible. Mountain streams and larger lakes may harbor otters. Remember, if you feel uncomfortable when encountering any critter, keep your distance and they will generally keep theirs.

Overhead, many raptors will be plying the skies for food, including bald eagles, hawks, peregrine falcons, and owls. Depending upon where you are, other birds you may spot range from kingfishers to woodpeckers. Songbirds are abundant during the warm season no matter the habitat.

The flora offers as much variety as you would expect with geographical and elevational range, as well as proximity to salt water. The glacially carved New Jersey Highlands give way to the Piedmont—roughly the now heavily populated corridor connecting New York City and Philadelphia—which in turn gives way to the famed Pinelands, which gives way to the Atlantic coast. This wide variety of topography is further enhanced by New Jersey's location at the confluence of northern and southern plant life zones, creating a land of biodiversity surprising for the size of the state. A little under 20 percent of the state is considered wetlands. This includes brackish coastal wetlands.

The Highlands are cloaked in hardwoods of maple, oak, and hickory, with plenty of pines and cedar adding an evergreen touch. Moister valleys add birch and rhododendron. A few hemlocks are still hanging on, or being preserved by land managers. New Jersey's Pinelands, aka Pine Barrens, is a fascinating area and much more than just pines, and is rife with blackwater streams and white cedar swamps. The Pine Barrens are heavily shaped by fire, especially the prevalent pitch pine and shortleaf pine and a host of scrub oaks. Blueberries and cranberries occur naturally and were later cultivated in the Pine Barrens. Brackish streams flow in and out with the tides on Jersey's coast, giving way to dunes and beaches with attendant plant life. Delaware Bay adds a huge fresh-to-salt water transitional zone.

Beauty in bloom at Wallkill National Wildlife Refuge

WILDERNESS RESTRICTIONS/REGULATIONS

Hikes on federal lands include Delaware Water Gap National Recreation Area and Gateway National Seashore, as well as the National Park Service–held Appalachian Trail corridor and national wildlife refuges. Other hikes occur at New Jersey state parks, forests, and preserves as well as county parks and to a lesser extent privately held preserves open to public use. On one hike you may traverse multiple public parcels of land, going from a state park to a state forest or from a state forest to a state reservation, and so on. Most

This boardwalk is another New Jersey Appalachian Trail surprise.

of the time you will not know the difference—the flora and fauna of New Jersey certainly don't. A couple of hikes edge into Pennsylvania and New York. The public lands are managed differently where fees are concerned and are noted in each hike's summary matter. Each unit will have its own backcountry camping regulations. The Appalachian Trail corridor in New Jersey allows camping only at specific designated sites.

Detailed trail and road maps are available of almost all public and private lands traveled in this guide. Download them—they come in handy in helping you get around.

GETTING AROUND

AREA CODES

New Jersey's large population is reflected in its large number of area codes, ten in all: 201, 551, 609, 640, 732, 848, 856, 862, 908, and 973.

ROADS

The hikes in this guide cover the entire state. Where possible, hike directions start from an interstate, including I-78, I-80, I-95, I-287, and I-295, the New Jersey Turnpike, and the Garden State Parkway, as well as a few other major highways.

BY AIR

New Jersey has plenty of airports serving the state and nearby cities of Philadelphia and New York. Newark Liberty International Airport, Trenton-Mercer Airport, Atlantic City International Airport, and Morristown Municipal Airport are the major landing destinations for planes here.

BY BUS

Most trailheads are not accessible via bus, but Greyhound serves some cities in New Jersey, including Newark, Atlantic City, Camden, and Mount Laurel. Visit www.greyhound.com for more information.

VISITOR INFORMATION

For general information on visiting New Jersey, go to www.visitnj.org.

HOW TO USE THIS GUIDE

Take a close enough look, and you'll find that this guide contains just about everything you'll ever need to choose, plan for, enjoy, and survive a hike in New Jersey. Stuffed with useful New Jersey hiking-specific information, *Hiking New Jersey* features forty-five mapped and cued hikes. I grouped the hikes into three units. "North Jersey" covers hikes in the northwestern part of the state, including Delaware Water Gap National Recreation Area, the Appalachian Trail, and hikes along the New York border. "North Central Jersey" harbors hikes south of the I-80 corridor, including the hikes of Morris County, and other preserves directly west of New York City, including the Great Swamp and Liberty State Park. "South Jersey" details hikes in the most southerly portion of the Garden State, roughly below a line running due east from the state capital in Trenton, including parks and preserves in the fabled Jersey Pinelands as well as coastal hikes all the way down to Cape May.

Each hike starts with a short summary of its highlights. These quick overviews give you a taste of the hiking adventures to follow. You'll learn about the trail terrain and what surprises each route has to offer.

Following the overview, you'll find the hike specs: quick, nitty-gritty details of the hike. The hike specs are explained below:

Start: Tells you exactly where you will begin your hike. For example, the hike might start at a picnic area within a state park, allowing you to look for a specific trailhead rather than just the state park. The name of the trailhead often corresponds to names found on mapping apps.

Distance: The total distance of the recommended route—one-way for loop hikes, round-trip on out-and-back or balloon loop hikes. Options are additional.

Difficulty: Each hike has been assigned a level of difficulty. The rating system was developed from several sources and personal experience. These levels are meant to be a guideline only and may prove easier or harder for different people depending on ability and physical fitness.

Easy—3 miles or less total trip distance in one day, with minimal elevation gain and paved or smooth-surfaced dirt trail.

Moderate—up to 8 miles total trip distance in one day, with moderate elevation gain and potentially rough terrain.

Difficult—more than 8 miles total trip distance in one day, with strenuous elevation gain and rough and/or rocky terrain.

Elevation change: This is the aggregate elevation gained and lost during a hike, whether it is a loop hike or an out-and-back hike. These numbers were found using GPS data obtained during the given hike loaded onto a mapping program.

Maximum grade: This details the steepest portion of the hike for a sustained distance, whether you will be going up or down that grade on the specific hike. The maximum grade is calculated by dividing the elevation gained or lost by the distance covered.

Hiking time: The average time it will take to cover the route. The number is based on the total distance, elevation gain, and condition and difficulty of the trail. Your hiking pace and fitness level will also affect your time.

Seasons/schedule: This details information on the best time of year to do the given hike and/or the specific hours a place is open/closed.

Fees and permits: Tells you whether you need to carry any money with you for park entrance fees and permits.

Dog friendly: This not only states whether or not dogs are allowed and/or gives specific regulations, but also lets you know if it makes sense to take your pet on the given hike.

Trail surface: General information about what to expect underfoot. Is the trail very rocky, smooth, wide, natural surface, etc.? Are parts of the path paved or concrete? This way you know what footwear to use and what conditions to expect.

Land status: Whether it is a state park, state forest, private preserve, or other entity.

Nearest town: Helps orient you to the hike's location and also helps you find out what amenities are in the nearest town, such as outfitters, restaurants, or an emergency clinic.

Other trail users: Such as horseback riders, mountain bikers, inline skaters, etc.

Maps to consult: This is a list of other maps to supplement the maps in this book. USGS maps can be a good source for accurate topographical information, but the local park map may show more recent trails. Use both.

Amenities available: Lets you know if restrooms, picnic areas, campgrounds, and other enhancements are at or near the trailhead. This way you can stop on the way to use the restroom en route if no restrooms are available at the trailhead, know whether to bring a picnic to the trailhead, etc.

Cell service: This gives you an idea of whether or not your phone will get reception on the hike. In elevationally varied areas such as the Highlands, you can have reception on a ridge but not down in the valley. Also, what carrier you use can have a lot to do with whether or not you have reception. In New Jersey expect to have service more often than not.

Trail contact: This is the location, phone number, and website URL for the local land manager in charge of the trails within the selected hike. Before you head out, get trail access information, or contact the land manager after your visit if you see problems with trail erosion, damage, or misuse.

The **Finding the Trailhead** section gives you dependable driving directions to where you'll want to park. **The Hike** is the meat of the chapter. Detailed and honest, it's a carefully researched impression of the trail. It also often includes lots of area history, both natural and human. Under **Miles and Directions**, mileage cues identify all turns and trail name changes, as well as points of interest.

HOW TO USE THE MAPS

Overview map: This map shows the location of each hike in the area by hike number.

Route map: This is your primary visual guide to each hike. It shows all of the accessible roads and trails, points of interest, waters, landmarks, and geographical features. The map also distinguishes trails from roads, and paved roads from unpaved roads. The selected route is highlighted, and directional arrows point the way.

TRAIL FINDER

To get our readers started on the hikes that best suit their interests and abilities, we include this simple trail finder that categorizes each of the hikes in the book into a helpful list. Your hikes can fall under more than one category. Please choose the categories that are most appropriate for your area.

HIKE #	HIKE NAME	BEST HIKES FOR WATERFALLS	BEST HIKES FOR GREAT VIEWS	BEST HIKES FOR CHILDREN	BEST HIKES FOR DOGS	BEST HIKES FOR WATER LOVERS	BEST HIKES FOR BACKPACKERS	BEST HIKES FOR NATURE LOVERS	BEST HIKES FOR HISTORY LOVERS
1	Mount Tammany Loop	*	*			*	*		
2	Pahaquarry Copper Mines Circuit	*			*			*	*
3	Paulinskill Valley Trail	*		*		*			*
4	Falls of Tillman Ravine	*		*	*	*		*	
5	Millbrook Village Van Campens Glen Loop	*	*			*			*
6	Kittatinny Vistas		*				*	*	
7	Steenykill Lake and High Point		*			*			*
8	Lake Rutherford Appalachian Trail Loop	*				*		*	*
9	Wallkill Refuge Loop	*	*	*				*	
10	Pinwheel Vista via Pochuck Valley		*			*		*	
11	Wawayanda Lake Loop		*		*	*			*
12	Terrace Pond		*			*	*	*	
13	Surprise Lake Loop		*			*			
14	Saffin Pond and Headley Overlook		*		*	*		*	
15	The Tourne		*	*	*				*
16	Pyramid Mountain and Tripod Rock		*		*			*	

HIKE #	HIKE NAME	BEST HIKES FOR WATERFALLS	BEST HIKES FOR GREAT VIEWS	BEST HIKES FOR CHILDREN	BEST HIKES FOR DOGS	BEST HIKES FOR WATER LOVERS	BEST HIKES FOR BACKPACKERS	BEST HIKES FOR NATURE LOVERS	BEST HIKES FOR HISTORY LOVERS
17	The Pequannock Highlands		*		*			*	*
18	Wyanokie High Point	*	*		*				*
19	Palisades Interstate Park	*	*		*	*			*
20	The Delaware Valley—Stockton to Lambertville Loop		*			*			*
21	The Delaware Valley—Stockton to Bulls Island Loop		*			*			*
22	Ken Lockwood Gorge		*	*	*	*			*
23	Schooley's Mountain	*	*	*	*			*	
24	Black River Gorge			*	*	*		*	*
25	Jockey Hollow				*			*	*
26	Lord Stirling Park			*	*	*		*	
27	South Mountain and the Rahway River		*					*	*
28	Liberty State Park		*	*		*			*
29	Cheesequake Loop		*	*	*				
30	Sandy Hook Loop		*			*			*
31	Clayton Park Loop			*	*			*	
32	Rancocas State Park			*	*	*		*	
33	Cattus Island		*	*		*		*	
34	Byrne State Forest Circuit			*	*			*	*
35	Franklin Parker Reserve		*	*		*		*	
36	Wells Mills			*	*			*	*
37	Batsto Lake Loop			*	*	*		*	
38	Bass River State Forest Loop			*	*			*	*
39	Fort Mott		*	*		*			*
40	Parvin Lake Loop			*	*				*
41	Maurice River Bluffs Preserve		*					*	*

HIKE #	HIKE NAME	BEST HIKES FOR WATERFALLS	BEST HIKES FOR GREAT VIEWS	BEST HIKES FOR CHILDREN	BEST HIKES FOR DOGS	BEST HIKES FOR WATER LOVERS	BEST HIKES FOR BACKPACKERS	BEST HIKES FOR NATURE LOVERS	BEST HIKES FOR HISTORY LOVERS
42	Belcoville and the South River			*		*		*	*
43	East Creek Trail				*			*	
44	Higbee Beach		*	*		*		*	
45	Cape May Point		*	*		*		*	*

MAP LEGEND

Municipal

🛣️ **95** Freeway/Interstate Highway

🛣️ **206** US Highway

🛣️ **94** State Road

🛣️ **607** County/Paved/Improved Road

= = = = Unpaved Road

├────┤ Railroad

- - - - - State Boundary

Trails

- - - - - - Featured Trail

- - - - - Trail or Fire Road

───── Paved Trail

Water Features

Body of Water

Marsh/Swamp

River/Creek

Intermittent Stream

Waterfall

Land Management

State Park/Forest

Preserve/Wildlife Management Area/ Reservation

Symbols

🛏 Bench

|||||| Boardwalk

➤ Boat Launch

≍ Bridge

■ Building/Point of Interest

✪ Capital

▲ Campground

† Cemetery

▬ Dam

🕯 Lighthouse

▲ Mountain/Peak

🅿 Parking

🪑 Picnic Area

🛈 Ranger Station/Park Office

🍴 Restaurant

🚻 Restroom

📷 Scenic View/Overlook

🗼 Tower

○ Towns and Cities

㉑ Trailhead

❓ Visitor/Information Center

1 MOUNT TAMMANY LOOP

This first-rate circuit hike climbs from the Delaware River along a sheer bluff, sporting eye-popping views while rising to Mount Tammany, a classic New Jersey destination with views of the Delaware River gorge below. From there, trek along the brow of Kittatinny Mountain, then drop to visit picturesque Sunfish Pond, a highland tarn, and descend into and through the deep cascade-rich gorge of Dunnfield Creek before completing the loop.

Start: Worthington State Forest I-80 trailhead
Distance: 10.5-mile loop
Difficulty: Difficult due to distance
Elevation change: +-1,872 feet
Maximum grade: 18% grade for 1.2 miles
Hiking time: About 6.0 hours
Seasons/schedule: March through November
Fees and permits: None
Dog friendly: Yes, on leash only
Trail surface: Forested natural surface, lots of rock

Land status: State forest, national recreation area
Nearest town: Columbia
Other trail users: None
Maps to consult: Worthington State Forest
Amenities available: Restrooms, picnic table at trailhead
Cell service: Good on most parts of hike
Trail contact: Worthington State Forest, (908) 841-9575, www.nj.gov/dep/parksandforests

FINDING THE TRAILHEAD

From Columbia, take I-80 west for 2.4 miles to the Dunnfield Creek/Appalachian Trail exit. Once off the interstate, continue past the picnic area parking to the Appalachian Trail parking. Trailhead GPS: 40.971643,-75.125440

THE HIKE

This hiking adventure first climbs to the precipices above Delaware Water Gap, one of New Jersey's natural wonders, where the Delaware River cuts a gorge of immense proportions as it forms the boundary between the Garden State and Pennsylvania. The first 1.2 miles of the hike—on the Mount Tammany Trail—climbs over 1,000 feet. But you will be partly mesmerized by the views from the rim of the gorge, with the muscle-bound Delaware River charging below, splitting around Arrow Island, and Mount Minsi rising with its gray talus slope striping the peak, all framed in pitch pines and scrub oaks.

After topping out on Mount Tammany, you will join the Mount Tammany Fire Road (unless you want to shorten the loop by taking the Blue Blaze Trail back to the trailhead for a 3-mile circuit) and run along the eastern brow of Kittatinny Mountain among fire-managed pines and oaks rising over ferns, swaying grasses, and blueberry bushes, with a perceptible steep slope falling away to your right. These days, the Mount Tammany

This spiller is sometimes known as Dunnfield Creek Falls.

Fire Road is but a slim path, more trail than road. By the way, Mount Tammany was named after Tamanend, a benevolent and wise Lenape chieftain in the Pennsylvania–New Jersey region. He gained the admiration and respect of early eighteenth-century settlers because of his fairness and goodwill.

The hiking remains nearly level until you join the Turquoise Trail. That path skims the headwaters of Dunnfield Creek then meets the fabled Appalachian Trail (AT) and Sunfish Pond, the most southerly glacial lake along the AT. The 41-acre, spring-fed tarn, ringed by glacial debris, is the centerpiece of the 285-acre state natural area. Hike along the shoreline, then pick up the Dunnfield Creek Trail, following the handsome brook as it gains volume and cuts a gorge into Kittatinny Mountain.

The stream, bastion of native brook trout, works its way over boulders and rocks, tumbling over stone breeches, then slows in crystalline pools, only to push on, urged by gravity, one lively cascade following another. Down toward the lower end of the gorge, you'll come to a fine waterfall that spills over a curved ledge, visible from a hiker bridge spanning Dunnfield Creek, as well as a series of slide cascades, aquatic highlights of Dunn-field Creek State Natural Area contained within greater Worthington State Forest.

The hike is a full 10 miles, so allow plenty of time to do the actual walking as well as enjoy the sights. Furthermore, the trailhead can be busy, as it is a parking area for the

Gazing south into the Delaware River Gorge

Appalachian Trail. The views from Mount Tammany draw in the crowds, as does Sunfish Pond, so plan appropriately.

MILES AND DIRECTIONS

0.0 Leave from the I-80 Appalachian Trail parking area on the Mount Tammany Trail, also known as the Red Dot Trail. Climb along a wooded ledge on wood and earth

Hiking the rocky shore of Sunfish Pond

steps, then meet an alternate path coming in on your right from the picnic area parking. Stay with the blazes on a wide, heavily used trail, ignoring non-blazed user-created paths, climbing all the while under tulip trees, beeches, and oaks.

0.4 Come to your first view into the Delaware River gorge, on the edge of a bluff, dotted with craggy cedars and oaks. Gaze south down the waterway, downstream, toward Arrow Island. Keep climbing along the edge of the headland.

0.7 Come to another major vista point, this one almost 500 feet higher than the first overlook. This overlook presents a better view upstream. The vehicles of I-80 below look like toys. Keep ascending among boulder gardens.

1.2 Emerge at the highest overlook and one of the finest vistas in the Garden State. Unofficial spurs go down to additional views. Just ahead, join the Blue Blaze Trail, aka the Pahaquarry Trail. Keep straight (northeast), bound on a rocky track along the rim of Mount Kittatinny.

1.6 Reach a trail intersection. The Blue Blaze Trail heads left and is a good option for a shorter loop. Our hike keeps straight, joining the trail-like Mount Tammany Fire Road. The crowds end as you enter fire-managed hickory-oak-pine woods. Gently undulate along the 1,500-foot mark, bisecting occasional fern glades.

3.2 Cross an open helicopter landing area labeled Helispot 2.

4.6 Head left on the singletrack Turquoise Trail. Descend northwest on a stony track, stepping over uppermost Dunnfield Creek.

5.2 Head left at the T intersection, joining trail-like Sunfish Fire Road, running conjunctively with the Turquoise Trail.

5.6 Split right on the Turquoise Trail.

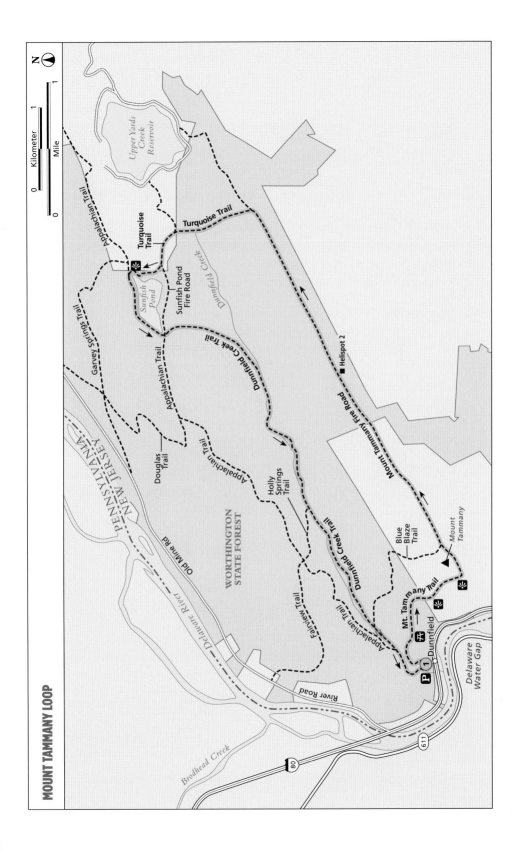

MOUNT TAMMANY LOOP

5.8 Emerge at a rock outcrop with a fine view of tannin-stained Sunfish Pond.

5.9 Join the AT. Head left, southbound along the north shore of the tarn. Relish more watery views and waterside hiking. The trail is very rocky in places.

6.4 Cross the outflow of Sunfish Pond.

6.6 Reach the west end of the tarn. Absorb a last view, then come to a stone monument acknowledging Sunfish Pond as a Registered Natural Landmark. Here, the AT splits right, but we head left for just a few feet on the Sunfish Pond Fire Road then split right on the singletrack Dunnfield Creek Trail. Climb on a rocky track over a knob in low, brushy woods, then descend. Step over a few trickling tributaries.

7.7 Come alongside Dunnfield Creek. Enjoy pretty stream scenes amid the evergreens and yellow birches.

8.0 Rock hop to the left bank of Dunnfield Creek, singing in shoals.

8.4 Rock hop the stream twice in succession. The trail widens.

8.9 Cross over to the right bank of Dunnfield Creek.

9.1 The Holly Springs Trail enters on your right, linking to the Appalachian Trail and beyond.

9.3 Cross over to the left-hand bank, then climb well above the creek.

9.9 Return to the stream. Look for stone bluffs above the water.

10.0 The Blue Blaze Trail enters on your left and the trail ahead is much more heavily used. Come to a hiker bridge over Dunnfield Creek, and above that tumbles a 10-foot waterfall, sometimes known as Dunnfield Creek Falls. Continue down the right-hand bank of the creek.

10.2 The AT comes in on your right. Keep down the valley on a wide and busy track.

10.5 Arrive back at the trailhead after bridging Dunnfield Creek one last time.

2 PAHAQUARRY COPPER MINES CIRCUIT

This fun hike deep in Delaware Water Gap National Recreation Area first takes you to an entrance to the old Pahaquarry Copper Mine and a waterfall. It then passes the stone relics of the mine processing area before climbing the west slope of Kittatinny Mountain. Top out then dive into the chasm of Mine Brook, passing more waterfalls and cascades. Visit a second mine entrance before completing the loop and returning to the trailhead.

Start: Old Mine Road
Distance: 2.6-mile balloon loop with spur
Difficulty: Moderate
Elevation change: +-793 feet
Maximum grade: 19% grade for 0.4 mile
Hiking time: About 1.4 hours
Seasons/schedule: April through December
Fees and permits: None
Dog friendly: Yes, on leash only

Trail surface: Forested natural surface
Land status: National recreation area
Nearest town: Columbia
Other trail users: None
Maps to consult: Coppermine Trail—National Park Service
Amenities available: None
Cell service: Not good
Trail contact: Delaware Water Gap National Recreation Area, (570) 426-2452, www.nps.gov/dewa

FINDING THE TRAILHEAD

From Columbia, take I-80 west for 3.2 miles to exit 1, Millbrook/Flatbrookville. Join River Road/Old Mine Road for 6.6 miles to the trailhead parking on your left. *Note:* Old Mine Road is closed during the winter, so call ahead to check before driving to the trailhead during the shoulder seasons. Trailhead GPS: 41.037831,-75.027227

THE HIKE

Once the site of Boy Scout Camp Pahaquarra, 1925–71, the trailhead and adjacent area have reverted back to nature, save for remains of mill processing buildings and barred mine shafts. The story goes back much further. Once home to the Lenape Indians, who occupied much of what became New Jersey, and later settled by Dutch colonists, what is now the Delaware Water Gap National Recreation Area was rich in natural resources—timber, water, iron ore, and even a little copper. Furthermore, the Delaware River availed relatively easy transportation to bring the resources to market.

Long about the mid-1700s, enter John Reading Jr., one of New Jersey's early Colonial governors. Mr. Reading purchased property along a tributary of the Delaware River, later to become Mine Brook, to mine copper. Turns out the mineral was low-grade and the end product remained low-grade using the primitive smelting operations of the time. However, a century later the Allegheny Mining Company restarted operations, digging shafts, but the ongoing glitch of poor-grade mineral spiked the operation. A final attempt was made in the early 1900s when the Pahaquarry Copper Company began a larger-scale

Find this cascade along Mine Brook.

operation that included open quarry as well as pit mining. They also built a sizable on-site ore processing operation, the backbone of the remaining ruins we see today.

Their investment was a complete failure. Then in came the Boy Scouts, using several of the buildings for their camp. Later, the land was bought as part of the never-to-be Tocks Island Dam project. Objections to flooding the Delaware River gorge proved a boon for New Jerseyites, as the to-be-flooded land became the foundation for Delaware Water Gap National Recreation Area—a place where the Delaware runs free and the

These stairstep falls tumble just upstream of a Pahaquarry Mine opening.

magnificent gorge and surrounding terrain, waters, and history fashion a fine place to hike and explore.

Our hike travels these preserved lands. First, head upstream along babbling Mine Brook to view the creekside barred entrance to one of the copper mines, as well as a 20-foot tiered cascade of a cataract. View ruins of the mine processing operation, stone walls, and building remains. Next, begin working up the side of Kittatinny Mountain, joining a series of old roads winding along the wooded slope, first in the form of the Kaiser Spur

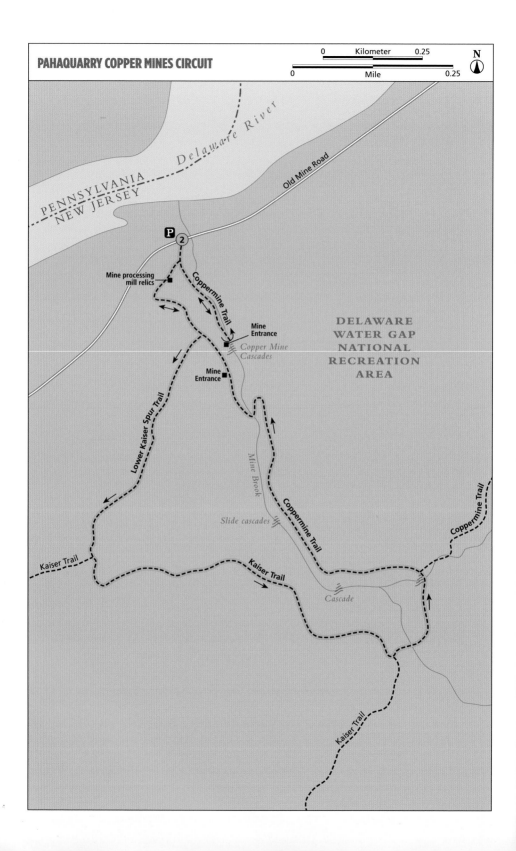

PAHAQUARRY COPPER MINES CIRCUIT

0   Kilometer   0.25

0   Mile   0.25

N

Delaware River

PENNSYLVANIA
NEW JERSEY

Old Mine Road

P
2

Mine processing
mill relics

Coppermine Trail

Mine
Entrance

Copper Mine
Cascades

DELAWARE
WATER GAP
NATIONAL
RECREATION
AREA

Mine
Entrance

Lower Kaiser Spur Trail

Mine Brook

Slide cascades

Coppermine Trail

Coppermine Trail

Kaiser Trail

Kaiser Trail

Cascade

Kaiser Trail

Trail, then the Kaiser Trail itself. Reach a high point, then work your way to the upper end of Mine Brook and join the Coppermine Trail. A pretty stream throughout as it cuts a sharp path down an incised vale, you will encounter several waterfalls, sluices, and cataracts. Many of the pourovers are difficult to reach, especially since the forest is transitioning away from hemlocks that once dominated the forest here.

User-created spurs travel to the more accessible spillers, yet some cataracts will have to be appreciated from a distance. Just before finishing the loop portion of the hike, you will pass a second mine entrance, also barred. As always, exercise caution around mines and mine openings. You then finally return to the trailhead flats, where Camp Pahaquarra stood, now just another chapter of the past, same as the Pahaquarry Mines themselves. *Note:* If you want to check out the Delaware River from the trailhead parking area, a short spur trail leads to the river at its confluence with Mine Brook, creating a viable water access option.

MILES AND DIRECTIONS

0.0 Leave south from Old Mine Road on the Coppermine Trail. The trail quickly splits. Stay left and begin walking along Mine Brook, climbing a platform, part of the old mine processing area. Look for other structure remnants. Cruise along Mine Brook.

0.2 Come to the lower copper mine opening, safely barred on a rock face. Work upstream a little more, coming to a tiered cascade rumbling 20 feet over rocks, then slowing in a pool. Backtrack, returning to the Coppermine Trail junction, then turn up the Coppermine Trail, passing relics of stone block structures, part of the ore processing infrastructure.

0.5 Reach the loop portion of the hike. Here, split right with the Lower Kaiser Spur Trail, climbing an old roadbed in woods. The trail then levels off and traverses rock slabs.

0.9 Meet the Kaiser Trail, coming in on your right from Old Mine Road. Split left, and resume climbing.

1.5 Reach a trail intersection. Here, split left with the spur to the Coppermine Trail as the Kaiser Trail stays right for the Appalachian Trail. Shortly rock hop a sparkling tributary of Mine Brook.

1.7 Rock hop Mine Brook, then reach another intersection. Here, the Coppermine Trail goes left and right. Go left, passing a 10-foot fall, first angling over a striated rock slide before dropping into a rhododendron-enshrouded grotto.

1.8 Pass a spur heading left to more falls, a pair of ledges. Keep heading deeper and steeper into the Mine Brook gorge. The sound of falling water echoes in the watershed. Slides, ledges, and other falls are common but difficult to access due to the deepness of the gorge and transitioning forest. The trail is dropping almost as sharply as the falls themselves.

2.2 Bridge Mine Brook, getting a fine look at the stream as well as slide cascades below the trail bridge.

2.3 A short spur heads left to another mine entrance, also barred.

2.4 Return to the intersection with the Lower Kaiser Spur Trail. You have completed the loop portion of the hike. Backtrack toward the trailhead.

2.6 Arrive back at the trailhead, completing the short but sweet hike.

3 PAULINSKILL VALLEY TRAIL

Follow this rail trail along a scenic river, crossing bridges and passing a pond. The former line, converted to a path, offers nearly level hiking in attractive woods as it leads you from tiny Marksboro, following the rapids and pools of the Paulinskill River to reach Footbridge Park in Blairstown. Your return trip will yield additional sights.

Start: Spring Valley Road trailhead
Distance: 6.6 miles out and back
Difficulty: Moderate
Elevation change: +-35 feet
Maximum grade: <2% grade for 3.3 miles
Hiking time: About 3.0 hours
Seasons/schedule: Year-round
Fees and permits: None
Dog friendly: Yes, on leash only
Trail surface: Pea gravel
Land status: State park

Nearest town: Blairstown
Other trail users: Bicyclers, occasional equestrians
Maps to consult: Kittatinny Valley State Park
Amenities available: Restrooms, picnic tables at Footbridge Park
Cell service: Good
Trail contact: Kittatinny Valley State Park, (973) 786-6445, www.nj.gov/dep/parksandforests

FINDING THE TRAILHEAD

From exit 12 on I-12, take Hop-Blairstown Road north for 0.4 mile, then turn right onto Silver Lake–Marksboro Road and follow it for 1.5 miles, keeping straight as it becomes Silver Lake Road. Stay with Silver Lake Road for 3.3 miles, then stay right, joining NJ 94 north. Follow NJ 94 for 0.3 mile to turn left on Spring Valley Road and follow it for 0.4 mile, turning left into the trailhead parking area just after bridging the Paulinskill River. Trailhead GPS: 40.992145,-74.910192

THE HIKE

Stand in the Paulinskill Valley Trail parking lot and imagine flagging down one of the five passenger trains that once ran daily over these cinders. Or smell the smoke of the milk-run train stopped at the Marksboro creamery. It's already picked up the milk cans at the creameries in Blairstown, Vail, and Hainesburg.

Approaching the deck girder bridge, you can almost hear the rattling of the rails from the two engines pulling twenty-five coal cars, racing at 30 miles an hour from the Pennsylvania coal fields to the industrial Northeast. The coal trains rumbled across this railroad bridge five times a day to the tune of 1.5 million tons of anthracite per year.

As the trail approaches the thru-plate girder bridge, can you picture the ice train on its way to Jersey City? Or might you be a vacationer on a special weekend express to Blairstown? Today, when you get there, imagine the ghost of a railway station, the freight yard, the water tanks, and the turntable as you hike through the parking lot of cinders. On the other hand, could you be an employee of the New York, Susquehanna & Western who is on a special company excursion train to Lake Susquehanna at Blairstown Airport with your family for the annual employees' picnic?

Trail bridges present fine views of the Paulinskill River.

What is now the Paulinskill Valley Trail was once part of the Delaware, Lackawanna & Western Railroad empire called the Lackawanna Cutoff, or the New Jersey Cutoff. A reroute, the new line opened in 1911 and offered a straighter track and less gradient, allowing faster trains to operate. Times changed, and by 1979 the cutoff saw its last train. In 2001, the State of New Jersey acquired the right-of-way through eminent domain and today we have a fine 24-mile rail trail to explore and enjoy.

Our particular trek follows the Paulinskill River between tiny Marksboro and Blairs-town. You are never far from water, and can hear the splashy stream even from the trail-head parking area. Speaking of splashing, a connector trail leads from the trailhead area to a nearby waterfall, part of the outflow from nearby White Lake, a natural resource area with trails of its own. So, when you start—if the waters are flowing—take the spur to the 16-foot angled stairstep cascade before joining the main trail.

Heading southwest, the trail trundles down the river valley, rarely far from water, and eventually returns to the riverbank where the river cascades over shelves of shale, drop-ping into long, straight, sleepy stretches where a family of mallards may be taking flight. The railroad bed travels through cuts, across fills, and on a shelf above the Paulinskill, all the while being canopied by 80- to 100-foot camouflage-colored, shaggy bark sycamores that thrive in damp, rich soil. The path comes back to the river and crosses it twice within the next 0.2 mile on railroad bridges, then skirts a pond formed by the Paulina Dam (the dam may be removed in the future). Here at Paulina Park you may find a single

The sign indicates you are 80 miles from Jersey City.

swan, a beaver lodge, a trout angler, and most likely, a romantic couple. The trail crosses another girder bridge and the Paulinskill River, works its way behind some backyards, and approaches NJ 94. The sound of the vehicles is a bit distracting, but the trail drops below the highway and the noise fades.

The path comes into Blairstown, where you can take advantage of the facilities at Footbridge Park. This municipal park has benches, restrooms, a picnic pavilion, and a playground, as well as a footbridge over the Paulinskill River to the main part of town, where you can obtain all manner of food and drink before backtracking to the trailhead in Marksboro.

MILES AND DIRECTIONS

0.0 Leave the trailhead and pass around a pole gate, heading southwest on the Paulinskill Valley Trail. Just ahead, a spur leads right, linking to White Lake Natural Resource Area, with its own set of trails, and a 16-foot stairstep cascade. Resume down the rail trail under a corridor of sycamore, maple, and tulip trees on a 10-foot-wide pea gravel path. The river stretches 50 to 60 feet wide. Spur trails lead to the water. Private rights-of-way occasionally bisect the trail.

0.5 Pass a stone marker labeled JC 80. This is left over from the railroad days, denoting the railroad is 80 miles from its Jersey City terminus.

PAULINSKILL VALLEY TRAIL

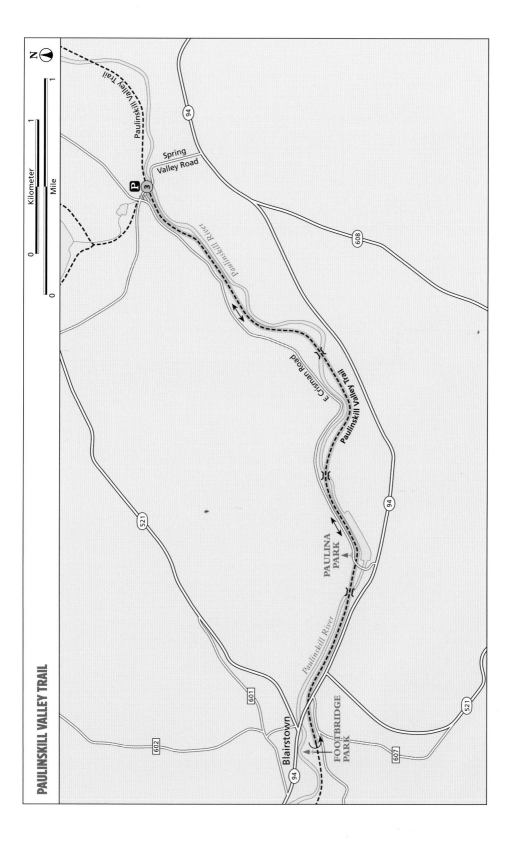

1.2 Cross the Paulinskill River on an old rail bridge. You are now on the left-hand bank heading downstream.

1.5 Pass the JC 81 stone marker. Just ahead, a tributary enters on your left and raucous rapids form on the Paulinskill.

1.9 Bridge the Paulinskill on a sturdy iron-truss span. Here, the river is being backed up by Paulina Pond, a small impoundment. The trail runs along the still shores of the tarn.

2.3 Reach small Paulina Park and an overlook at the Paulina Dam. Go out to the dam for a view, then cross East Crisman Road, continuing on a berm in woods.

2.5 Bridge over to the left-hand bank of the river. You now come along NJ 94 and beside backyards of houses pinched between NJ 94 and the rail trail. Ahead, enter a high-canopied forest.

3.1 Pass under NJ 94, cut through a parking area, then briefly follow Foot Bridge Lane.

3.3 Reach Footbridge Park, with its amenities. Cross the footbridge over the Paulinskill River to Blairstown for food and drink if desired. Backtrack to the trailhead.

6.6 Arrive back at the trailhead, completing the rewarding rail trail.

4 FALLS OF TILLMAN RAVINE

This fun little hike, great for water lovers, explores Tillman Ravine Natural Area on a series of interconnected nature trails within Stokes State Forest. Leave the parking area, heading to a series of long cascades and the Tea Cup, a swirling pool in the middle of the falls. Continue down the incised gorge of Tillman Brook, then visit Wallpack Cemetery. Backtrack up the ravine, then make a loop, crisscrossing Tillman Brook numerous times as you traverse the gorge.

Start: Lower Tillman Road parking lot
Distance: 1.8-mile double loop with spur
Difficulty: Easy
Elevation change: +-371 feet
Maximum grade: 9% downhill grade for 0.3 mile
Hiking time: About 1.0 hour
Seasons/schedule: April through November
Fees and permits: None
Dog friendly: Dogs permitted on leash, but some parts of trail are over slick rock

Trail surface: Forested natural surface, rock slab, gravel
Land status: State forest
Nearest town: Branchville
Other trail users: None
Maps to consult: Stokes State Forest, Stokes State Forest South
Amenities available: Restroom at trailhead
Cell service: Poor
Trail contact: Stokes State Forest, (973) 948-3820, www.nj.gov/dep/parksandforests

FINDING THE TRAILHEAD

From Branchville, take US 206 north for 4.3 miles to turn left on Struble Road. Follow Struble Road for 2.4 miles and stay left with the main road as it becomes Dimon Road. Stay with Dimon Road for 1.5 miles, then veer right onto Tillman Road and follow it for 0.5 mile, passing the Tillman Ravine upper parking lot on the way. Park in the lower Tillman Ravine lot. **Note:** Call ahead to make sure access roads are open from December 15 to April 15. Trailhead GPS: 41.156994,-74.862230

THE HIKE

Tillman Ravine Natural Area is a protected 525-acre parcel of Stokes State Forest. According to the New Jersey Natural Areas directive, the tract was preserved because "it contained anticline geologic forms, the effects of water erosion on exposed rocks, a near natural habitat, and unusual and outstanding forest types composed of hemlocks, mixed hardwoods and mixed oaks." It also contains a 25-acre plot of old-growth forest. Today, you can see why Tillman Ravine is the pride of big Stokes State Forest, over 16,000 acres of outdoor New Jersey, with a variety of activities contained within, from hiking to camping to swimming, paddling, hunting, fishing, and more.

The effects of water erosion—in common parlance—means waterfalls, cascades, and cataracts as Tillman Brook dives off Kittatinny Mountain toward the flats of Flat Brook, a tributary of the Delaware River. A series of slides and chutes will quicken your pulse as you near Tillman Brook, following it to the Tea Cup, a swirling circular pool. The

One of many falls on lively Tillman Brook

steep gorge cut by Tillman Brook was formed by post-glacial water erosion cutting along a fault in the rock. This narrow vale creates a microclimate of its own, often cool on the hottest summer day. Unfortunately, many of the hemlocks that once graced Tillman Ravine have fallen prey to the exotic insect from China known as the hemlock woolly adelgid. However, forest personnel are preserving some of the evergreens, treating them with an in-ground insecticide absorbed through the roots of the hemlocks.

Below the Tea Cup, the path takes you past more slide cascades then traces Tillman Brook as its valley widens past former farms returned to forest to reach Brook Road. Follow this country lane a short distance to discover historic Wallpack Cemetery, the burial ground for nearby Wallpack Center, a former agricultural community of the New Jersey Highlands. Residents of Wallpack Center were bought out when the Tocks Island Dam was to be erected. The project never came to be, then Delaware Water Gap National Recreation Area was established and the building cluster was preserved, including a small museum in the Rosenkrans House as well as the Methodist church and post office. The worth-a-look hamlet is just a short drive from this hike's trailhead.

From the cemetery, backtrack up Tillman Brook to the falls around the Tea Cup, then continue up the slot gorge with its everywhere-you-look beauty, including wildflowers, mosses, and the contrasts of rock and moving water. You will know the stream intimately, bridging it numerous times while working your way up the ravine. The hike then pops

Tapered faucet-like falls characterize Tillman Brook.

out at the Tillman Ravine upper parking area. A little more walking leads you back to the trailhead.

If you desire more waterfall action beyond this short but rewarding hike, visit Buttermilk Falls, within Delaware Gap National Recreation Area, not far from the trailhead. Also, Stokes State Forest offers 63 miles of pathways within its confines. Back in 1905, New Jersey governor Edward Stokes, desirous to establish parks and forests within the

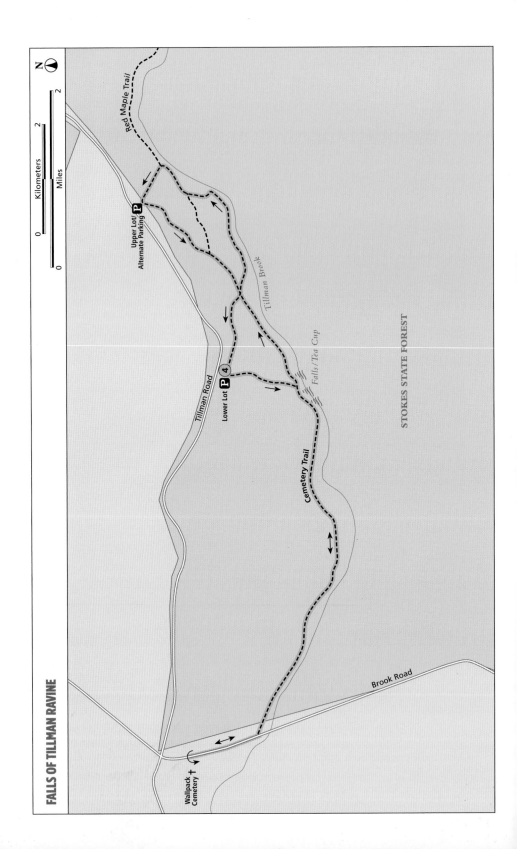

FALLS OF TILLMAN RAVINE

Red Maple Trail

Upper Lot / Alternate Parking

Tillman Road

Tillman Brook

Lower Lot

Falls / Tea Cup

Cemetery Trail

STOKES STATE FOREST

Brook Road

Wallpack Cemetery

N

Kilometers

Miles

Garden State, donated his own 500 acres to form the nucleus of what became Stokes State Forest. Additional purchases enlarged the forest to the 16,000 acres we appreciate today.

Camping at Stokes State Forest is another fine option, with five distinct overnighting areas. The forest also has rustic cabins and lean-tos for overnight stays. The regal scenery in the state forest, home of Sunrise Mountain, New Jersey's second-highest peak, is complemented by the stonework, trail building, tree planting, and more of the Civilian Conservation Corps (CCC), who were stationed in the forest from 1933 to 1942.

The CCC also dammed streams here, creating Lake Ocquittunk and Skellinger Lake, adding to the fishing and paddling opportunities on the forest, which also includes Lake Ashore. Only electric motors are allowed on the waters, making for a serene experience. Visiting Sunrise Mountain is a must-do New Jersey experience. A road leads to the peak, leaving you a short walk to the top of the naked stone mount presenting 360-degree views. The stone pavilion up there is another contribution of the CCC. Although the hike at Tillman Ravine Natural Area may be short, there's plenty of opportunities to complement it with other nearby outdoor endeavors.

MILES AND DIRECTIONS

0.0 Leave from the lower parking area and hike through a planted red pine grove before descending quickly to Tillman Brook. Stay with the trail blazes and avoid user-created trails.

0.1 Come to Tillman Brook. You are looking headlong at a series of cataracts and the swirling pool of the Tea Cup. Turn right, downstream, on a potentially slick stone slab, parallel to slide cascades, joining the Cemetery Trail in a tight, thickly wooded ravine.

0.3 The singletrack trail leads to where the ravine opens. Come along former farmed lands, bisected by stone walls, now forested terrain.

0.5 Reach gravel Brook Road. Turn right here, down the country lane, to soon reach Wallpack Cemetery, a fairly large internment with many ornate headstones of days gone by. After respectfully visiting, backtrack to the Cemetery Trail.

0.7 Rejoin the Cemetery Trail, climbing into the closing ravine.

1.1 Continue past the falls around the Tea Cup, trekking new pathway.

1.3 Stay right at the four-way intersection with the Tillman Ravine nature trails. Drop back to the stream and begin crossing the translucent waterway numerous times on small bridges in a tight ravine.

1.4 Stay right at another nature trail intersection.

1.5 Intersect the signed Red Maple Trail. It continues up the Tillman Brook valley, linking to other pathways in Stokes State Forest. Stay left with the nature trail, heading away from the stream.

1.6 Pop out at the upper Tillman Ravine parking area. Stay left, back on footpath, heading southwest in woods. Roll through woods, passing a trail cutting back left.

1.7 Return to the four-way intersection where you were earlier. Stay right, aiming for the lower parking area.

1.8 Arrive back at the lower parking area, completing the fun nature trail/waterfall hike.

5 MILLBROOK VILLAGE VAN CAMPENS GLEN LOOP

Start your hike at historic Millbrook Village, worth a little hiking tour of its own. Travel old farm roads and quiet lanes, climbing to Hamilton Ridge with its gorge views. From there, descend to the Delaware River, cruising near the big waterway before heading up gorgeous Van Campens Brook, with its numerous waterfalls, chutes, and slots. Pass near the restored Watergate wetlands, then loop back to Millbrook Village. The circuit is a full 6 miles but the trails are wide and without excessive elevation change.

Start: Millbrook Village
Distance: 6.2-mile loop
Difficulty: Moderate
Elevation change: +-820 feet
Maximum grade: 11% downhill grade for 0.6 mile
Hiking time: About 3.2 hours
Seasons/schedule: Year-round; summer weekends for touring village
Fees and permits: None
Dog friendly: Yes, on leash only
Trail surface: Forested natural surface, old asphalt in places, short road walk

Land status: National recreation area
Nearest town: Blairstown
Other trail users: None
Maps to consult: Delaware Water Gap NRA—National Park Service
Amenities available: Restrooms, picnic tables at Millbrook parking area
Cell service: Very little
Trail contact: Delaware Water Gap National Recreation Area, (570) 426-2452, www.nps.gov/dewa

FINDING THE TRAILHEAD

From Blairstown, take Millbrook Village Road north for 7.3 miles to Millbrook Village and Old Mine Road. The parking area is on the right at the intersection with Old Mine Road. Trailhead GPS: 41.073709,-74.963280

THE HIKE

Millbrook Village is the site of a small community situated along Van Campens Brook. Established in the 1830s, the hamlet slowly grew, peaking around 1875, and included around nineteen buildings. Later, residents drifted away for better opportunities, leaving just a handful of residents to usher Millbrook into the twentieth century. Then, in the 1960s, when the Tocks Island Dam threatened several historic buildings in what became Delaware Water Gap National Recreation Area, those structures were moved to Millbrook Village, concentrating the historical structures in one place, since Millbrook was above the proposed lake waterline. Though not the actual replicated Millbrook Village, the old buildings collectively represent a New Jersey way of life gone by. Nevertheless, on summer weekends lifeways of old times gone are demonstrated for today's residents. Check the Delaware Water Gap National Recreation Area website for dates and times of demonstrations. The hike undertaken from Millbrook Village also traverses former farms

Van Campens Brook presents numerous cascades as it cuts through a gorge.

and lands that have reverted back to nature, yet evidence of farm days remains—a stone fence here, a crumbled road or a squared-off foundation there.

Additionally, the natural side of things is well represented on this hike when you turn up Van Campens Brook, with its rocky gorge, cascades, and everywhere-you-look beauty. This area can be very busy, from the Van Campens Glen parking area to Lower Van Campens Falls. However, the park service has reinforced the path here to withstand heavy use. No wonder it is busy, as the trail meanders along Van Campens Brook, with its

Millbrook Village presents a peaceful aura.

national park–level scenery, as well as the stony gorge through which it flows. Exercise caution around the numerous waterfalls to be found; many of them are difficult to access. The last part of the hike travels around the restored Watergate wetlands. Hopefully on your hike you will be able to view these wetlands, returned to their original state, after once being turned into a series of ponds.

Even if you don't undertake this hike to coincide with a historic demonstration at Millbrook, the hike alone is worth it, plus you can simply take a self-guided tour of the historic buildings that provide a glimpse into yesterday's life in New Jersey's Highlands.

MILES AND DIRECTIONS

0.0 Cross Old Mine Road from the north end of the Millbrook Village parking area, joining the Orchard Trail, an old woods road. Climb past stone walls under white pine, cedar, maple, beech, cherry, and tulip trees rising above berry bushes and other brush.

0.3 Pass a bench at an old homesite with a fast-disappearing view south down the Van Campens Brook valley.

0.5 Reach the Hamilton Ridge Trail. Head left on a crumbled asphalt track, much of which is covered with moss.

1.2 Split right on the Pioneer Trail, a more primitive path, trundling under cedars and white pines. Pass a spur on the right to an old limekiln before turning left, now running left along the rim of the Delaware River gorge. Partial views open into the

A roaring slit-like cataract on Van Campens Brook

chasm below and Pennsylvania beyond. Soon turn down a drainage to the Delaware River bottoms.

1.9 Reach the bottoms, curving north, then abruptly turn northwest, crossing stone fences.

2.1 Turn sharply left, heading westerly on an old roadbed. The river is visible below you. Pass some obvious old homesites into brushy woods that were once productive farmlands under cultivation and pasturage for ages. Ahead, turn away from the river, paralleling more rock walls.

MILLBROOK VILLAGE VAN CAMPENS GLEN LOOP

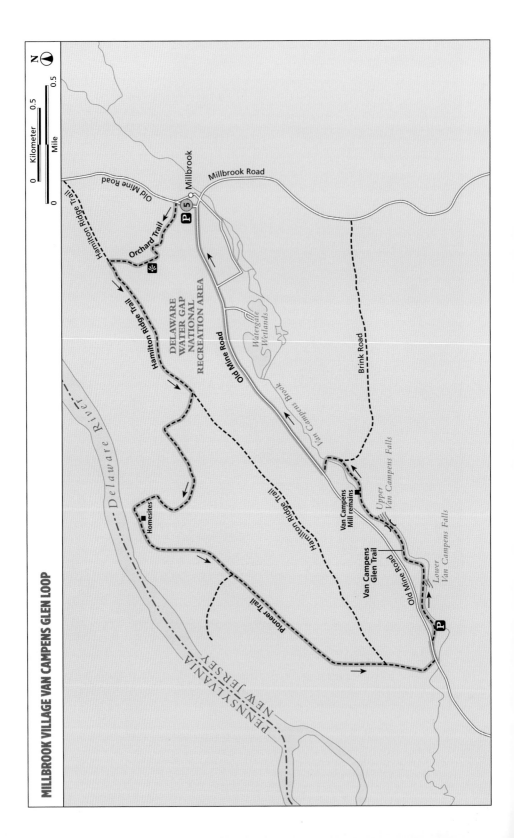

2.6 Pass under massive power lines, then stay straight at an intersection with an agricultural road splitting right to access still-cultivated fields along the Delaware River bottoms. Continue along the margin between the bottoms and the rising river gorge. This part of the hike recalls trekking a country lane.

3.4 Meet the other end of the Hamilton Ridge Trail, then cross a tributary of Van Campens Brook.

3.7 The Pioneer Trail pops out on Old Mine Road. Walk left along Old Mine Road for a few hundred feet, then split right toward the Van Campens Glen parking area. Pass through the parking area, with restrooms and picnic tables, and begin the Van Campens Glen Trail, entering a deep wooded ravine rich with preserved hemlocks. Elaborate trail work takes you directly along the swishing stream bordered by pink rock.

4.1 Come to Lower Van Campens Falls, a narrow 16-foot chute drop where the stony gorge pinches in Van Campens Brook. Here, the trail rises well above the stream, offering additional looks at the cataract. Ahead, the trail drops you at the head of Lower Van Campens Falls. If the rock isn't wet, peer over the falls for a top-down view.

4.4 Bridge over to the right-hand bank of Van Campens Brook.

4.5 Reach Upper Van Campens Falls. Here, the stream makes a 30-foot angled fan-shaped dive, widening as it descends, then slows in a large plunge pool, one of the widest, most open parts of the stream, bordered on its lower end by loose rock and gravel. The trail swings around the right side of the pool then ascends a stone slab to come along an incredible mini slot canyon through which Van Campens Brook flows. More cascades and cataracts lie immediately upstream.

4.8 Pass the remains of Van Campens Mill, constructed in the 1750s.

4.9 Stay left as old Brink Road, a crumbled asphalt path-turned-hiking trail, enters on your right. Stay left to again bridge Van Campens Brook on an old road bridge, then emerge at Old Mine Road. Head right, walking easterly on Old Mine Road, working around the old Watergate wetlands, once the country home of a man named George Busch.

6.2 Arrive back at the Millbrook trailhead, completing the hike. Hopefully you have enough energy for a tour of the village buildings.

6 KITTATINNY VISTAS

This loop hike at Stokes State Forest takes the inimitable Appalachian Trail along the crest of Kittatinny Mountain, passing outcrops delivering first-rate panoramas into Delaware Water Gap and beyond to Pennsylvania. The trek also visits a historic observation tower before descending along Stony Brook, sporting a few melodic cascades. Next, pay a visit to Stony Lake, a popular recreation area, before closing the loop with the Coursen Trail and a brief walk along acclaimed Sunrise Mountain Road.

Start: Culvers Gap parking area
Distance: 6.2-mile balloon loop with spur
Difficulty: Moderate
Elevation change: +-870 feet
Maximum grade: 8% grade for 1.2 miles
Hiking time: About 3.2 hours
Seasons/schedule: Year-round; winter can be frigid
Fees and permits: None
Dog friendly: Yes, on leash only

Trail surface: Forested natural surface, a little paved road
Land status: State forest
Nearest town: Branchville
Other trail users: None
Maps to consult: Stokes State Forest, Stokes State Forest North
Amenities available: Restroom at trailhead
Cell service: Good on ridgetops
Trail contact: Stokes State Forest, (973) 948-3820, www.nj.gov/dep/parksandforests

FINDING THE TRAILHEAD

From Branchville, take US 206 north for 3.4 miles to turn right on Upper North Shore Road. Follow it 0.2 mile, then turn left onto Sunrise Mountain Road and immediately turn left again into the Culvers Gap parking area. Trailhead GPS: 41.180272,-74.787851

THE HIKE

This hike employs one of New Jersey's more scenic stretches of the Appalachian Trail (AT). Furthermore, the trail here through Stokes State Forest is one of the older footpaths in the state. The trail segment was built soon after the State of New Jersey acquired the tract and was used by rangers to access the fire tower lookout near the summit of the ridge. It was later adopted as a section of the AT.

The Culver Fire Tower, originally called the Normanock Lookout Tower, was part of a series of forest fire lookout towers established by the State of New Jersey early in the twentieth century. By 1928, the system consisted of nineteen fire towers across the state. Nowadays, fire watching is done by strategically placed cameras, along with watching by plane when conditions warrant. There was an observation platform here as early as the 1880s, and a wooden fire observation tower had been erected by 1919. The original wooden Culver Fire Tower had become a popular visitors' spot by the 1920s.

A visitor in 1928 noted that over a thousand people had signed the visitors' register by that time, most from New Jersey and New York, but some from as far away as Florida,

An outcrop opens views west into Pennsylvania.

Colorado, Puerto Rico, and even Russia. The current 47-foot steel tower was erected in 1934 by Civilian Conservation Corps (CCC) Camp S-51 in Stokes State Forest. The tower was originally located near the village of Blue Anchor, in the Pine Barrens of Winslow Township, down in Camden County. The tower was dismantled, trucked north, and hauled up the mountain to this spot where the "CCC boys" reassembled it. The Aermotor Company of San Angelo, Texas, established in 1888, built the fire tower itself; their primary business was (and remains) building windmills. They stake claim as America's only windmill manufacturer.

Stony Lake, now a popular swimming area, was originally home to Camp Madeleine Mulford, built for the Girl Scouts of Montclair in 1927. Mulford was a leader in Girl Scout activities; her husband, wealthy publisher and investor Vincent S. Mulford, donated the camp in her memory. The camp was the first real effort to develop Stokes State Forest for recreation, and not simply timber management.

You will visit both the Culver Fire Tower and Stony Lake on this hike. For a hike of its length and scope, the trek is on the easy side. Elevation changes aren't drastic. The trails are well signed and maintained, and not too rocky. After starting, it isn't long before you open to your first view, and the vista is a dandy. Here, an open outcrop, bordered in grasses and framed in pines, opens forth to the west, with the chasm of the Delaware River and the Pocono Plateau rising in the distance. Kittatinny Lake lies in the near.

You are now atop the crest of Kittatinny Mountain, trending southwest–northeast. Run along the rock ridge, with partial views opening along the slender hogback under

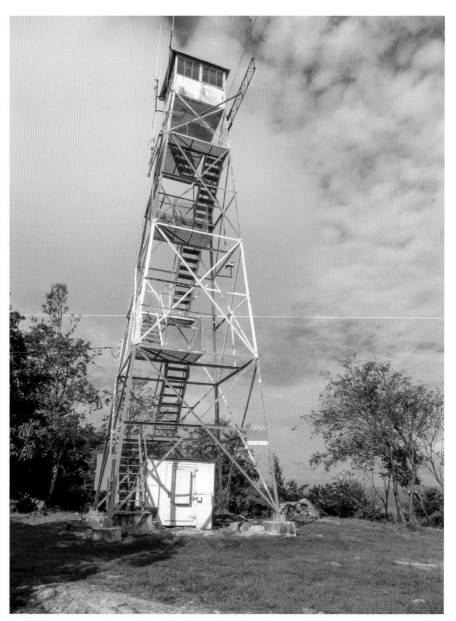

The historic observation tower on Kittatinny Mountain

shade of hardwoods rising from the forest floor. Another vista opens before reaching a grassy clearing and the Culver Fire Tower at the hike's apex. The painted metal structure rises overhead and a stone outcrop opens to the west, providing a natural overlook. The spot is enhanced by a picnic table, making for a fine picnicking locale.

Beyond the tower, another view opens at the intersection with the Tower Trail. You ease down Kittatinny Mountain in bucolic woodlands before picking up the Stony Brook Trail, leaving the AT behind. Roughly parallel the stream as it dives for the lowlands,

The Appalachian Trail takes you to this view.

passing a few splashy cataracts that sing through the forest and in your ears. The hike becomes easy once again as it picks up an old woods road, passing former farmlands-turned-forest in a wide segment of the Stony Creek vale. You then come to Stony Lake, 15 acres in size, complemented by a swim beach. Consider extending your trip by about a mile with a loop around the lake. From Stony Lake, you take the Coursen Trail as it winds through rich woods, gently undulating back to reach Sunrise Mountain Road. A brief road walk takes you back to the trailhead.

MILES AND DIRECTIONS

0.0 Leave from the northwest corner of the large parking area and walk a short distance on a slender path to reach the Appalachian Trail. Head right, northbound, in maples, oaks, and other hardwoods.

0.2 Reach Sunrise Mountain Road. Walk left 100 feet then split right, staying with the white blazes. The AT immediately climbs a rocky hillside.

0.6 Reach the crest of Kittatinny Mountain and a fine view as the AT switchbacks to the left. Open outcrops and low grasses clear a distant panorama. After absorbing the view, continue north in windswept oaks, pines, and hickories. Gently climb along the crest of the ridge.

1.5 A short spur leads left to an outcrop and a fine view across the Delaware River into Pennsylvania, with the New Jersey Highlands in the fore.

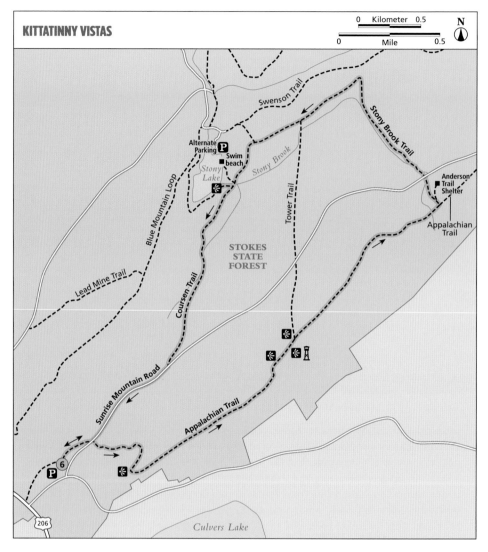

0 Kilometer 0.5

0 Mile 0.5

N

Swenson Trail

Stony Brook Trail

Alternate Parking

Swim beach

Stony Lake

Stony Brook

Blue Mountain Loop

Anderson Trail Shelter

Appalachian Trail

Tower Trail

STOKES STATE FOREST

Lead Mine Trail

Coursen Trail

Sunrise Mountain Road

Appalachian Trail

6

206

Culvers Lake

1.7 Reach the Culver Fire Tower with another natural view to the north, after circling around a cell tower. Return to woods on a stony path. Descend a bit, then meet the Tower Trail. Head left and follow it a short piece to an enriching overlook. Backtrack then return to the Appalachian Trail, northbound.

2.7 Turn left on the Stony Brook Trail after crossing the upper reaches of Stony Brook. Descend northwesterly, shortly passing the spur trail leading right to the Gren Anderson trail shelter. The Stony Brook Trail descends through tulip tree-heavy hardwoods, while the treadway becomes soft and framed by ferns.

2.9 Reach Sunrise Mountain Road. Walk left on the road then turn right, descending the left bank of Stony Brook. Shortly bridge the brook. Ahead, the trail and stream steepen, resulting in falls along Stony Brook.

3.5 The trail swings west, joining a woods road, paralleling wetlands while under white pines and lined by stone walls. Look for homesite foundations along the road.

3.9 The Tower Trail splits left, climbing to the Culver Tower. Our hike keeps on the Stony Brook Trail on an easy path.

4.1 A spur trail leads right to meet the Blue Mountain Loop. This general locale was the site of the historic Madeline Mulford Girl Scout Camp.

4.4 A leg of the Stony Lake Trail leads right to Stony Lake parking and beach. Cross Stony Creek then split right with the Stony Lake Trail, curving along the south shore of the impoundment for a view, then backtrack and pick up the Coursen Trail south in rocky woods.

5.5 The Coursen Trail ends at Sunrise Mountain Road. Turn right onto Sunrise Mountain Road (one-way, coming at you).

6.0 Split right with the AT, leaving the road.

6.2 Arrive back at the trailhead, completing the worthwhile circuit hike.

7 STEENYKILL LAKE AND HIGH POINT

What a highlight-rich hike! Make a loop through New Jersey's loftiest terrain at one of its most historic state parks, starting at striking Steenykill Lake. Trek along the shore, gaining views of the High Point Monument, then work your way to the crest of Kittatinny Mountain, detouring to loop through a protected highland cedar swamp before reaching New Jersey's highest spot, replete with 360-degree panoramas of three states. From there, descend past marvelous Lake Marcia before returning to Steenykill Lake.

Start: Steenykill Lake boat ramp
Distance: 6.0-mile balloon loop with additional inner loop
Difficulty: Moderate
Elevation change: +-880 feet
Maximum grade: 14% downhill grade for 0.3 mile
Hiking time: About 3.1 hours
Seasons/schedule: April through November
Fees and permits: None if starting at Steenykill Lake boat ramp; fee if driving up to High Point Monument
Dog friendly: Yes, on leash only

Trail surface: Forested natural surface, a little pavement
Land status: State park
Nearest town: Sussex
Other trail users: None
Maps to consult: High Point State Park
Amenities available: Restrooms, fountain at High Point parking area
Cell service: Good
Trail contact: High Point State Park, (973) 875-4800, www.nj.gov/dep/parksandforests

FINDING THE TRAILHEAD

From Sussex, take NJ 23 north for 9.4 miles, then turn right into the signed right turn for the Steenykill Lake boat launch. Follow the road for 0.2 mile to end at the boat launch and two smallish parking areas. Trailhead GPS: 41.320877,-74.677148

THE HIKE

This is simply one of the best hikes in New Jersey, a trek of superlatives—state high point, world's highest cedar swamp, and highest lake in the state, among other accolades including the most sublime vistas from the High Point Monument, as well as other overlooks scattered throughout the loop.

The hike first treks along Steenykill Lake, crossing its dam, one of many projects undertaken by the Civilian Conservation Corps (CCC) in High Point State Park. The construction of Steenykill Lake was begun by the state in the late 1920s but stopped due to the Great Depression. In 1935 the CCC restarted the project, a three-year effort that included the dredging of the lake and construction of the 1,200-foot-long, 45-foot-high dam. Make a mental note of Steenykill Lake so when you arrive at Dryden Kuser Natural Area—still in its untamed state—you can compare what were two white cedar swamps.

High Point Monument

Additionally, you can gaze up at the High Point Monument from the lake's edge, presenting a picture-postcard scene.

Hiking up the Steenykill Trail beyond Steenykill Lake, you are now on another project built by the CCC, reflected in the trail stonework. Once on the Monument Trail, there continues to be evidence of the CCC handiwork in rock cribs and stone steps. Once you climb up through the hardwoods, you are now experiencing scrub oak and pitch pine during your ridge walk. From various vistas looking west, views of the Delaware

Looking out to the Delaware River valley from New Jersey's High Point Monument

River, Pocono Plateau, and the city of Port Jervis and Matamoras lay out before you. Descending off the ridge, you will encircle the Dryden Kuser Natural Area, containing the highest-elevation (1,500 feet) white cedar swamp in the world, with Atlantic white cedar, Eastern hemlock, and sphagnum moss. A nature guide, obtained online, will enhance your experience.

Leaving this natural Shangri-la, emerge on the east ridge with periodic views (east) of the New Jersey Highlands, revealing how much green still exists in the most densely populated state in the union. There will also be one vista looking west where most of the hike can be visually traced. Arriving at the High Point Monument complex, you will find restrooms and a water fountain (seasonal). The 221-foot-tall monument was built in 1928–30 to honor New Jersey veterans of all wars and modeled after the Bunker Hill Monument. The monument interior, with the option to climb 291 steps to the top, is open on weekends and holidays from Memorial Day weekend until Columbus Day, staff and weather permitting, from 9:00 a.m. to 3:45 p.m.

The loop hike also passes Lake Marcia, the highest lake in New Jersey, as well as near the gorgeous stone structure that is the Interpretive Center. This handsome stone building has gone through many transitions. Originally built in 1930 as a restaurant for park visitors, it was later converted to the park Interpretive Center. From here, the hike goes back down the mountain to Steenykill Lake and dam, our starting point. Enjoy an encore view of High Point Monument, where you were earlier.

High Point Monument as seen from Steenykill Lake

MILES AND DIRECTIONS

0.0   Leave from the boat ramp at the edge of Steenykill Lake, the dammed headwaters of Clove Brook, on the Steenykill Trail. Head northeast, with the shoreline to your right. Soon emerge on the grassy shore and lake dam, with a small picnic area.

0.2   Reach the dam's end and outflow of Steenykill Lake. Quickly enter woods of birch, cherry oak, and maple, climbing on stone steps through a boulder garden.

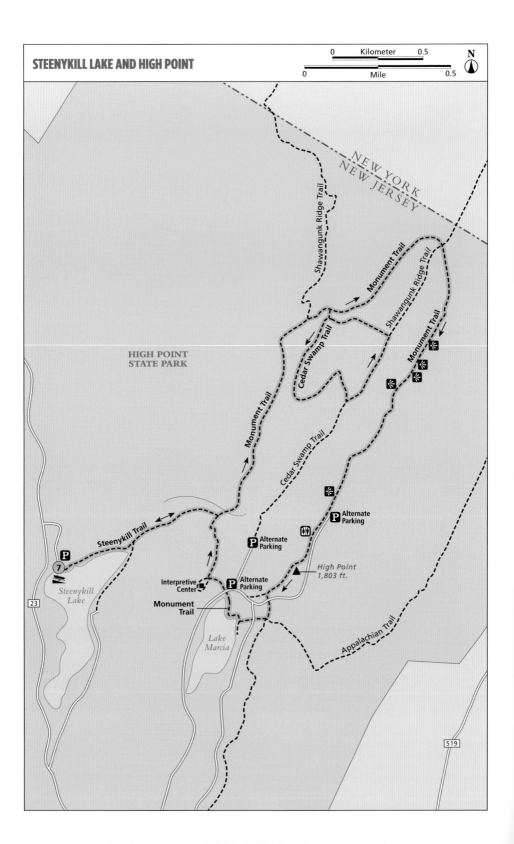

STEENYKILL LAKE AND HIGH POINT

0   Kilometer   0.5

0   Mile   0.5

N

NEW YORK
NEW JERSEY

HIGH POINT
STATE PARK

Shawangunk Ridge Trail

Monument Trail

Cedar Swamp Trail

Shawangunk Ridge Trail

Monument Trail

Monument Trail

Cedar Swamp Trail

Monument Trail

P

Alternate
Parking

P

Alternate
Parking

P
Alternate
Parking

High Point
1,803 ft.

Steenykill Trail

P

7

Interpretive
Center

P
Alternate
Parking

Monument
Trail

Steenykill
Lake

23

Lake
Marcia

Appalachian Trail

519

0.6 Meet the Monument Trail. Head left, bridging a tributary of Clove Brook. Keep northeast in rocky woods, sometimes nearing the rocky mountain edge with partial views among young chestnuts. Join a ridge with stunted xeric hardwoods and pines.

1.4 The Shawangunk Ridge Trail enters on your left. Stay right.

1.5 Head right with the inner loop that is the Cedar Swamp Trail. Once meeting the loop of the Cedar Swamp Trail, head right, circling the swamp on a level track. Pass interpretive signage astride the world's highest white cedar swamp.

2.1 Pass an arm of the Cedar Swamp Trail, formerly Cedar Swamp Drive, on the right where it enters Dryden Kuser Natural Area, marked by a stone and bronze plaque on the left honoring Dryden Kuser, an ardent naturalist and ornithologist. Continue to circle the swamp counterclockwise.

2.4 The Shawangunk Ridge Trail leaves right, while the Cedar Swamp Trail stays left, crossing 100 yards of boardwalk.

2.6 Complete the inner loop of the Cedar Swamp Trail then head right, rejoining the Monument Trail, northeast bound.

3.1 Come to a four-way intersection very near the New York state line. Cross the Shawangunk Ridge Trail one last time, then climb to the nose of Kittatinny Ridge and turn south, once again on a rocky ridge with stunted oaks and hickories.

3.5 A spur trail leads left to an easterly vista of the New Jersey Highlands. Ahead, pass other spur trails that lead left to outcrops with similar views.

4.3 Reach the north end of the large High Point Monument parking area. Keep south through the lot, passing restrooms and a fountain.

4.6 Reach the High Point Monument. Walk up it if it is open. Circle the area for 360-degree views, then head south on the Monument Trail, descending from the west side of the monument, passing power lights illuminating the monument.

4.7 Stay left as you descend, as a wide trail heads right. Quickly cross Monument Drive and reenter woods.

4.8 Meet the Appalachian Trail at a four-way intersection in rocky woods. Stay right, still on the Monument Trail. Descend to cross Scenic Drive. Ahead, meet Lake Marcia, the highest impoundment in the Garden State, elevation 1,572 feet. Stay right along the lake, keeping the shore to your left, absorbing looks into the water and beyond at this popular summertime swimming destination.

5.0 Reach the north end of Lake Marcia. Cross Kuser Road, then take the paved road uphill toward the Interpretive Center.

5.1 Split right with the natural-surface Monument Trail with the rustic stone Interpretive Center to your left. Surmount then descend a hill in forest.

5.4 Complete the loop of the Monument Trail. Head left on the Steenykill Trail, backtracking.

6.0 Arrive back at the trailhead, completing the hike of superlatives.

8 LAKE RUTHERFORD APPALACHIAN TRAIL LOOP

This highly recommended hike at High Point State Park first uses the fabled Appalachian Trail, winding westerly atop Kittatinny Ridge past warm-up westerly views before reaching the best vistas along the upper edge of Dutch Shoe Rock, where you can scan easterly down on your next highlight—Lake Rutherford—as well as a wave of ridges in the distance. Visit Lake Rutherford, taking the Iris Trail—a fine footpath designed by the prestigious Olmstead design firm—on your return trip to the trailhead.

Start: Appalachian Trail overnight parking area
Distance: 6.5-mile balloon loop
Difficulty: Moderate
Elevation change: +-1,034 feet
Maximum grade: 13% downhill grade for 0.2 mile
Hiking time: About 3.8 hours
Seasons/schedule: April through November
Fees and permits: Parking permit required only if overnight backpacking

Dog friendly: Yes, on leash only
Trail surface: Forested natural surface
Land status: State park
Nearest town: Sussex
Other trail users: None
Maps to consult: High Point State Park
Amenities available: None
Cell service: Good
Trail contact: High Point State Park, (973) 875-4800, www.nj.gov/dep/parksandforests

FINDING THE TRAILHEAD

From Sussex, take NJ 23 north for 7.9 miles, then turn left into the signed Appalachian Trail parking area. Trailhead GPS: 41.302754,-74.667551

THE HIKE

High Point State Park protects over 16,000 acres of Garden State highlands in its northwest boundary with Pennsylvania and New York. Laced with 50 miles of trails—including 18 miles of the Appalachian Trail (AT)—the park offers a wealth of hiking opportunities as well as camping, paddling, swimming, fishing, and picnicking. This particular hike incorporates the AT as it travels New Jersey's rooftop that is Kittatinny Mountain.

Your southbound trek first offers views of Sawmill Pond below and the Pocono Plateau as well as the gorge of the Delaware River in the distance, a westerly perspective. After traversing a slow, rocky trail section, the views open to the east where the AT leads along the upper edge of Dutch Shoe Rock, a massive stone slope, scant of vegetation, that delivers sweeping vistas to the east for 0.3 mile. Serene Lake Rutherford lies below, while wooded ridges meld with farms and woods in the distance.

You'll return via the Iris Trail. This broad path was part of the Olmsted Brothers' plan for High Point Park. When High Point Park was created in 1923, its commissioners knew they had to develop a plan for it, and they went to the crème de la crème of

Soak in views of Sawmill Pond in the foreground and the Delaware River gorge in the distance

park designers: the Olmsted Brothers of Brookline, Massachusetts. The firm's founder, Frederick Law Olmsted, co-designed New York's Central Park, the US Capitol grounds, and numerous other city and state parks; his sons continued the tradition. The Olmsteds proposed a broad development plan for High Point, but only a portion of it had been implemented by the early 1930s when the economic crunch caused by the Great Depression put an end to park development plans.

Luckily, the Iris Trail was completed by the Civilian Conservation Corps (CCC). Hiking along it, you'll perhaps expect to see irises in season, but you won't. So how did it get the name? High Point State Park headquarters (off NJ 23 not far from the current parking area for this hike) is located in a building built by the park in 1941 in the CCC style of the era. Originally intended to be a visitor center and "teahouse" (i.e., serving light refreshments), it was originally called the "Iris Inn," after the blue flag irises that grow (even now) in the pond in front of it.

A major highlight of the hike is Lake Rutherford, originally dubbed "Sand Pond" in the 1800s. When John Rutherfurd, a wealthy businessman from Bergen County, started buying up tens of thousands of acres in the Kittatinny Mountains in the mid-1800s, it was perhaps inevitable that a lake should be named after him. "Sand Pond" became "Lake Rutherfurd" in 1897. By the mid-twentieth century, most of the Rutherfurd family had changed the spelling to the more modern "Rutherford," and so too did the lake's name change. This is a natural lake raised by a dam in the late 1800s to supply extra

Looking out from Dutch Shoe Rock

waterpower to mills operating on Clove Brook in the valley below. Most lakes in these mountains were home to a summer colony or hotel, and this was no exception. So, as you walk by, think of the lake's past as first a smaller natural tarn, then a summer home colony, and now a park, preserving New Jersey's natural heritage.

Gazing down the shore of Lake Rutherford

MILES AND DIRECTIONS

0.0 Leave south from the Appalachian Trail parking area on a blue-blazed connector trail. Pass a little wetland, then enter hickory, oak, and maple woods. Pass rock fences.

0.2 Meet the Iris Trail. This will be your return route. For now, stay straight on the blue-blazed connector, still climbing toward the top of Kittatinny Mountain.

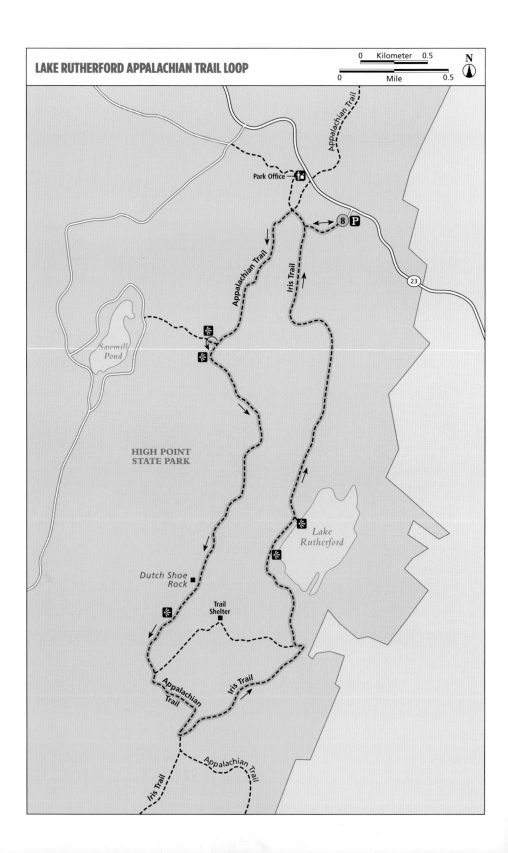

LAKE RUTHERFORD APPALACHIAN TRAIL LOOP

0   Kilometer   0.5

0   Mile   0.5

N

Appalachian Trail

Park Office

8 P

23

Appalachian Trail

Iris Trail

Sawmill
Pond

HIGH POINT
STATE PARK

Lake
Rutherford

Dutch Shoe
Rock

Trail
Shelter

Appalachian
Trail

Iris Trail

Iris Trail

Appalachian Trail

0.3 Meet the Appalachian Trail at a four-way intersection. A trail goes straight for the park office, but we head left on the AT, southbound, in oaks and hickories with a ferny understory. Soon skirt alongside a sheer bluff.

1.0 The Blue Dot Trail comes in on your right. Follow it downhill to a rock outcrop where you can gaze down on Sawmill Pond and its camping area, with the gorge of the Delaware River and Pennsylvania's Pocono Plateau in the distance. Backtrack, then resume the AT southbound. Shortly pass a second view to the west.

1.4 Skirt a mean boulder field, then climb a bit.

2.4 Come to your first view from Dutch Shoe Rock. Here, the rock slab clears a vista of Lake Rutherford below and a wealth of forested ridges and farm valleys beyond. Continue along the AT as it skirts the top of Dutch Shoe Rock, opening other vistas.

2.7 Pass the last view from Dutch Shoe Rock. Walk out on the sloped outcrop to experience this geological phenomenon. Ahead, the trail starts descending.

3.0 A spur trail leads left to the Rutherford trail shelter. It you want to overnight, make sure to contact the state park beforehand to obtain an overnight parking permit.

3.4 Reach a trail intersection. Turn left on the foot-friendly wide and easy Iris Trail. Begin a half-mile descent, crossing a few wet springs.

4.1 Make a sharp left, avoiding private property. Ahead, a spur trail leads left to the Rutherford trail shelter. Stay right with the Iris Trail, aiming for Lake Rutherford.

4.6 Bridge a stream and approach Lake Rutherford, seen through the trees. Ahead, pass an outcrop on the right, affording a partial vista of the 66-acre natural lake, augmented through impoundment.

4.8 A spur trail leads right and downhill to the shoreline of Lake Rutherford. This user-created path affords your best direct access of the lake from this hike. After viewing Lake Rutherford, resume northerly on the Iris Trail, gently yet sporadically gaining elevation as you turn away from the water.

5.6 Pass near a cluster of squarish glacial boulders.

6.3 Return to the blue-blazed connector after crossing a small stream. Turn right here, backtracking toward the parking area.

6.5 Arrive back at the trailhead, completing the ridge and lake loop.

9 WALLKILL REFUGE LOOP

This circuit hike at Wallkill National Wildlife Refuge offers a variety of attractions. A good family day hike, you begin in the upper Wallkill River valley, cruising past distant views of the Wallkill River below and hills beyond. Descend to river bottoms for watery looks and birding opportunities. The last part of the hike traverses fields and woods to visit a surprising waterfall before climbing back to the trailhead.

Start: Refuge visitor parking
Distance: 2.5-mile loop
Difficulty: Easy–moderate
Elevation change: +-369 feet
Maximum grade: 6% downhill grade for 0.4 mile
Hiking time: About 1.3 hours
Seasons/schedule: Year-round; summer can be hot
Fees and permits: None
Dog friendly: No, pets not allowed
Trail surface: Grass, forested natural surface

Land status: National wildlife refuge
Nearest town: Hamburg
Other trail users: None
Maps to consult: Dagmar Dale Trail Map
Amenities available: Restrooms at refuge parking area
Cell service: Good
Trail contact: Lenape National Wildlife Refuge Complex, (973) 702-7266, www.fws.gov/refuge/Wallkill_River

FINDING THE TRAILHEAD

From Hamburg, take NJ 23 north for 3.1 miles, then turn right on Glenwood Road and follow it for 1.5 miles to turn left into the refuge. Follow the main road a short distance to a large visitor parking area with a restroom building. Trailhead GPS: 41.200688,-74.565150

THE HIKE

This excellent short hike—an ideal family hike—leads you through both the uplands and the bottomlands of the Wallkill River valley, within the preserved scenic confines of Wallkill National Wildlife Refuge, an important natural spot in this part of New Jersey. In fact, the refuge has been identified as a priority focus area for waterfowl management in the Garden State, from teal to ducks to swans, as well as forest and grassland birds such as meadowlarks and sparrows.

Additionally, the Wallkill River valley has a long history of providing humans with what they need, going all the way back to the Paleo-Indian Period some 10,000 years ago. Archaeologists have discovered prehistoric chert quarries along the Wallkill, where indigenous New Jerseyites came to obtain the very fine-grained stone they used to fashion spear points, scrapers, knives, and arrowheads. Native American occupation of the Wallkill River valley was continuous up to the 1700s, when the first Europeans started to settle in the valley. A number of prehistoric sites exist within the wildlife refuge.

Early settlers, too, utilized the chert deposits—not for arrowheads but for flints for their muskets and pistols. They also obtained fish from the river, using weir-nets to trap

Clouds loom over the Wallkill River valley.

eels and other fish by the barrelful. They were then salted down and shipped out to the city for sale. The uplands were fine farming areas—good, deep, rich soils—and they were cleared by the mid-1700s. But early farmers had a hard time farming this soggy bottomland: Though the earth was rich, it flooded both regularly and severely, which led the agriculturists to give the area the mournful appellation "The Drowned Lands." The lower areas on this hike were routinely under 3 to 5 feet of water in the 1700s and early 1800s.

In the late 1700s, settlers tried to un-drown the land by digging drainage canals, but with minimal effect. It was not until the mid-1800s, with the construction of a huge drainage canal near Denton, New York, toward its mother stream the Hudson River, that the Wallkill was effectively drained. These flat farmlands then became a growers' paradise, with the northern portion of the region, around Pine Island, New York, remaining a preeminent onion-producing region today.

Rich, prosperous farms dotted the Wallkill Valley, like the one occupied as refuge headquarters today. Though the large dairy barn burned in the 1990s, the farmhouse—now headquarters—remains. Industrialist Gustav Nyselius, a Swedish émigré, owned the farm in the 1950s; an avid avocational farmer, he bottled and sold his own milk. He named the farm Dagmar Dale Farm after his wife, Dagmar Nyselius. Dagmar Dale Farm was the last farm in Vernon Township to bottle and deliver its own milk, and the history behind the name is preserved with the Dagmar Dale Trail.

This wildlife refuge also includes wildflowers in season.

On this hike you will see the valley below from on high, as well as views of the Wallkill River up close. Grab more views of the upper valley where you started, crossing open meadows and rich woods, where you will find a perky little waterfall tumbling over a stone ledge before returning to the trailhead. ***Note:*** Bring a hat, as much of the hike is in open, exposed terrain. Also, the hike is better done in drier conditions, as the grassy trails and meadows can soak your pants and shoes to the bone.

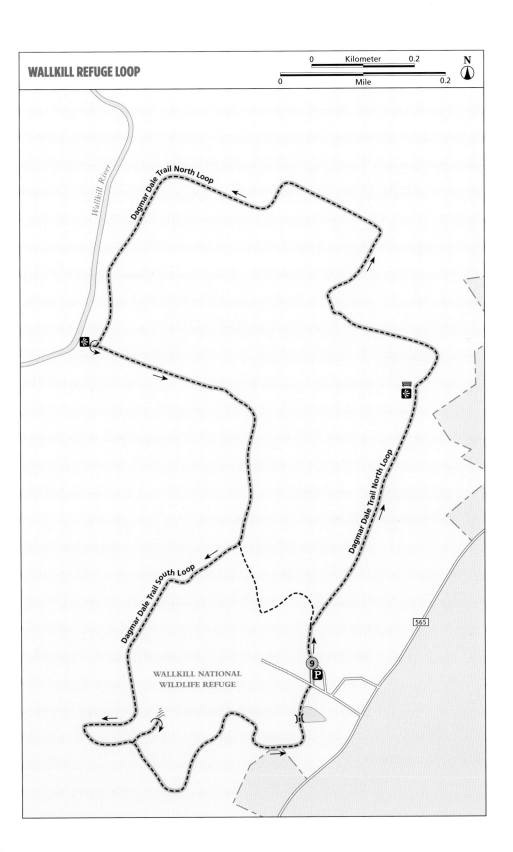

WALLKILL REFUGE LOOP

0   Kilometer   0.2

0   Mile   0.2

N

Wallkill River

Dagmar Dale Trail North Loop

Dagmar Dale Trail North Loop

Dagmar Dale Trail South Loop

WALLKILL NATIONAL
WILDLIFE REFUGE

565

9

P

MILES AND DIRECTIONS

0.0 Leave from the north end of the visitor parking area on the Dagmar Dale North Loop on a wide grassy path traveling north. Just ahead, the other end of the North Loop goes left. Stay straight with a grassy hill to your right and woods to your left. Interpretive signage enhances the hike.

0.4 Reach a bench and a view. Here, panoramas open of the Wallkill River valley below, with the Kittatinny Mountains and High Point State Park in the distance. Continue the hike, turning west downhill along a line of woods where walnut trees grow big. More views open as you descend.

1.0 Turn left, southerly, in partly wooded bottoms of the Wallkill River.

1.2 A spur trail goes right to the Wallkill River and an old bridge site. Today, only the abutments remain. After the up-close look at the Wallkill, turn away from the river, eastbound along a willow-bordered stream running to your right and a field to your left. Soon enter full-blown woods.

1.6 Come to a trail intersection. Here, the Dagmar Dale North Loop leaves left but we stay right, joining the Dagmar Dale South Loop. Continue trekking through tall woods.

1.9 Bridge a rocky stream, then open onto a field. Turn sharply left on a U-turn.

2.0 Split left, taking the spur trail to a waterfall, dropping 10 or so feet down a tiered ledge, bordered by preserved hemlocks. Backtrack and rejoin the South Loop, ascending into a drier woodland of cedar and walnut. Come within sight of Glenwood Road.

2.4 Bridge the creek of the waterfall.

2.5 Arrive back at the trailhead, completing the wildlife refuge hike.

10 PINWHEEL VISTA VIA POCHUCK VALLEY

Join the Appalachian Trail for a hiking adventure low and high. First, traverse the wetlands of the Vernon Valley atop thousands of feet of boardwalk that are not only fun to hike but present unique vistas across these eye-pleasing land- and waterscapes. Next comes the large suspension bridge over Pochuck Creek, replete with views. Return to terra firma, walking through woods and occasional boardwalks to cross the iron bridge over Wawayanda Creek. Work through more wetlands, then cross a pasture with big views of Wawayanda Mountain before making the extremely rocky ascent on the famed Stairway to Heaven, first to Annie's Bluff then rising through more boulder gardens to an outstanding panorama from Pinwheel Vista.

Start: NJ 517 trailhead
Distance: 7.2 miles out and back
Difficulty: Moderate, does have 600-foot climb
Elevation change: +-988 feet
Maximum grade: 20% grade for 0.4 mile
Hiking time: About 3.8 hours
Seasons/schedule: Year-round; boardwalks can be icy in winter
Fees and permits: None
Dog friendly: Yes, on leash, if your dog likes boardwalks

Trail surface: Boardwalk, natural surface
Land status: National scenic trail, state park
Nearest town: Vernon
Other trail users: None
Maps to consult: Appalachian Trail Map—Pochuck Boardwalk
Amenities available: None
Cell service: Good
Trail contact: Wawayanda State Park, (973) 853-4462, www.nj.gov/dep/parksandforests

FINDING THE TRAILHEAD

From Hamburg, take NJ 94 North for 2.4 miles, then stay left on McAfee Glenwood Road and follow it for 3.9 miles. Turn left on CR 517, staying with CR 517/McAfee Glenwood Road for 1.6 more miles to a roadside parking area on your right. This is a limited parking area, so be considerate. Trailhead GPS: 41.235020,-74.480714

THE HIKE

This hike makes for a memorable Appalachian Trail (AT) experience, one of New Jersey's greatest contributions to the greatest hiking trail of them all. Most of the AT passes through the "green tunnel" of the mountains, but here you get to experience a genuinely pastoral walk through meadowlands, farm fields, and pastures—mostly flat and easy—as well as an extensive segment of elevated boardwalk, a high suspension bridge, traditional stream spans, and low, narrow bog walkways. It begins on CR 517, known in the early 1800s as the Pochuck Turnpike.

"Pochuck" was the name for most of this area in years gone by, though exactly where "Pochuck" was or what it means remains a subject of debate. There's Pochuck Mountain

Long boardwalks lead through flowery wetlands.

(immediately to the west of this hike) and Pochuck Creek (which we cross); most of the area between or around the two at one time was called "Pochuck." Some sources claim it's a Native American Lenape word meaning "an out-of-the-way place; a corner or recess," referring to the mountains being easterly outliers of the New Jersey Highlands to the west. Ask an old-timer around here where or what "Pochuck" is, and they'll say: Pochuck is a state of mind.

For the first sixty years of the Appalachian Trail's existence here, it followed old country roads across the Vernon and Wallkill Valleys between Wawayanda Mountain and High Point. But such road walks were not always safe and became less bucolic as the decades passed and housing development boomed. By the late 1970s, efforts were under way to move the AT to its own corridor, but this required massive trail rerouting. It was a cooperative effort involving volunteers and staff from the New York–New Jersey Trail Conference and the Appalachian Trail Conference working in conjunction with the land-managing agencies, the New Jersey Department of Environmental Protection and the National Park Service. The old route up Wawayanda Mountain (a boulder scramble) was abandoned and an alternate route laid out. The reroute up Wawayanda Mountain has been dubbed "The Stairway to Heaven" and is a rugged trek through a big, bewildering, and beautiful boulder garden.

The valley route was even more difficult to navigate and build, involving the crossing of wetlands and rivers. The Pochuck Creek meadowlands were bridged in 1995 with a 150-foot suspension bridge that you will savor on this hike. The adjacent meadowlands

This boardwalk is another New Jersey Appalachian Trail surprise.

were spanned with 1.5 miles of boardwalk built on nearly 900 metal piers sunk as deep as 20 feet into the mire. The three-year project involved some 9,000 hours of volunteer labor, and it's spectacular—more boardwalk, seemingly, than Atlantic City!

Near Wawayanda Creek, the hike passes through an area rich in Native American archaeological significance (a few miles north of here is the Black Creek Site State and National Prehistoric District, a major archaeological site now part of Wawayanda State Park). The limestone rock here contains deposits of chert that the Native Americans quarried to make tools.

The trail also passes through active farm fields and pastures. The Rickey family has been farming near here since the Revolutionary War, and the Van Dokkenburg farm adjacent to it is likewise one of the oldest and most beautiful in the region. A boardwalk leads you across a large cow pasture, while Wawayanda Mountain looms ever closer on the horizon. They may swim with the dolphins in Florida, but in this part of New Jersey we hike with the bovines. Then you start your ascent from the base of the peak, working through the stony slope, seeming all forest from a distance and all rock in the near. The view from Annie's Bluff warms you up, then Pinwheel Vista delivers the final reward. And you can look back where you've been—and the route of the AT—in amazement.

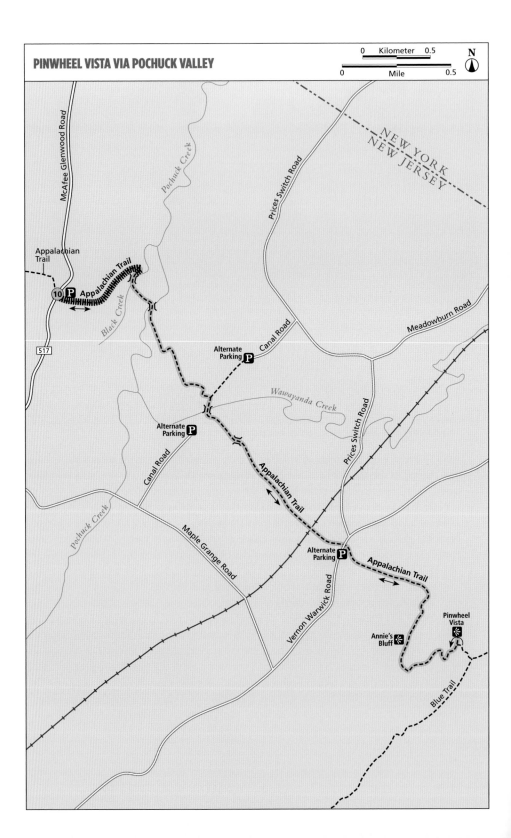

PINWHEEL VISTA VIA POCHUCK VALLEY

0   Kilometer   0.5

0   Mile   0.5

N

McAfee Glenwood Road

Pochuck Creek

Prices Switch Road

NEW YORK
NEW JERSEY

Appalachian
Trail

Appalachian Trail

10 P

Black Creek

Meadowburn Road

Canal Road

Alternate
Parking P

517

Wawayanda Creek

Alternate
Parking P

Canal Road

Prices Switch Road

Appalachian Trail

Pochuck Creek

Maple Grange Road

Alternate
Parking P

Appalachian Trail

Vernon Warwick Road

Annie's
Bluff

Pinwheel
Vista

Blue Trail

MILES AND DIRECTIONS

0.0 From the parking area, leave north, walking along the shoulder of CR 517, then reach the Appalachian Trail. Head right, northbound, traveling east into the Pochuck Marsh. Soon join the famed boardwalk, meandering through the wetlands, pocked with tree islands.

0.4 Join dry land in forest for a bit.

0.5 Rejoin the boardwalk.

0.6 Traverse the small bridge over Black Creek. Continue in the marsh, going on and off boardwalks.

0.8 Cross the elevated span over Pochuck Creek. Enjoy looks across the marsh from the perch.

1.0 Enter woods and dry ground in forest. Curve past old rock walls.

1.4 Come to gated Canal Road, now a trail with alternate parking. Head right on the wide grassy track, then cross the iron bridge over Wawayanda Creek. Head left, still with the AT, just after crossing the stream. Cruise a mix of wetland and woods.

1.7 Bridge an unnamed small branch, still crossing wetlands and land, often using low plank boardwalk bridges. Ahead, roll through lightly hilly woods.

2.2 Cross railroad tracks, then reach an open pasture, opening up vistas of Wawayanda Mountain. Cross the pasture on a long, low plank walkway.

2.4 Come to Vernon Warwick Road and another alternate parking area, holding about ten cars. Continue the AT toward Wawayanda Mountain, rising through cedar-dominated woods, also crossing a power line en route.

2.8 Reach the rocky base of the mountain and begin climbing an extremely rocky path. This section is known as the Stairway to Heaven but it could also be called the "Boulder Garden from Hell."

3.1 Reach Annie's Bluff, where an outcrop delivers a westerly view. Continue surmounting the stony mountainside.

3.5 Reach a trail intersection. Here, split left with a blue-blazed trail near a huge rock pile.

3.6 Come to Pinwheel Vista, an open-ledge perch with an outstanding view of the Wawayanda Creek valley through which you hiked, with the New Jersey Highlands rising in the background. Backtrack to the trailhead.

7.2 Arrive back at the trailhead, completing the rewarding Appalachian Trail trek.

11 WAWAYANDA LAKE LOOP

This enjoyable trek encircles big Wawayanda Lake, rolling through regal woods along friendly trails. Start at the busy swim beach end of the lake, then circle the west shoreline to the impoundment's upper reaches. Return via the east side, appreciating the many lake views you get as the trail travels along the shore. Elevation changes aren't bad, making it an "easy-ish" longer hike. Additionally, the state park features numerous other offerings to enhance your hiking adventure.

Start: Large swim beach parking area
Distance: 5.2-mile loop
Difficulty: Moderate
Elevation change: +-471 feet
Maximum grade: 5% downhill grade for 0.3 mile
Hiking time: About 2.6 hours
Seasons/schedule: Year-round
Fees and permits: Entry fee charged Memorial Day through Labor Day
Dog friendly: Yes, on leash, but keep dog off beach
Trail surface: Forested natural surface

Land status: State park
Nearest town: West Milford
Other trail users: None
Maps to consult: Wawayanda State Park
Amenities available: Restrooms, picnic area, playground near parking area
Cell service: Good
Trail contact: Wawayanda State Park, (973) 853-4462, www.nj.gov/dep/parksandforests

FINDING THE TRAILHEAD

From West Milford, take White Road north for 1.7 miles, then veer left onto Warwick Turnpike and follow it for 4.2 miles to turn left into Wawayanda State Park. Follow the main park road for 2 miles, then take the signed left turn for Wawayanda Lake and shortly dead-end in the very large Wawayanda Lake parking area. The hike starts in the northwest corner of the parking area, on the north side of the restroom building. Trailhead GPS: 41.190557,-74.429267

THE HIKE

Big Wawayanda State Park encompasses over 35,000 acres of ridges, lakes, streams, marshes, and more, delivering a lot of greenspace and helping New Jersey to retain its moniker as the Garden State.

Wawayanda Lake, with over 5 miles of shoreline, was originally two smaller ponds called the Double Ponds and was first dammed in the 1790s to power a sawmill and gristmill. Local forests fed the sawmill, and mountain farms grew grain for the mill. Where you will hike was once remote country farms, the settlers extracting a living from the steep, stony soils. One mountain settlement—the village of Cherry Ridge—was located near the southern end of Wawayanda Lake. Between land acquisitions for the state park and watershed, it's virtually vanished today. There was iron in these mountains, too, the first mines being opened during the Revolutionary War.

The Double Ponds were raised again in 1845. That year, William L. Ames, a Massachusetts industrialist, bought the property and built an iron furnace (located just a

Looking upon a cove in Wawayanda Lake

little ways off this loop), a new gristmill and sawmill, and other structures, forming an industrial village. Wawayanda Furnace consumed roughly an acre of timberland a day as fuel, with ore coming from the nearby mines. Ames, and later his family, owned the property until 1869, when it passed through a variety of other owners. These included the Thomas Iron Company of Pennsylvania and, briefly, Standard Oil Company.

By 1900, most of Wawayanda's industry had faded away, but now the property was becoming more and more popular as a place for recreation. This included one of the first YMCA summer camps in US history, Camp Wawayanda, which operated here from the 1880s through 1918. The Wawayanda tract was later owned by the New Jersey Zinc Company, which harvested mine props here for the Franklin and Ogdensburg mines. Lake Wawayanda was for years ringed with summer cabins leased by the zinc company to its employees, torn down after it became a state park.

The property was purchased by the State of New Jersey in 1963, one of the first acquisitions of the Green Acres program. In the 1960s, Wawayanda's water resources were tapped by the city of Newark. Droughts in the 1960s led the city to get permission to construct a pump house and pipeline, which drew water from Lake Wawayanda and deposited it in streams feeding Canistear Reservoir. Last used around 1980, the pump house sites and the pipeline remain interesting reminders of long-ago water emergencies. Similarly, the old furnace, stone foundations, and archaeological remains of Wawayanda Village are fascinating relics of the site's industrial heritage.

Wawayanda Lake is a time-honored New Jersey recreation destination.

The modern-day legacy of Wawayanda Lake State Park is its emphasis on outdoor recreation and preservation. The refuge is home to three designated state natural areas and around 60 miles of hiking and bicycling trails that course through hill and dale. The big swim beach, featuring a fine panorama up Wawayanda Lake, is open from Memorial Day weekend through Labor Day. Paddling enthusiasts can bring their own kayak, canoe, or sailboard, or you can rent one during the warm season. A large picnic area near the trailhead makes a pre- or post-hike meal an easy, enticing experience. Anglers can vie for landlocked salmon and rainbow, brown, or lake trout, as well as pickerel, perch, and bass. Of course, you may just want to relax along the shore of Wawayanda Lake and watch everybody else have a good time—after you had yours.

MILES AND DIRECTIONS

0.0 Start in the northwest corner of the large beach parking area near the restrooms. Begin following the orange blazes of the Wawayanda Lake Trail. Head across the grass toward the lake, then follow the orange blazes right, entering woods near a small shaded picnic area (tracing the old Pump House Trail route), gently climbing away from the lake on a wide trail under oaks, beeches, and maples.

0.2 Stay left as a spur leads right to Wawayanda Road. Mountain laurel and bracken ferns border the path.

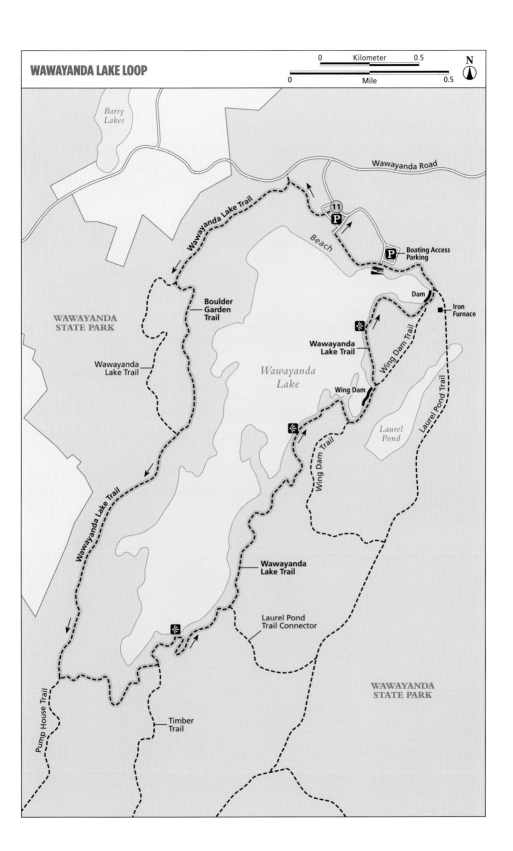

WAWAYANDA LAKE LOOP

Barry Lakes

Wawayanda Road

11 P

Boating Access Parking

P

Beach

Dam

Iron Furnace

Wawayanda Lake Trail

Boulder Garden Trail

WAWAYANDA STATE PARK

Wawayanda Lake Trail

Wawayanda Lake

Wawayanda Lake Trail

Wing Dam Trail

Wing Dam

Laurel Pond

Laurel Pond Trail

Wing Dam Trail

Wawayanda Lake Trail

Laurel Pond Trail Connector

WAWAYANDA STATE PARK

Pump House Trail

Timber Trail

N

0   Kilometer   0.5
0   Mile   0.5

0.7 Split left on the more difficult Boulder Garden Trail as it skirts around then bridges a feeder branch of the lake, bordered in marsh. The path may be wet in places here. Ahead, climb, gaining glimpses of the lake to your left.

1.2 The Boulder Garden Trail takes you beside a remarkable upended glacial boulder.

1.3 Rejoin the Wawayanda Lake Trail. The hiking becomes easier due to the foot-friendly trail bed. Keep south in woods, back from the lake.

1.9 A closed trail leads left. This is one of a few now-closed paths that went to pump house sites.

2.1 The Pump House Trail keeps straight while we stay left with the Wawayanda Lake Trail, now heading easterly in swampy woods, rich in yellow birches and evergreens, and scads of mountain laurel.

2.4 Rock hop a tributary of Wawayanda Lake, then step over a huge pipeline, once used to pump water to Newark long ago.

2.7 The Timber Trail splits right. Stay left with the orange blazes.

2.8 Come to a small stream feeding into Wawayanda Lake. Enjoy your first good look into the impoundment since the trailhead. Hike north along a wooded slope with the impoundment visible through the trees to your left, crossing occasional intermittent tributaries flowing toward the lake.

3.2 The Laurel Pond Trail Connector leaves right, but we stay left with the orange-blazed Wawayanda Lake Trail. Travel a rocky hillside on a singletrack footpath.

3.9 Return to the shoreline and begin a segment with views aplenty of the nearby lake islands as well as the swim beach to the north. Ahead, circle around a cove.

4.1 Stay left as a leg of the Wing Dam Trail splits right. Ahead, cross the outflow of the wing dam as a waterfall flows below the trail.

4.2 Split left with the Wawayanda Lake Trail, cruising along the shore as the Wing Dam Trail stays straight. Ahead, relish more lake panoramas.

4.7 Meet the other end of the Wing Dam Trail after passing through where cabins once stood. Cross the main lake dam (to reach the historic iron furnace, split right after the dam), then stay left along the shore, passing more lake views before reentering woods then curving around the north shore of the lake.

5.0 Pass by a boat launch, boathouse, and restroom as well as a boating access parking area. Continue along the shore, passing through a wooded picnic area.

5.2 Arrive back at the beach parking area, ending the hike after passing between a picnic area, playground, and the beach.

12 TERRACE POND

Make a rewarding loop among the hills, bogs, and outcrops of specially designated Bearfort Natural Area, part of Wawayanda State Park. Work your way through deep woods to a highland bog, then begin trekking along the striated ridges that define Bearfort Mountain to reach mystical Terrace Pond, one of the finest aquatic destinations in the Garden State. Soak in the tarn's serenity, then work your way over rock ridges, with some outcrops presenting views as they jut above the forest roof.

Start: Clinton Road trailhead	**Trail surface:** Forested natural
Distance: 4.7-mile loop	surface, naked rock segments
Difficulty: Moderate, does have short	**Land status:** State park
ups and downs	**Nearest town:** West Milford
Elevation change: +-623 feet	**Other trail users:** None
Maximum grade: 12% downhill grade	**Maps to consult:** Abram S. Hewitt
for 0.4 mile	State Forest
Hiking time: About 2.7 hours	**Amenities available:** None
Seasons/schedule: Year-round	**Cell service:** Good
Fees and permits: None	**Trail contact:** Wawayanda State Park,
Dog friendly: Yes, on leash only	(973) 853-4462, www.nj.gov/dep/
	parksandforests

FINDING THE TRAILHEAD

From West Milford, take White Road north for 1.7 miles, then veer left onto Warwick Turnpike and follow it for 1.8 miles to turn left onto Clinton Road. Stay with Clinton Road for 1.7 miles to reach the parking area on your right, with the actual trail to the left side of the road. The parking lot is signed P-7. **Note:** If your vehicle is here after 6:00 p.m. it is subject to towing. Trailhead GPS: 41.142926,-74.407374

THE HIKE

The Terrace Pond West Trail is your conduit throughout this hike. In 2020, the trails of Wawayanda State Park and adjoining Abram S. Hewitt State Forest (the two units are managed together) were rehabbed, reblazed, and renamed, resulting in a more favorable situation for hikers like us. The two units—despite having dense human populations on parts of their boundaries—are important habitats for all sorts of wildlife, including the specially designated Bearfort Mountain Natural Area. Large unbroken forests are a key component of this part of New Jersey being so critical to wildlife. A large blue heron rookery calls Wawayanda State Park home. Barred owls, Cooper's hawks, and red-shouldered hawks find this medley of naked rock striations, bogs, mixed hardwood forests, and scrub oaks a fine place for a home.

Of course, predatory birds are just a part of the web of life here. It is always exciting to spot a porcupine. You may have a ruffed grouse startle you while flying away. Black bears are prevalent in this area, and beavers are found near the ponds and wetlands, along with otters. Foxes and coyotes are elusive but can be seen in the morning or evening.

This highland bog is part of the Bearfort Natural Area.

Pileated woodpeckers will alert you to their presence with their hammering on trees in search of insects.

Interestingly, these highlands are a vital home to bobcats, listed as endangered in New Jersey. Decades back, with the state's bobcat population in peril, bobcats were captured in Maine and successfully relocated in Bearfort Mountain Natural Area to bolster the state's numbers. (They still meow with that funny Maine accent!) Although listed as an endangered species in the state, the bobcat population in New Jersey is recovering from its low a half century back.

So what do bobcats eat? They hunt rabbits, turkeys, squirrels, and mice using their exceptional hearing and vision, as well as soft footpads to sneak up on these critters that also inhabit the state park and state forest. Typically, elusive bobcats will den in small rock shelters or under fallen trees. A bobcat litter is normally two or three kits, usually breaking out on their own after ten to twelve months. In the wild, bobcats can live a dozen years. Northern New Jersey is the state's feline stronghold, with a population varying between 200 and 400 animals. Central and southern New Jersey have far fewer bobcats. Most unnatural bobcat deaths are caused by vehicle "interactions," primarily young cats, two years or younger, getting hit while seeking out territory of their own. Therefore, when driving this area, especially at night, be aware.

Terrace Pond can be a tranquil place.

MILES AND DIRECTIONS

0.0 Cross over to the east side of Clinton Road and reach the signed trailhead. Here, the Terrace Pond West Trail goes right or left. Go right, southeasterly, making a counter-clockwise circuit. Enter chestnut oaks and mountain laurel and soon cross your first bog on a boardwalk. Roll over wooded hills broken by wooded wet areas.

0.9 Join the first open linear rock striation. You are walking southbound, then pull away from the stone spine in rolling woods. The hiking is easy and mostly level.

1.5 Abruptly turn left, joining an old woods road. Begin circling by a large wetland to your left.

1.7 The Terrace Pond West Trail turns left, now northbound, still keeping the wetland, rife with tree snags, to your left.

2.1 Reach an intersection. Stay left with the Terrace Pond West Trail, as a connector trail keeps straight to the Terrace Pond North Trail.

2.2 Leave the wetland behind, then climb back into xeric sassafras, oak, maple, and blueberry woods. Ahead, pass the end of the Terrace Pond Red Trail entering on your right.

2.5 Make a short but steep descent into an uber-rocky streambed, then climb back out to a rocky ridgeline of puddingstone with a view to the south. Work along an angled stone ledge. Use caution in wet weather hereabouts.

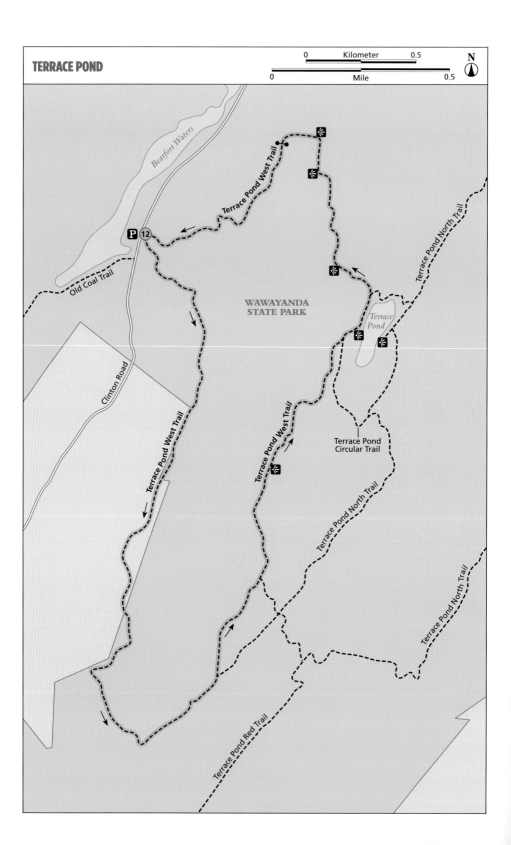

TERRACE POND

0   Kilometer   0.5

0   Mile   0.5

N

Beaufort Waters

Terrace Pond West Trail

P 12

Old Coal Trail

Terrace Pond North Trail

WAWAYANDA
STATE PARK

Terrace
Pond

Clinton Road

Terrace Pond West Trail

Terrace Pond West Trail

Terrace Pond
Circular Trail

Terrace Pond North Trail

Terrace Pond North Trail

Terrace Pond Red Trail

3.0 The trail makes a short but steep climb up a boulder-strewn ledge, then cuts through an almost funnel-like spot between low ledges. Descend sharply, gaining glimpses of Terrace Pond to your right.

3.2 Reach a trail intersection at the base of a rock ridge. Here, the Terrace Pond Circular Trail splits right and is a good addition to this hike if you want to add a little mileage. Our hike stays left.

3.3 Emerge at Terrace Pond after crossing more lichen-covered ridges. This spot offers a fine view of the lake and access to its shore. However, No Swimming signs are posted. Help keep this popular spot, perhaps the most visited backcountry locale in the area, clean and pristine. Continue along the shore, passing more outcrops with rewarding water views.

3.5 The other end of the Terrace Pond Circular Trail enters on the right, but we stay straight with the Terrace Pond West Trail. Begin a demanding section, surmounting ledges, going against the grain.

3.6 Emerge at an upthrust stone knob, rising above the forest. It offers a good look to the west. Work your way north and west, going off and on linear ridges.

3.9 A spur left leads up to another stone upthrust and a northerly view. Descend once back on the main trail.

4.0 Open onto a gas line clearing. Head left, downhill along the clearing, relishing more views.

4.1 Leave the clearing, left, aiming for the trailhead. Shortly pass around a pole gate. Roll through level, somewhat swampy woods on stepping stones.

4.7 Arrive back at the trailhead, completing the varied hike.

13 **SURPRISE LAKE LOOP**

Savor this rewarding circuit hike at Abram S. Hewitt State Forest. Trek up from Greenwood Lake onto a series of open rock ridges with some of the best vistas in the Garden State. Continue along the ridges to find charming Surprise Lake nestled between them. Clamber westerly over rocks and small vales to discover smaller West Lake. Finally, pick up a segment of the Appalachian Trail as part of your return route. The going is slow on this challenging trek, so take your time and enjoy every footfall.

Start: Lakeside Road near New York border
Distance: 4.0-mile balloon loop
Difficulty: Moderate, does have slow, tough sections
Elevation change: +-1,130 feet
Maximum grade: 15% grade for 0.8 mile
Hiking time: About 3.0 hours
Seasons/schedule: Year-round
Fees and permits: None
Dog friendly: Yes, on leash only

Trail surface: Forested natural surface, lots of naked rock
Land status: State forest
Nearest town: West Milford
Other trail users: None
Maps to consult: Abram S. Hewitt State Forest
Amenities available: None
Cell service: Good
Trail contact: Abrams S. Hewitt State Forest, (973) 853-4462, www.nj.gov/dep/parksandforests

FINDING THE TRAILHEAD

From West Milford, take Marshall Hill Road for 0.6 mile to keep straight, joining Lincoln Avenue for 1 mile. Turn left onto Greenwood Turnpike and follow it for 0.7 mile, then turn right and follow Lakeside Road for 2.5 miles to the trailhead parking area on your left, just across from Greenwood Lake Marina and just before reaching the New York state line. **Note:** The road that is the left turn into the trailhead has state forest parking on the left side and Greenwood Lake Marina equipment on the right side. Parking is limited, so be considerate and don't park on the marina side of the road no matter what. Trailhead GPS: 41.185782,-74.331830

THE HIKE

Abram S. Hewitt State Forest safeguards a series of northeast-to-southwest-running ridges poking their rock ribs between and above popular Greenwood Lake and Upper Greenwood Lake, holding fast against the New York state line. An overhead view of the forest reveals lush woodlands striped with gray lines, the glacially originated bare rock striations that run parallel to one another, collectively known as Bearfort Mountain. They are a major characteristic of this preserve that is also dotted with marshes and bogs as well as moving streams. Stunted pines and hardwoods rising along the naked rock and the geologically fascinating puddingstone formations are two more aspects that distinguish this New Jersey jewel.

Hiking is easily the primary activity at Hewitt State Forest, and the trails are well marked and maintained—and popular. In 2020, the trail system of the 2,000-acre state

Greenwood Lake reflects the morning sunshine.

forest was rehabbed and improved, making a good thing even better. The forest is also an important wildlife corridor, linking the wild highlands of northwest New Jersey with the forests of New York's Hudson River valley, including for black bears, which are numerous in the forest. You would think a high population of the bruins to be a given, since the primary mountain in Hewitt Forest is called Bearfort Mountain. Although the name "Bearfort" might seem apt given New Jersey's very real population of bruins, the name doesn't refer to them. Dating back to the mid-1800s, it is said to originate with a family named Beresford, who owned land on the mountain and had a home near its base. The name had a silent *s*, which led to it later being corrupted to Bearfort.

As you traverse the stone ridges of Bearfort Mountain, bordered with pitch pine–scrub oak forest, you view one of the favorite subjects of leading Hudson River School artist Jasper Francis Cropsey (1823–1900). With his brushes, he depicted Greenwood Lake and its surrounding mountains. One such sunny landscape painting won Cropsey a membership in the National Academy of Design (1844). During this period, he also won the hand of his wife, Maria Cooley, a young woman from Greenwood Lake, and for a period they lived in neighboring Warwick. Over the next forty years, he returned and painted numerous works of this region. So, as you reach various outlooks on Bearfort Mountain, picture yourself entering Cropsey's *View of Greenwood Lake, New Jersey* (1845), and experience all its "primordial essence."

Looking west toward Sawmill Pond and the Delaware Water Gap gorge

In addition to viewing Greenwood Lake from afar, the two smaller bodies of water you visit—Surprise Lake and West Pond—are also treats. Surprise Lake, 11 acres, bordered by marsh and stone, is nestled between rock ridges and truly does come as a surprise as you slowly work up and down the ridges, going against the northwest–southwest grain of the terrain. West Pond is the smaller of the two tarns, and is 4 acres in size. You can enjoy a subtle view of it from an outcrop.

Just know that the going is likely slower than you expect. The trek starts with a 600-foot climb. The multiple views will then slow you down, but it's the east–west travel on the circuit that makes the going sluggish—up over a rock ridge, down into a small moist, wooded valley, then up and down the next striated rock ridge. And hiking along the stone ridges can be challenging, too, as you climb or descend along bare stone. Avoid this hike during wet conditions if you can, due to the naked rock.

MILES AND DIRECTIONS

0.0 Join the State Line Trail, immediately crossing a rocky brook. Ascend, leaving busy Greenwood Lake behind in rocky woods. Pass by cabins near the forest boundary.

0.5 Switchbacks mitigate the steady climb. Large outcrops mix with lesser rocks, pocking the oak forest.

Marsh Pond on a still morn

0.7 Meet the yellow-blazed Ernest Walter Trail. Head left, still climbing. Ahead, open to your first view of Greenwood Lake with the woods, hills, and towns of New Jersey and New York stretching toward the horizon.

0.8 Level off at another view, then keep southwesterly over a linear open rock slab presenting stupendous scenes. Note teardrop-shaped Fox Island in Greenwood Lake. Pines border the rock slabs. Continue walking the open slab, savoring first-rate panoramas. Drift in and out of small tree copses. More views lie ahead.

1.0 Turn westerly into woods. Cross a small bog, typical of what lies between the parallel rock striations. Keep west.

1.2 A short spur leads right to a view of Surprise Lake below. Backtrack and continue the hike, then meet the Bearfort Ridge Trail. It heads left. Stay right with the Ernest Walter Trail, keeping the shore of Surprise Lake to your right, traveling in rhododendron thickets.

1.5 Cross Cooley Brook, then surmount a ridge with a modicum of scrambling. Drop and climb over more ridges divided by boggy forests. The going is slow.

1.6 Emerge at an outcrop with a view at a trail junction. Here, the other end of the Bearfort Ridge Trail splits left. Stay right, westerly, surmounting more rock ridges and little vales on the Ernest Walter Trail.

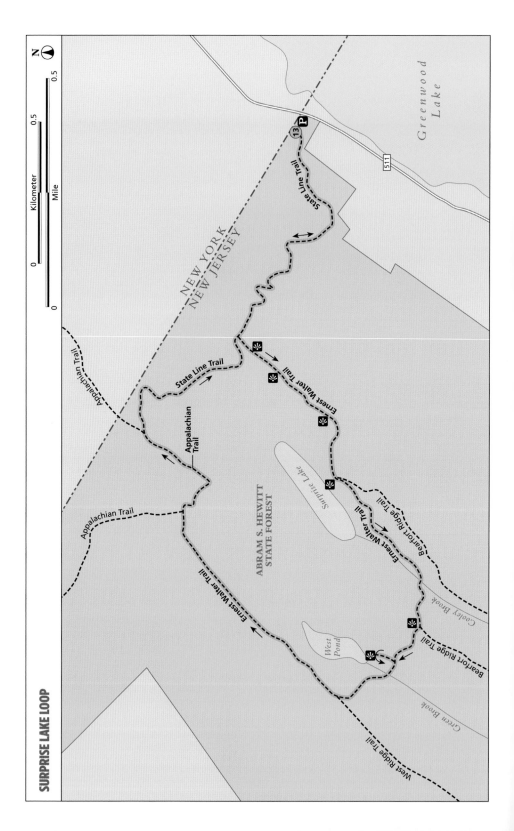

SURPRISE LAKE LOOP

1.7 Stay right with the spur to an outcrop and fine view of marsh-bordered West Pond, and a fine relaxation spot. Backtrack then continue west, stepping over Green Brook, then work over more rock ridges, going against the grain.

2.0 Meet the pink-blazed West Ridge Trail on a stone striation. Stay right, still with the yellow-blazed Ernest Walter Trail. Now, go with the grain along slender, partially vegetated stone avenues. You can see West Pond to your right through the trees.

2.6 Meet the Appalachian Trail (AT). Start beating your way east on the AT, once again going against the grain of the ridges, up and down, then turn north along the grain.

2.9 Leave the AT at a trail intersection on an open rock slab, joining the State Line Trail just before the AT enters New York. Split right, once again fighting the grain downhill toward the marshes north of Surprise Lake.

3.3 Complete the loop portion of the hike upon meeting the Ernest Walter Trail. Stay straight here, backtracking, beginning the descent toward Greenwood Lake.

4.0 Arrive back at the trailhead, completing the vista-rich undulating circuit hike.

14 SAFFIN POND AND HEADLEY OVERLOOK

This double-loop hike takes you through a historic segment of the New Jersey Highlands, now returned to nature as part of Morris County's Mahlon Dickerson Reservation. Start the hike by tracing an old railroad grade past pretty Saffin Pond, with its swim beach, then cross its dam to climb into hills. Pass the reservation's recommended tent campground before curving out to a bluff, where views open of lands and waters to the east and southeast, including Lake Hopatcong, from Headley Overlook. Return through rich woods that reflect the marsh and hill nature of this locale.

Start: Saffin Pond trailhead
Distance: 3.7-mile double loop
Difficulty: Moderate
Elevation change: +-532 feet
Maximum grade: 5% grade for 0.3 mile
Hiking time: About 2.0 hours
Seasons/schedule: Year-round
Fees and permits: None
Dog friendly: Yes, on leash only
Trail surface: Forested natural surface, gravel

Land status: County park
Nearest town: Wharton
Other trail users: None
Maps to consult: Mahlon Dickerson Reservation
Amenities available: Restrooms at trailhead
Cell service: Good
Trail contact: Mahlon Dickerson Reservation, (973) 326-7616, www.morrisparks.net

FINDING THE TRAILHEAD

From exit 34B on I-80 near Wharton, take NJ 15 north for 5 miles to exit right on Weldon Road. Follow Weldon Road for 2.8 miles to the Saffin Pond trailhead on your right. Trailhead GPS: 41.007918,-74.586533

THE HIKE

This hike encompassing water, woods, and overlooks also brings together a number of past historical developments that shaped this part of the New Jersey Highlands—iron, railroads, and canals. After you learn of this past it will come as no surprise that this park was named after early New Jersey titan Mahlon Dickerson (1770–1853), who was involved with all three. Dickerson was a Morris County lawyer, writer, businessman, and politician. Few men in the history of New Jersey filled as many roles as he, including virtually every office from legislator and Supreme Court judge to governor and US senator. The family business was iron mines, and Dickerson named his hilltop Morris County estate "Ferromonte"—Iron Mountain.

Dickerson likely would be happy that the county park named after him includes some of the old Ogden Mine Railroad. Our hike starts out on the rail bed of this once-important railroad, built in 1865. It shipped iron and zinc ore from Sussex County to Nolans Point on Lake Hopatcong. Lake Hopatcong had been dammed and raised to

Come relax at Saffin Pond.

feed the Morris Canal, with its numerous locks and inclined planes. It was a "thirsty" canal that needed a vast water supply. Loaded onto boats, the ore was tugged across the lake to the Morris Canal, where it was shipped out by canal boat. A huge tonnage of ore was shipped this way—over 70,000 tons in 1873 alone. Dickerson would be happy about this, too: The construction of the Morris Canal was a project he advocated while governor. This unique system of shipping (railroad/lake/canal) worked for years.

But in 1881, the Central Railroad of New Jersey acquired and connected with the Ogden Mine Railroad, ending the canal use. The loss in revenue to the canal was but another blow in its long decline. In later years, the Ogden Mine Railroad shipped out the zinc briquettes produced by fabled New Jersey resident Thomas A. Edison's concentrating works near Ogdensburg. By the late 1940s, however, the railroad line saw little use and was scrapped (a part of the old line is a trail, and this hike uses part of it). In 1960, the first parcels of what became Mahlon Dickerson Reservation were purchased. Today the preserve boasts not only trails aplenty but also fine campgrounds for tents and RVs. I've overnighted here and recommend the experience.

The reservation also includes traditional county park–type amenities such as ball fields and picnic areas. The park boasts almost 25 miles of trails within its 3,500-acre boundary. A radio-controlled car track, as well as waters for radio-controlled boats, adds even more possibilities for visitors.

The trail system uses color-coded blazes for different paths. Make sure to download the latest trail map onto your phone. The trails and their markings have changed over time,

Headley Overlook provides a distant view.

but overall the pathway network continues to improve. Despite the plethora of names and color-coded blazes, the hike is easy to follow on the ground.

MILES AND DIRECTIONS

0.0 Leave from the northwest corner of the Saffin Pond parking area and pass around a pole gate, then join a southwesterly track, the old Ogden Mine Railroad Trail.

SAFFIN POND AND HEADLEY OVERLOOK

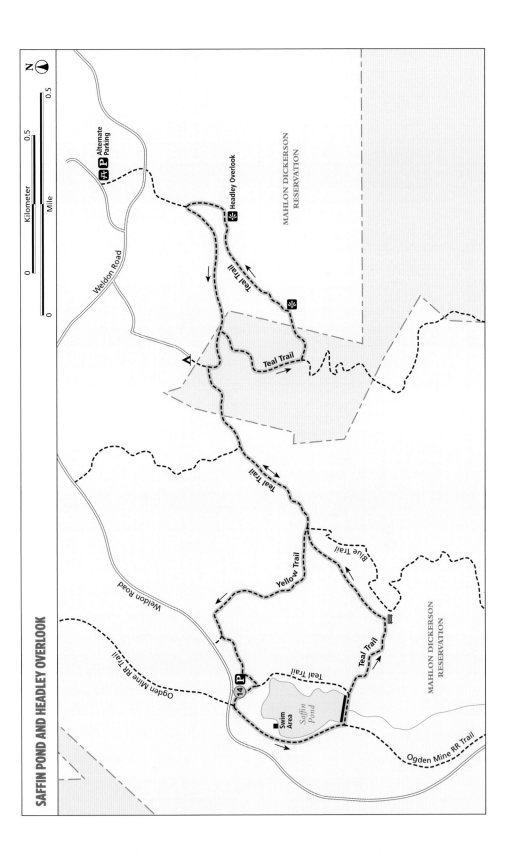

0.2 Pass the swim beach on your left after coming along Saffin Pond.

0.3 The Ogden Mine Railroad Trail keeps straight, southbound, while we turn left. Cross the Saffin Pond arched dam bridge over the pond spillway and quickly reach another intersection. Here, a trail splits left along the pond toward the Saffin Pond parking lot while we keep straight, easterly, climbing away from the pond on the Teal Trail. Climb in rocky hardwoods, heavy in oaks, sugar maples, and beeches.

0.6 Reach a bench and former intersection. Here, a closed trail leaves right and a user-created trail goes straight, climbing a hill. Stay left with the official park path.

0.9 Come to an intersection. Here, the Yellow Trail cuts back acutely left, while the Blue Trail goes right as a singletrack. Stay straight with the Teal Trail, cruising past bouldery areas.

1.1 An unblazed spur heads left to Weldon Road. Stay straight on an old woods road.

1.3 Cross a small brook, then come to another intersection. Here, a short spur leads left to the reservation's tent campground near campsite 8. Stay right, climbing a bit.

1.5 Reach yet another intersection. Stay right here with the Teal Trail, beginning your easterly loop.

1.7 Stay left with the Teal Trail at another intersection. Turn easterly, climbing along a bluff. Gain glimpses through the trees.

1.9 A view opens to the east along the edge of the escarpment in chestnut oaks and hickories interspersed among the stone slabs.

2.1 Come to Headley Overlook after passing through mountain laurel thickets. Gaze south to view Lake Hopatcong and lower-elevation lands east and south. After enjoying the cliffside overlook, follow the path north, away from the overlook.

2.2 Cut a hard left on a doubletrack path. If you go straight—the wrong way—you will soon emerge at Weldon Road.

2.6 Complete the easterly loop and begin backtracking toward the trailhead, shortly passing the spur to the tent campground.

3.1 Split right at a trail intersection, joining the Yellow Trail, turning westerly. Work through wetlands and woods, coming near to Weldon Road. Ahead, a spur goes right to Weldon Road.

3.7 Arrive back at the Saffin Pond trailhead, completing the double-loop hike.

15 THE TOURNE

This undulating loop hike is not only on the top ten New Jersey best hike names list, it also snakes through hill and dale, over glacially landscaped terminal moraine, kettle holes, and puddingstone erratics. Strategically placed benches make for a relaxing tramp. Enjoy the impressive views of the Highlands as well as the Manhattan skyline from the Tourne. Meander through the Wildflower Trail Area or along the banks of lily-covered Birchwood Lake and beside Rattlesnake Meadow, where trails lead through adjacent Richard Wilcox Municipal Park.

Start: McCaffrey Lane trailhead off Norris Road
Distance: 4.4-mile loop
Difficulty: Moderate
Elevation change: +-662 feet
Maximum grade: 15% grade for 0.5 mile
Hiking time: About 2.6 hours
Seasons/schedule: Daily 7:00 a.m. to dusk
Fees and permits: None
Dog friendly: Yes, on leash only

Trail surface: Natural
Land status: Mostly county park, some municipal park
Nearest town: Boonton
Other trail users: Mountain bikers in some areas
Maps to consult: Tourne County Park
Amenities available: Restrooms, picnic area, playground at trailhead
Cell service: Excellent
Trail contact: Tourne County Park, (973) 326-7600, www.morrisparks.net

FINDING THE TRAILHEAD

From exit 45 on I-287 near Boonton, head west on Wooton Street and follow it 0.9 mile to turn right onto Oak Street. Follow Oak Street for 1.1 miles to turn left onto Powerville Road and follow it 0.2 mile to turn right onto Old Denville Road. Follow Old Denville Road 1.1 miles and stay with it 0.2 mile farther as it becomes Norris Road, then turn left onto McCaffrey Lane, entering the park. The trailhead is 0.3 mile ahead on your left, where McCaffrey Lane is gated to prevent thru-traffic. Trailhead GPS: 40.909709,-74.441714

THE HIKE

Like some other hikes in this book, this is a walk through a green oasis on the edge of the great megalopolis. The Tourne is just that: an island of forest at the edge of the great metropolitan sprawl of northeastern New Jersey.

Tourne is Dutch for "tower," and in the 1700s it was almost a generic term for a high promontory with a good view. The Boonton Tourne is particularly associated with Clarence A. DeCamp (1859–1948), the legendary owner of the property who spent his life developing it with roads and trails, and generally making it pleasant for public recreation. Everybody knew who DeCamp was: small, gruff, eccentric, outspoken, and often with an ax in his hand. He was a descendant of Morris County ironmasters, and he poured

Cat toe wildflowers grace the trail.

the same energy into his Tourne property that his ancestors did into mines and forges. It was a de facto public park, and DeCamp had frequent bonfire parties at the summit, where he built a tower. He kept hiking his beloved hill right up until the day before his death at eighty-nine.

Just as today this area is a tangle of highways, so too in the late 1800s was it a tangle of transportation systems, mainly the Morris Canal and railroads (the Delaware, Lackawanna & Western, mainly). The White Trail, also known as the Ogden Trail, which our hike crosses, was originally a railroad spur that was to go from Boonton to Denville. Clarence DeCamp, in fact, worked on the construction of the railroad bed in 1898–99. But though the rail bed was built, no tracks were ever laid, mystifying both DeCamp and others— another failed business scheme, it seems.

The summit of the Tourne, when cut back, has excellent views of New York Harbor and Manhattan, and the trails here are pleasant, easy walking. Like so many parks with a fine view of the city, it has become a memorial for those who died in the Twin Tower attacks on 9/11.

As for the hiking itself, the route follows color-coded trails throughout. The trail system can be a tangle of paths in a small area, so stay abreast of your position. Beware

A southwesterly view from the Tourne

unblazed user-created shortcuts and the like. Although the vast majority of the hike is in Tourne County Park, part of the trek travels through adjacent Richard Wilcox Municipal Park, though the delineations are not signed and you'll be hard-pressed to find evidence you switched properties.

MILES AND DIRECTIONS

0.0 From the parking area, cross McCaffrey Lane and head south on the Red Trail, going away from the Tourne in oak and hickory woods. Run a ridge.

0.4 Cross the Pink Trail in a gap. Stay straight with the Red Trail.

0.5 Cross the Purple Trail at a four-way intersection. Work up a rocky wooded knob. Surmount the rocky knob, then descend by switchbacks.

1.1 Stay with the Red Trail as the Purple Trail splits left twice in a row. Descend toward Birchwood Lake, passing the Pink Trail.

1.5 Come to an intersection near Birchwood Lake and stay left with the Red Trail. Ahead, the White Trail and Purple Trail spur away. Stay with the Red Trail, skirting

You are likely to find a 9/11 memorial atop the Tourne.

around the north side of pretty Birchwood Lake on a gravel track. You are now in Richard Wilcox Municipal Park.

1.7 Split left with the Red Trail, northbound, back on natural-surface track.

2.1 Split left with the Blue Trail, aiming for Rattlesnake Meadow.

2.3 An elevated spur cuts left across Rattlesnake Meadow. Stay with the Blue Trail, passing the remnants of an old springhouse. Work the margin between the meadow to your left and hilly woods to your right.

2.6 Rejoin the Red Trail, still northbound, aiming for a large parking area. Pass through a gate, reentering Tourne County Park. Ahead, stay with the Red Trail as spurs go left and right in a trail nest near an alternate parking area on McCaffrey Lane.

3.0 Reach a large parking area and McCaffrey Lane. Head left on McCaffrey Lane and follow it downhill to cross the stream draining Rattlesnake Meadow. Here, split right, cut through a gate, and enter the Wildflower Trail Area. Explore at your leisure, then keep east to meet the Yellow Trail, a wide gravel road. This is also known as the DeCamp Trail. Begin an extended ascent.

3.4 The Orange Trail splits right and circles the lower slopes of the Tourne.

3.8 Reach the top of the Tourne. Here, an outcrop presents views of the New York skyline to the east as well as westerly vistas. The peak is enhanced with picnic tables.

4.1 Pass the other end of the Orange Trail on the descent. Ahead, reach an intersection. Split right with the Red Trail, a gravel road.

4.4 Arrive back at the trailhead, completing the fine day hike.

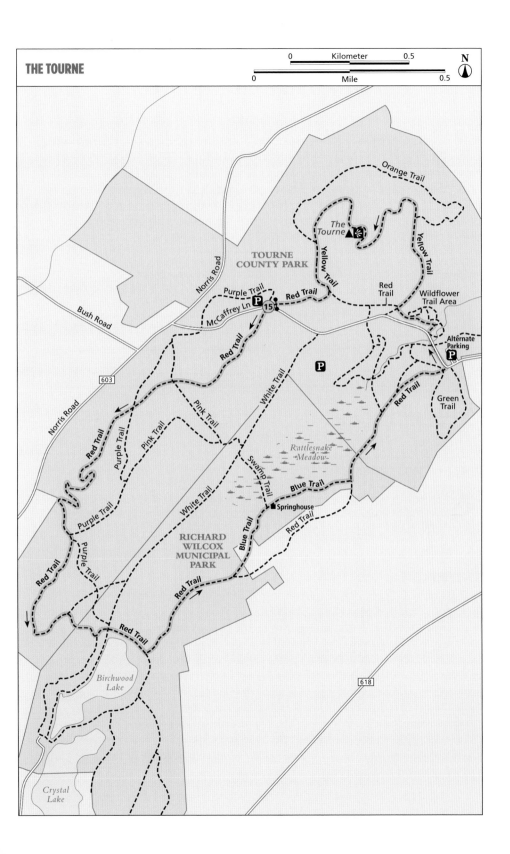

THE TOURNE

0   Kilometer   0.5

0   Mile   0.5

N

Orange Trail

The Tourne

Yellow Trail

Yellow Trail

TOURNE COUNTY PARK

Norris Road

Bush Road

Purple Trail

Red Trail

Red Trail

Red Trail

Wildflower Trail Area

McCaffrey Ln

15

Alternate Parking

603

Red Trail

White Trail

Red Trail

Green Trail

Norris Road

Red Trail

Purple Trail

Pink Trail

Pink Trail

Rattlesnake Meadow

Swamp Trail

Blue Trail

Purple Trail

White Trail

Blue Trail

Springhouse

Red Trail

RICHARD WILCOX MUNICIPAL PARK

Purple Trail

Red Trail

Red Trail

Red Trail

Red Trail

Birchwood Lake

618

Crystal Lake

16 PYRAMID MOUNTAIN AND TRIPOD ROCK

Take an extraordinary jaunt through a natural glacier-sculptured garden. Pass some remarkable erratic boulders: Bear Rock, possibly New Jersey's largest; Whale Head Rock, directly out of *Moby Dick*; and Tripod Rock, a balanced pedestal rock claimed by some to have links to the solstice and prehistoric congregations. Along with views of the Newark Basin and the New York skyline, there are side trips to the Morgan Place foundations and Lucy's Overlook.

Start: Pyramid Mountain Boonton Avenue trailhead
Distance: 4.4-mile balloon loop
Difficulty: Moderate, does have rocky trails
Elevation change: +-672 feet
Maximum grade: 9% grade for 0.4 mile
Hiking time: About 2.4 hours
Seasons/schedule: Daily sunrise to sunset
Fees and permits: None
Dog friendly: Yes, on leash only

Trail surface: Natural
Land status: County park
Nearest town: Boonton
Other trail users: None
Maps to consult: Pyramid Mountain Natural Historic Area
Amenities available: Restrooms at trailhead
Cell service: Excellent
Trail contact: Pyramid Mountain Natural Historic Area, (973) 334-3130, www.morrisparks.net

FINDING THE TRAILHEAD

From exit 45 on I-287 near Boonton, head left on Wooton Street and follow it 0.6 mile to turn right onto Boonton Avenue. Follow Boonton Avenue 2 miles to turn right onto Rockaway Avenue, then make a quick left on the continuation of Boonton Avenue and follow it 0.8 mile to the Pyramid Mountain parking area on your left. Trailhead GPS: 40.946633,-74.388520

THE HIKE

Bear Rock and Tripod Rock are two of the many outstanding features of this hike through the Pyramid Mountain Natural Historic Area. They are both incredible, but in different ways. Bear Rock is alleged to be the largest boulder in New Jersey, and it could well be. Known early on as "Bare Rock," the origin of its name is unclear. Some say it looks like a bear, or perhaps a bear lived there, or perhaps it was bare. Whatever the case, the Lenape found a use for this colossal rock next to a stream and a swamp, as rock shelters exist on both sides of it, used as transient camps by hunting and foraging parties. Archaeologist Max Schrabisch excavated them back in 1909.

Tripod Rock has a different story. The old proverb says, "Don't bring up religion or politics unless you want to start a fight." In New Jersey hiking and history communities, you might add one more to that proscribed list: balanced boulders. Few things are both as fascinating and as controversial as Tripod Rock.

The strange but fascinating Tripod Rock

As you will see visiting the site, Tripod Rock is a 160-something-ton boulder, roughly triangular, balanced at an angle on three smaller boulders, at a height of some 2 feet. Looking like a precarious joke left by an ancient race of giants, it is one of the great wonders of New Jersey. A geological wonder, most would say—the last ice age deposited untold glacial erratics across the mountains of northern New Jersey, so it stands to reason that some of them would end up in unusual configurations. Tripod Rock is a monument to the power (albeit random) of natural geological forces.

"Pshaw!" says another camp. How can anything so obviously artificial be dismissed as a work of nature? Over the past several decades, some researchers have advanced a belief that North America is filled with ancient, huge rock monuments—megaliths—placed by ancient cultures to mark important dates in the calendar: a summer or winter solstice, or a spring or fall equinox. Three boulders near Tripod Rock form a triangle that points (kinda, sorta) to the summer solstice. It is a calendar stone, an ancient astrological site, indeed, a spiritual energy vortex, they say.

"Phooey!" (accompanied by serious rolling of the eyes), say the geologists and historians. There's no archaeological evidence of any culture, Native American or otherwise, having been at Tripod Rock, and the notion that it points to the solstice requires wishful (and creative) thinking. It's a geological wonder—a natural one—period!

A third camp represents a bit of a compromise and posits that while Tripod Rock may indeed be natural, it nevertheless could have attracted the attention of aboriginals who could have worshipped there.

Can you see the whale in Whale Rock?

The difference of opinion will surely continue. Every year in June, Tripod Rock is a busy place to be for the summer solstice. Some come to enjoy the beauty of the scene, some come to ponder the mysteries of geology and ancient civilizations, and some are probably waiting for a call from the mother ship. Any way you look at it, Tripod Rock is a good place to ponder the imponderables.

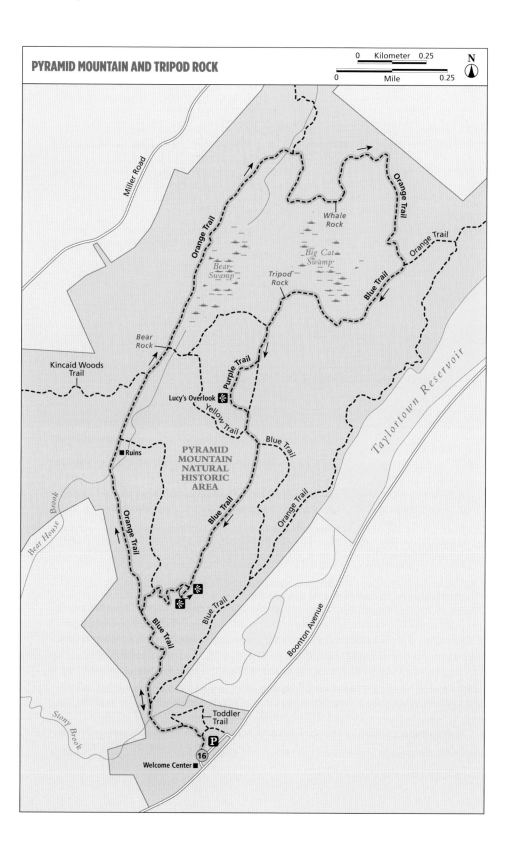

PYRAMID MOUNTAIN AND TRIPOD ROCK

0   Kilometer   0.25
0   Mile   0.25

N

Miller Road

Orange Trail

Whale Rock

Orange Trail

Bear Swamp

Big Cat Swamp

Tripod Rock

Orange Trail

Blue Trail

Bear Rock

Kincaid Woods Trail

Purple Trail

Lucy's Overlook

Yellow Trail

Blue Trail

Taylortown Reservoir

Ruins

PYRAMID MOUNTAIN NATURAL HISTORIC AREA

Blue Trail

Blue Trail

Orange Trail

Bear House Brook

Orange Trail

Blue Trail

Boonton Avenue

Blue Trail

Stony Brook

Toddler Trail

P

16

Welcome Center

MILES AND DIRECTIONS

0.0 From the corner of the parking lot near the welcome center, join the Blue Trail, at this point a wide gravel track bordered in stones. Cruise rocky woods as a spur of the Toddler Trail goes right. Ahead, pass a second spur of the Toddler Trail.

0.2 Bridge the outflow of Taylortown Reservoir, Stony Brook. Just ahead, the Blue Trail splits. Stay left, beginning up the slope of Pyramid Mountain, cutting under and then running along a power line clearing.

0.5 Reach a trail intersection. Here, the Blue Trail goes right and is your return route. For now, stay left, joining the Orange Trail, swinging around the west side of Pyramid Mountain and staying parallel to the power line in rocky woods. Boardwalks lead over occasional wet spots and small streams.

0.8 Bridge Bear House Brook, then pass the basement of the old Morgan Place. Supposedly during the late 1800s, the Morgans—Boonton bad boys—used it as a hideout. Ahead, an unblazed trail comes in on your right.

1.0 Come to an intersection. Here, a trail leads left to Kincaid Woods. Keep straight.

1.1 Reach Bear Rock, New Jersey's largest freestanding stone, and a trail junction. Stay straight on the Orange Trail, soon climbing above the stream and wide, marshy Bear Swamp.

1.7 Cross Bear House Brook again. Here, a spur goes left to Miller Road. Stay right and begin climbing an uber-rocky hillside.

2.0 Come to unmistakable Whale Rock. Roll through hills, then come near the park boundary. Descend, passing an ephemeral pond.

2.5 Come to an intersection on the east brow of the mountain above Taylortown Reservoir. Head right on the Blue Trail, circling around mountaintop Big Cat Swamp.

2.9 Reach Tripod Rock, to the right of the trail. Make your own guess as to its origination. Ahead, pass a spur leading right toward Bear Rock. Stay straight, southerly.

3.0 Take the purple-blazed loop right to Lucy's Overlook, delivering a southwesterly view. Return to the Blue Trail, keeping south.

3.2 Stay straight on the Blue Trail as the Yellow Trail leaves right toward Bear Rock.

3.3 Stay right as the Blue Trail splits left and right. Climb the slope of Pyramid Mountain.

3.6 Reach a spur left to a stellar view, open to the east with mountains in the near and the Big Apple skyline in the distance. Take another spur going to the south end of Pyramid Mountain and another superlative vista. From there, backtrack to the main trail then descend by switchbacks, ignoring user-created erosive shortcuts.

3.9 Complete the loop portion of the hike. Backtrack left on the Blue Trail toward the trailhead.

4.4 Arrive back at the trailhead, completing the geologically fascinating hike.

17 THE PEQUANNOCK HIGHLANDS

This short ramble at Silas Condict Park goes a long way. It offers some fine, lesser appreciated views, including vistas in nearly all directions. The hike abounds with glacial erratics and also includes a small, charming lake. Stroll through the picnic groves and around the "Casino," allegedly a former speakeasy.

Start: Parking lot on east side of Cantys Lake
Distance: 2.7-mile loop
Difficulty: Easy–moderate
Elevation change: +-505 feet
Maximum grade: 8% downhill grade for 0.2 mile
Hiking time: About 1.3 hours
Seasons/schedule: Daily sunrise to sunset; clear days for best views
Fees and permits: None

Dog friendly: Yes, on leash only
Trail surface: Natural, a little gravel
Land status: County park
Nearest town: Kinnelon
Other trail users: None
Maps to consult: Silas Condict Park
Amenities available: Picnic area, restrooms nearby
Cell service: Excellent
Trail contact: Silas Condict Park, (973) 326-7600, www.morrisparks.net

FINDING THE TRAILHEAD

From exit 52 on I-287 near Riverdale, take NJ 23 north for 3.3 miles to the Kinnelon Road exit. Take Kinnelon Road west for 1.1 miles to turn right onto William Lewis Arthur Drive and follow it for 0.6 mile to reach the parking lot just as you open onto the Cantys Lake area. The hike starts in the southwest corner of the very large parking area. Trailhead GPS: 41.003639,-74.383983

THE HIKE

In times of war and turmoil, some people get to be heroes without ever dodging a bullet; Silas Condict was such a man. Born in Morristown in 1738, he was a farmer and surveyor, with large landholdings in Morris County. But he was an ardent patriot, too, and lent his hand to political causes. He was on the committee that drafted the New Jersey state constitution, and in 1776 became his county's representative in the state legislature. In 1777–78 he served on the Revolutionary Council of Safety, and from 1781 to 1784 he was a member of the Continental Congress.

Condict's home in Morristown was the site of numerous meetings during the Revolution, and for his wisdom he was commonly called "Counselor" Condict. After the Revolution, he was elected to the New Jersey Assembly eight times, serving as speaker twice, and served as a Morris County justice of the peace and judge. He had no children of his own but adopted his deceased brother's sons. One of them, Lewis Condict (1773–1862), was a congressman and prominent physician who promoted early efforts at smallpox vaccination.

Silas Condict died in 1801, one of Morris County's busiest and most ardent patriots of the Revolution. His home in Morristown was torn down a century ago, but Silas Condict Park, dedicated in 1964, helps preserve his name and legacy.

Looking at the Casino across Cantys Lake

Here at Silas Condict Park you will see the glacial geology of the Highlands every-where in evidence. Exposed bedrock testifies to the force of the three glaciers that passed over these mountains over time. Huge puddingstone boulders dropped here and there like toys similarly tell of the ice-age journey of the ice sheet, and the rocks it picked up like curios and left behind as it retreated a hundred centuries ago.

But the hike also tells of a more genteel history. Silas Condict Park was originally the Canty estate, one of many in this area of Morris County in the early 1900s. At that time,

Views like this can be found in the Pequannock Highlands.

estates often featured a separate building just for entertaining. Such buildings were often architecturally ornate and included features like a dance floor or a bandstand. These entertainment buildings were in the tradition of the English banqueting hall, or the contemporary Italian custom of the "little house" near the main house, called the casina. In English, this was generally rendered "casino," even though gambling wasn't necessarily involved.

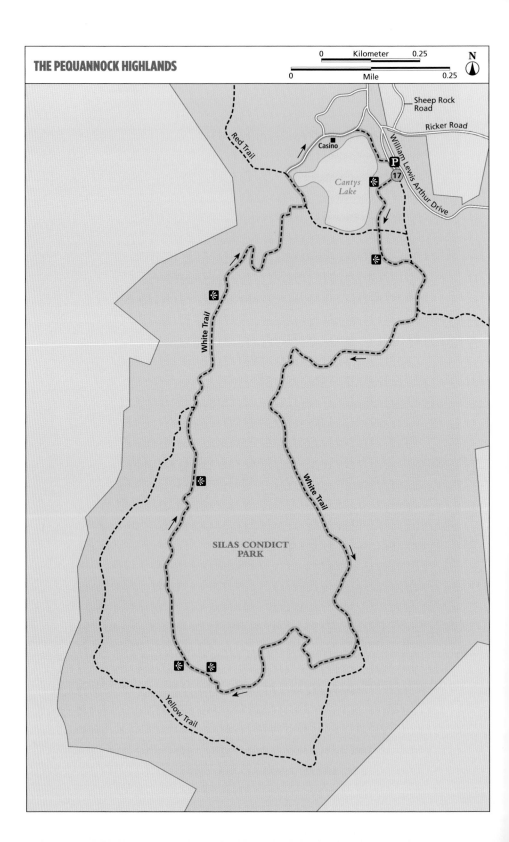

THE PEQUANNOCK HIGHLANDS

0   Kilometer   0.25

0   Mile   0.25

N

Sheep Rock
Road

Ricker Road

Red Trail

Casino

P

17

Cantys
Lake

William Lewis Arthur Drive

White Trail

White Trail

SILAS CONDICT
PARK

Yellow Trail

The "Casino" at Silas Condict Park, which we pass on this hike, was one such structure, originally serving the Canty estate. With its mahogany bar, bandstand, murals, ornate woodwork, and mirrors, the handsome stone building radiated charm and fun (and still does). In the 1920s it became the site of one of the area's more famous Prohibition-era speakeasies. Restored to its historic splendor by the Morris County Park Commission in the 1990s, the Casino is a popular place for weddings and special events.

MILES AND DIRECTIONS

0.0 From the southwest corner of the large parking area east of Cantys Lake, join the White Trail as it skirts the side of the lake, where you can savor a fine view of the Casino, backed by rising hills. Ahead, gravel tracks spur away, but stay with the white blazes, as you will throughout the trek. Pass a small picnic area while trekking amid oaks, scraggly mountain laurel, and blueberry bushes.

0.2 Come to a westerly view on a rocky knob, stretching across the outflow of Cantys Lake. Drop off the knob for the outflow stream of the lake. Ahead, a track splits left; stay right and cross the Cantys Lake outflow stream. Bridge a second small stream.

0.7 Cross some open rock slabs on the wooded hillside. The trail is rocky and slow.

1.0 Reach an intersection in a flat. Here, the Yellow Trail splits left and makes a wider loop. Stay with the White Trail. Generally rise in rocky woods, working around boulders and a jagged cliff line.

1.5 Reach an open rock slab and a view to the southwest and west. Cruise a lightly wooded linear ridge, passing a second view to westerly ridges.

1.8 Come to a northwesterly panorama after descending from a high point. This vista reaches toward the Pequannock River valley.

1.9 Meet the other end of the Yellow Trail. Stay straight with the White Trail, rolling through a few more hills and amid boulders.

2.1 Come to an easterly view where you can see the New York City skyline between a gap in the next ridge east. Drop toward Cantys Lake in some rugged terrain.

2.5 Split left, beginning to circle around Cantys Lake, now on a gravel track. Pass a play area and picnic shelter, then circle around the Casino.

2.7 Arrive back at the large parking area, a surprisingly fine hike under your belt.

18 WYANOKIE HIGH POINT

Grab one of the best vistas in the Garden State from Wyanokie High Point, a rocky prominence above Wanaque Reservoir, where vistas extend east to the New York City skyline. Located inside the bounds of Norvin Green State Forest, you can also stop by historic Roomy Mine and Blue Mine. You will also be well acquainted with Blue Mine Branch, as you cross it several times, on both its upper and lower stretches. Additional rewarding trails and destinations will tempt you to revisit this beautiful slice of the Garden State.

Start: New Weir Center
Distance: 5.4-mile balloon loop
Difficulty: Moderate, does have plenty of ascent/descent on rock paths
Elevation change: +-1,157 feet
Maximum grade: 12% grade for 1.0 mile
Hiking time: About 2.7 hours
Seasons/schedule: Daily dawn to dusk
Fees and permits: None

Dog friendly: Yes, on leash only
Trail surface: Natural
Land status: State forest
Nearest town: Wanaque
Other trail users: None
Maps to consult: Norvin Green State Forest
Amenities available: None
Cell service: Good
Trail contact: Norvin Green State Forest, (973) 962-7031, www.nj.gov/dep/parksandforests

FINDING THE TRAILHEAD

From exit 55 on I-287, take Ringwood Avenue north for 3.9 miles, then turn left on Westbrook Avenue and follow it for 1.9 miles. Turn left onto Snake Den Road and follow it for 0.7 mile to the large parking area on your right just before the official entrance to the New Weis Center. Do not park inside the New Weis Center unless you are going there only. Trailhead GPS: 41.069844,-74.321752

THE HIKE

The view from Wyanokie High Point, elevation 1,015 feet, is clearly the star of the show on this hike. On a clear day the panoramas extend near and far—near to adjacent peaks of the forest, down to the reservoir below, where watercraft look like little toy boats, and beyond as far as the clarity of the sky allows. Plan to linger atop Wyanokie High Point, walking around the mountain and finding outcrops with additional views of their own. Additionally, you can also visit a couple of historic mines. The Roomy Mine (probably named after a local family, originally spelled Roome) was also known as the Laurel or the Red Mine and operated from 1840 to 1857. The nearby Blue Mine (aka the London, Iron Hill, or Whynockie Mine) is much older, having been opened by German iron entrepreneur Peter Hasenclever in 1765. It operated intermittently until 1905, when it closed for good. But unlike the Roomy Mine, the Blue Mine is today little more than a great flooded hole in the ground.

This hike may get you to thinking: Is it Wyanokie, Wanaque, Whynockie, or what? The original Native American Lenape name for the region was something like

This vista reveals waters in the near and New York City in the distance.

"Wah–NAH–kay" or "Why–hah–NAH–key." As with so many Native words, there are variant opinions on its meaning: "rest and repose," says one source; "place of sassafras," say a number of others. It appears the first European to write down the name was a Frenchman, who rendered it phonetically in French: "Wa–na–que." Ever after, the name has frequently been pronounced "Wanna-cue," even though old-timers will insist it's "Wa–NA-key." And there are myriad other spellings: Wynokie, Wynocky, Wynoky, Wyn-ockie . . .

MILES AND DIRECTIONS

0.0 From the parking area, follow the green-blazed Otter Hole Trail into the New Weis Center, staying with Blue Mine Branch to your left and facilities to your right. Ahead, walk past the Natural Pool swimming area and climb. Cross Blue Mine Branch.

0.4 Reach an intersection and kiosk. Stay straight with the yellow-blazed Mine Trail.

0.5 Stay left with the Mine Trail in very rocky woods with scattered rock slabs, as the blue-blazed Hewitt Butler Trail goes right.

1.0 Reach an intersection. Head left with the orange-blazed Roomy Mine Trail. Dip to cross Blue Mine Branch at Wyanokie Falls, a spiller tumbling into and through a boulder jumble. Climb, then stay left toward Ball Mountain.

A northeasterly view from Wyanokie High Point

1.4 Reach an outcrop and warm-up view. Turn south on Ball Mountain as a leg of the Roomy Mine Trail descends left for Townsend Road. Pass another pair of rock outcrop views before descending.

1.9 Come to Roomy Mine, an old iron mine that extends into the mountainside. Continue down the Blue Mine Branch valley. Ahead, the Highlands Trail leaves left.

2.2 Reach flooded Blue Mine. Here, cross the hiker bridge westbound. Look for old pit holes and tailings. Pass a pair of intersections, including the white-blazed Lower Trail heading left just after a second creek crossing. Climb westerly on the Wyanokie Circular Trail.

3.2 After passing a warm-up view, open onto the top of Wyanokie High Point, with panorama-delivering rock slabs all about. Some of New Jersey's best vistas (one of my favorites) can be had from here—Wanaque Reservoir below, hills and habitations in the middle, and the New York City skyline to the east. Wow! Note other outcrops visible from here. Ahead, join the blue-blazed Hewitt Butler Trail, northbound, and cruise atop rock slabs with lesser views interspersed with woods.

3.5 Reach another intersection, as the white-blazed Macopin Trail splits left. For now, continue a short distance on the Hewitt Butler Trail to grab another rock outcrop view, this one to the northwest, then backtrack and join the westbound Macopin Trail. Descend in skimpy trees growing in shallow soils. Traverse a boulder field and small shallow stream.

WYANOKIE HIGH POINT

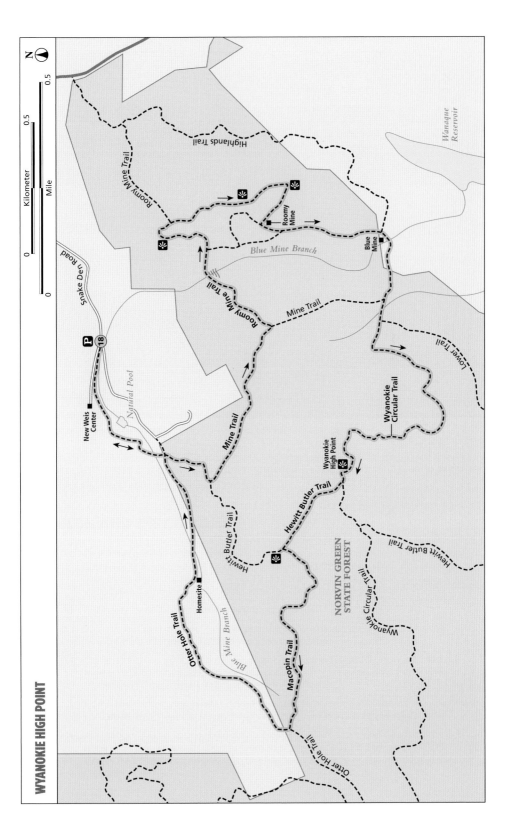

4.1 Come to another intersection. Here, meet the green-blazed Otter Hole Trail. Split right on the Otter Hole Trail, tracing an old roadbed, crossing the headwaters of Blue Mine Branch. Pass old stone walls indicating this as former farmland. Ahead, pull away from the old road, working around wet sections. Walk beneath bluffs before returning to the roadbed.

4.6 Pass the site of a former homesite just to the right of the trail. Look for the old well, yard, and homesite foundations. Continue downstream along Blue Mine Branch, then rock hop the creek at the site of a washed-out bridge.

5.0 Complete the loop portion of the hike. Backtrack past the Natural Pool and the New Weis Center facilities.

5.4 Arrive back at the parking lot just outside the New Weis Center, completing the hike.

19 PALISADES INTERSTATE PARK

This scenic loop hike traverses the top of the famed Palisades of the Hudson River and beside the banks of the big river. Due to its challenges, this adventure needs a heads-up approach. The trail fluctuates between serious stone steps, zigzagging dirt trails, wide meandering paths, abandoned highway, and trailer-size rock talus. The hike should not be attempted in wet or icy weather. Children need to be closely in tow and pets left at home! The hike, representing another special New Jersey hike unimagined by others around the nation, has its challenges, but the incredible views are some of the best around and worth your time and effort.

Start: State Line Lookout, off Palisades Interstate Parkway
Distance: 4.0-mile loop
Difficulty: Strenuous due to extended rock garden scrambles
Elevation change: +-802 feet
Maximum grade: 17% downhill grade for 0.4 mile
Hiking time: About 2.9 hours
Seasons/schedule: Daily 6:00 a.m. to 9:00 p.m.; best during dry conditions
Fees and permits: None
Dog friendly: Leashed dogs permitted, but rock scrambles are decidedly dog-unfriendly

Trail surface: Mostly natural surface, some gravel, very little concrete
Land status: State park
Nearest town: Alpine
Other trail users: Bicyclers, joggers on old Highway 9
Maps to consult: Palisades Interstate Park
Amenities available: Restrooms, restaurant at parking lot
Cell service: Excellent
Trail contact: Palisades Interstate Park, (201) 768-1360, www.njpalisades.org

FINDING THE TRAILHEAD

From exit 72 on I-95 just before entering New York City, join the Palisades Parkway north via Fletcher Avenue, then drive 9 miles to exit right at the signed State Line Lookout exit. Continue for 0.6 mile from the exit to reach the State Line Lookout parking area. The hike begins in the northwest corner of the parking lot, near the State Line Cafe/Bookstore. Trailhead GPS: 40.989046,-73.907191

THE HIKE

There may be ghosts of people, but what about of places? Some places are so special they seem to have souls, harboring beautiful memories. Though later abandoned and forgotten, their hold on the human imagination survives. You will pass two such places on our hike along the base of the Palisades: Forest View and Mary Lawrence Tonetti's waterfall and gardens. They make the walk a special one indeed.

The first ghost-place of the Palisades on our ramble is the huge, overgrown riverside area at the base of the steps down to the river. In the early days of Palisades Interstate Park, when cars were less common, it didn't seem odd to have a recreation area you walked to, and this was one: Forest View. It included a pavilion, restrooms, water fountains, picnic areas, boat docks, a marina, and a ball field. You got here either by walking the Shore

Peanut Leap Cascades

Trail a few miles north from the Alpine Boat Basin or by hiking down the stairs from the Women's Federation Monument above (or possibly by taking a boat).

For decades, Forest View was happy with the sound of games, cookouts, swimming, and laughter. But two things were working against it by the late 1940s: River pollution made swimming less popular or safe, and the centrality of the automobile to American life meant more people wanted to just drive to—not walk to—their fun spot. By the early 1960s, the park stopped maintaining Forest View, and in short order it was over-grown with weeds, vines, and poison ivy. Now only the stone-and-timber ruins of a few

Looking north up the Hudson River

old picnic benches here and there, peering out under the brush-like Mayan ruins, testify to the happy days once enjoyed here.

The other special spot is centered around Peanut Leap Cascades. Mary Lawrence came from an old New York family who established a summer home at nearby Sneden's Landing in the 1870s. The waterfall on our hike, by the name Peanut Leap Cascade or Half Moon Falls, was on the southern end of their property. Mary, born in 1868, developed into a sculptor of considerable talent. By the early 1890s, she was an assistant to famed American sculptor Augustus Saint-Gaudens. While in his employ, she executed the statue

New Jersey boundary monument

of Columbus that stood in front of the Administration Building at the 1893 World's Columbian Exposition in Chicago.

Mary had visited Italy in the late 1880s and was particularly impressed by the Capuchin Monastery at Amalfi, whose columned pergola overlooks the Gulf of Salerno. She determined to create a similar structure at the waterfall on the Hudson. With the assistance of prestigious architects, she designed and constructed a terrace, bench, and columned pergola on the edge of the river, with a pool, grotto, niches, and gardens at the base of

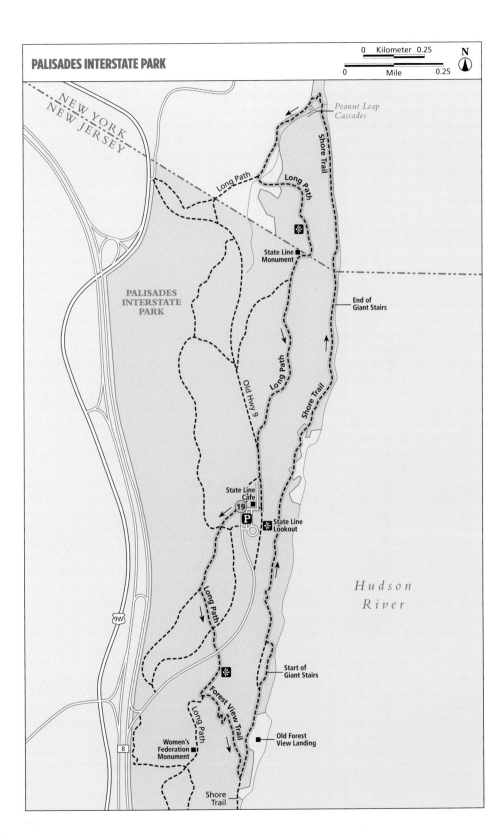

PALISADES INTERSTATE PARK

0   Kilometer 0.25

0   Mile   0.25

N

NEW YORK
NEW JERSEY

Peanut Leap
Cascades

Long Path

Long Path

Shore Trail

State Line
Monument

PALISADES
INTERSTATE
PARK

End of
Giant Stairs

Long Path

Old Hwy 9

Long Path

Shore Trail

State Line
Cafe

19

State Line
Lookout

Hudson
River

Long Path

Start of
Giant Stairs

Forest View Trail

Long Path

Old Forest
View Landing

9W

Women's
Federation
Monument

8

Shore
Trail

the waterfall. Decorated with sculptures, potted flowers, and shrubs and lit with Chinese lanterns, the waterfall and gardens were the Lawrences' favorite spot for summer parties.

Mary and her husband, sculptor Francois Tonetti, had a large family and many friends. Their circle included a stellar array of those in the arts, architecture, and Broadway theater. They frequently held post-theater parties, arriving from Manhattan by boat up the Hudson. Sadly, in the years after Mary Lawrence Tonetti's death in 1945, the magical falls, pool, grotto, and pergola fell into decay. Now it's not an imitation ruin but a real one—a sad reminder of a family's rich vision and imagination, yet remarkably compelling even to this day. Have lunch here, sit on the stone bench overlooking the Hudson, and envision the statues, the pools, the flowers . . .

The majesty and beauty of the Hudson and the Palisades are everywhere evident on this hike—small wonder that the preservation of these historic cliffs was one of the first great conservation victories in the region.

MILES AND DIRECTIONS

0.0 From the northwest corner of the parking lot, with the State Line Cafe and the Hudson River to your right, join the Long Path southwest and immediately enter a nest of trails. Stay with the green blazes of the Long Path, the 358-mile trail linking New York City to Albany.

0.4 Cross the entrance road, old Highway 9, and resume footpath. Ahead, pass some outcrops with extraordinary panoramas east toward New York. Descend steeply.

0.6 Bridge a stream, then reach an intersection. Here, the Long Path continues right toward the Women's Federation Monument, but we dive left onto the Forest View Trail. Descend sharply and steeply on stone steps cut into an incredibly steep slope.

0.9 Reach the bottoms of the Hudson River and the Shore Trail in big trees. Split left, northbound along the Shore Trail. Hike through the once-busy, now-abandoned Forest View Landing.

1.1 A trail splits left and reconnects to the Shore Trail ahead.

1.2 Begin the Giant Stairs, an extended trek through an incredible jumbled boulder garden. Do not take this segment lightly. The hike becomes slow and exhausting, despite limited elevation changes. Some parts of the boulder garden are partly wooded, while others are completely open to the sun overhead. Take your time and make every step count.

2.2 End the Giant Stairs, though you do have limited rocky segments ahead. Continue along the shore, then enter New York State after passing through a rusty fence.

2.6 Reach Peanut Leap Cascades and the old gardens. Note the old ruins as well as natural splendor of the 80-foot cataract. Climb up Skunk Hollow, grabbing more views of the cataract.

2.9 Come to an intersection. Head left, rejoining the Long Path, southbound, and continue climbing.

3.2 Pass some more outcrops with distant views east, south, and north. Savor the moment.

3.3 Take the short spur to the New Jersey state line monument. Ahead, stay with the green-blazed Long Path as nature trails spur right, away from the river.

3.8 Split left and join old Highway 9, now a concrete trail of sorts.

4.0 Arrive back at State Line Lookout, completing the challenging yet superlatively scenic circuit hike.

20 THE DELAWARE VALLEY—STOCKTON TO LAMBERTVILLE LOOP

This historic hike travels canal towpaths and rail beds along the Delaware River, an important waterway for the people of New Jersey and all the other states along its banks. This segment leaves south from Stockton to fun, active Lambertville. After crossing the Delaware River from Lambertville into New Hope, Pennsylvania, you travel north on the D&L Trail, a towpath, to Centre Bridge, finally recrossing the river into Stockton.

Start: Bridge Street in Stockton
Distance: 7.1-mile loop
Difficulty: Moderate–difficult due to distance
Elevation change: +-10 feet
Maximum grade: N/A
Hiking time: About 3.4 hours
Seasons/schedule: Year-round; river bridges can be icy in winter
Fees and permits: None
Dog friendly: Yes, on leash only
Trail surface: Pea gravel, concrete and wood on bridges

Land status: New Jersey state park, Pennsylvania state park
Nearest town: Stockton
Other trail users: Bicyclers
Maps to consult: Delaware and Raritan Canal State Park
Amenities available: All manner of amenities in Stockton, more so in Lambertville
Cell service: Excellent
Trail contact: Delaware and Raritan Canal State Park, (609) 924-5705, www.dandrcanal.com

FINDING THE TRAILHEAD

From the intersection of Main Street/NJ 29 and Bridge Street (leading to Pennsylvania) in Stockton, travel west on Bridge Street for 0.1 mile and at the former Stockton Railroad Station (now a market/deli) and just prior to the rail trail, turn left to the public parking areas along Railroad Avenue. If these spots are full, drive a short distance northwest on NJ 29 to the Prallsville Mills, part of the state park. Trailhead GPS: 40.405148, -74.976987

THE HIKE

This is a historical hike that delivers big views and broad perspectives into New Jersey's past. It is not a wilderness trek. You will experience quaint Stockton and the rising tourist destination of Lambertville, along with New Hope, Pennsylvania, which tends toward the hip tourist side of things. Along the way you will hear cars and other signs of civilization.

Now that the potential negatives are out of the way, go for this hike because of what it is—a historical path along the master river of the Northeast, with a foot-friendly tread and peerless views of the Delaware. The interpretive information scattered along the path is first-rate, turning the trek into an excursion through a living outdoor museum.

A deer grazes in the canal alongside the D&L Trail.

You will parallel the Delaware River the whole way, meandering along rail beds and towpaths and passing through river towns, reflecting the early growth of America's transportation industry. In the 1700s, Colonial settlements sprang up on both sides of the river near ferry landings. By the early 1800s, bridges replaced the ferries, funneling equestrian traffic through the growing villages. In the 1830s, boom years came to the hamlets with the arrival of Delaware & Raritan (D&R) Feeder Canal in New Jersey and the Delaware Canal in Pennsylvania. The Belvidere & Delaware Railroad in New Jersey and the Reading Railroad in Pennsylvania came chugging into the area in the 1850s, furthering industrial expansion. Just imagine the pungent odors produced by the paper mills, sawmills, sausage factories, breweries, potteries, cotton mills, ironworks, and rubber factories (this was home of the "Snag-Proof Boot") that once operated here. Now we smell creamy lattes, quiche Lorraine, and red wine.

A unique historical feature of the river crossings was their locations: all a day's journey from New York City and Philadelphia via the stagecoach along the Old York Road. To provide the weary traveler lodging and grub, hostelries sprang up on either side of the river: the Stockton Inn, Centre Bridge Inn, Lambertville House, and Ferry Tavern (today, Logan Inn), still open for business and waiting for hungry, well-dressed trampers.

Our journey begins in Stockton, the site of the early eighteenth-century Reading's Ferry. Originally worked by John Reading and family, it was sold to other entrepreneurs and later sold to the Centre Bridge Company. In the spring of 1814, they opened the 950-foot wooden covered bridge across the river. Centre Bridge derived its name from being equidistant between the Trenton and Phillipsburg bridges on the Delaware. The

Pennsylvanian side of the span claimed Centre Bridge for the town's name, while the Jersey side took Stockton after Senator Robert Field Stockton. His grandfather was a signer of the Declaration of Independence, and his father was also a US senator. Robert, as an accomplished naval officer, battled the Barbary pirates, negotiated for the creation of Liberia, and annexed California from the Mexicans. As a US senator, he introduced a bill to end flogging in the Navy. As a businessman, he promoted the Delaware & Raritan Canal, eventually becoming its president.

Where Lambertville, New Jersey, and New Hope, Pennsylvania, stand today was the Colonial site of Wells' Ferry, operated by John Wells and later by the Coryell family, hence the settlement name: Coryell's Ferry. The hamlet on the Jersey side became Lambertville in 1810, when New Jersey state senator John Lambert persuaded "the powers that be" to open up a post office with his nephew as postmaster. Hence, Lambertville . . . much to the chagrin of the local Coryells. Coryell's Ferry on the Pennsylvania side had a name change after the 1790s, when fire destroyed three mills. When the owner rebuilt several mills, it gave "New Hope" to the Pennsylvanians and a new name to the now-thriving tourist berg.

The demise of the ferry service occurred in 1814 with the construction of the New Hope–Lambertville Bridge, a wooden covered bridge extending 1,050 feet over the Delaware. But like all the other bridges spanning this river, it came under yearly attacks by the natural elements: flooding, ice floes, debris, and lightning. As a prime example, in the Flood of 1841, Centre Bridge broke loose and floated off its piers. Traveling down the raging river, the toll collector was "on board" the breakaway structure as it crashed into and removed the arches and piers of the New Hope–Lambertville Bridge. The woebegone toll collector continued on his terrifying 13-mile odyssey until rescued among the flotsam in Yardleyville. Here is hoping that your journey along the Delaware River and across the rehabilitated steel-span bridges is far less arduous than the toll collector's adventure!

MILES AND DIRECTIONS

0.0 From the former Stockton railroad station at Bridge Street, now a market/deli, head southeast on the Delaware and Raritan (D&R) Trail.

0.6 Pass over a deck-girder bridge, crossing over the Delaware & Raritan Feeder Canal into the section of town called Brookville, where the famous Deats plow was invented. You are now traveling southeasterly, roughly parallel to NJ 29, with the feeder canal to your left and the Delaware River to your right.

0.9 Cross over a bridge, which passes over the wickets that allow for the drainage of the canal into the Delaware River.

1.7 Coming in on your left and crossing the canal is the Mount Gilboa railroad siding, which leads to an adjacent stone quarry. Just ahead, another bridge crosses the canal to NJ 29.

2.3 Pass under the US 202 bridge and turn left (east), crossing a bridge over the canal. At the end of the bridge, turn right (south), staying on the D&R Trail.

2.5 Proceed over the Alexauken Creek aqueduct and continue straight (south) along the towpath. Shortly enter Lambertville.

2.6 Pass under a railroad girder-bridge and continue to parallel the canal. Come along numerous trail access points to the left: Elm Street, Buttonwood Street, Perry Street, Delevan Street, and York Street.

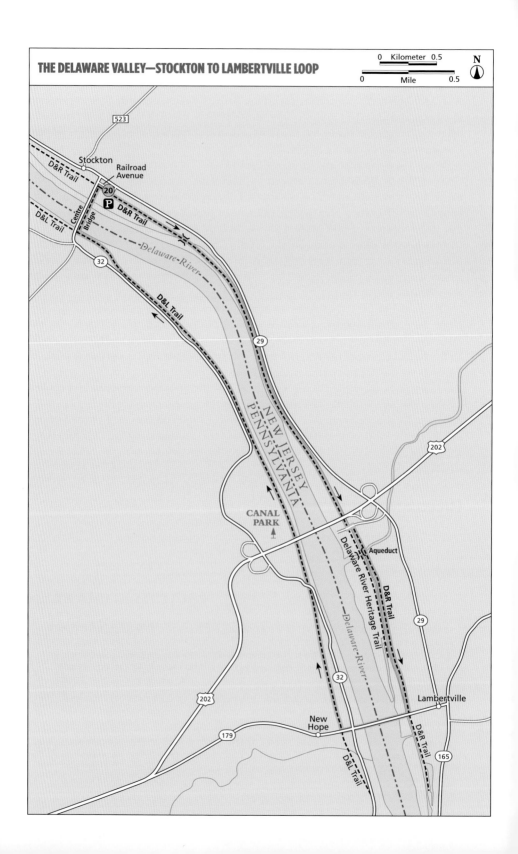

THE DELAWARE VALLEY—STOCKTON TO LAMBERTVILLE LOOP

0   Kilometer   0.5

0   Mile   0.5

N

523

Stockton

Railroad
Avenue

D&R Trail

20

P   D&R Trail

D&L Trail

Centre
Bridge

32

Delaware River

D&L Trail

29

NEW JERSEY
PENNSYLVANIA

CANAL
PARK

202

Aqueduct

Delaware River Heritage Trail

D&R Trail

Delaware River

29

202

32

Lambertville

179

New
Hope

D&L Trail

D&R Trail

165

3.4 At the junction with Bridge Street, cross the street and turn right (west) onto the sidewalk, paralleling Bridge Street, passing over the canal and passing by the former Lambertville Railroad Station on your left (south). You have arrived in Lambertville, the land of bistros, galleries, and boutiques.

3.5 Cross over the New Hope–Lambertville Bridge, built in 1904 and rebuilt in 1955 and 2004.

3.6 Upon reaching New Hope, proceed straight (west) along East Bridge Street on the sidewalk one block until you hit Main Street (PA 32). Cross over Main Street and onto West Bridge Street (PA 179), continuing straight up the hill along the sidewalk.

3.7 Before the bridge over the Delaware Canal, turn right (north), cross West Bridge Street, and descend to the D&L Trail, part of Pennsylvania's Delaware Canal State Park. Heading out of town, the towpath will take you along the backyard gardens and several street accesses.

4.5 Pass under Rabbit Run Bridge, River Road, where the towpath becomes co-aligned with driveways of houses to your right between you and the river.

4.8 Pass under US 202. Ahead, a bridge leads left to parking at Canal Park. Pass more private bridges ahead.

6.8 Before the auto bridge over the canal at Centre Bridge, turn right (east), climbing the stairs to the roadway. Turn right (east), crossing the Delaware River on Centre Bridge and its sidewalk, a beautiful place to view the river during sunset.

7.0 Upon arriving back in New Jersey, continue straight (east) on the sidewalk along Bridge Street, passing over the Delaware & Raritan Feeder Canal and by the Stockton Post Office.

7.1 Arrive back at the old Stockton Railroad Station and the Railroad Avenue parking area, completing the history-filled loop.

21 THE DELAWARE VALLEY—STOCKTON TO BULLS ISLAND LOOP

The serenity of the canals, the flow of the river, and the views from the bridges make this a magnificent hike. With its Old World charm, you amble along the Delaware River, the Delaware & Raritan Feeder Canal, and the Delaware Canal, passing the brownstone homes, backyard gardens, and canal-side cafes, but above all, bucolic scenes along the river and canals. Laden with historical railroad, canal, and mill structures, this circuit is ripe for exploration. From Stockton, head north to Bulls Island Recreation Area. After crossing the Delaware River into Lumberville, Pennsylvania, via a picturesque pedestrian bridge, you travel south on the D&L towpath to Centre Bridge, recrossing the river into Stockton, with water never far away.

Start: Bridge Street in Stockton
Distance: 7.4-mile loop
Difficulty: Moderate–difficult due to distance
Elevation change: +-20 feet
Maximum grade: N/A
Hiking time: About 3.7 hours
Seasons/schedule: Year-round; river bridges can be icy in winter
Fees and permits: None
Dog friendly: Yes, on leash only
Trail surface: Pea gravel, concrete on bridges

Land status: New Jersey state park, Pennsylvania state park
Nearest town: Stockton
Other trail users: Bicyclers
Maps to consult: Delaware and Raritan Canal State Park
Amenities available: All manner of amenities in Stockton
Cell service: Excellent
Trail contact: Delaware and Raritan Canal State Park, (609) 924-5705, www.dandrcanal.com

FINDING THE TRAILHEAD

From the intersection of Main Street/NJ 29 and Bridge Street (leading to Pennsylvania) in Stockton, travel west on Bridge Street for 0.1 mile and at the former Stockton Railroad Station (now a market/deli) and just prior to the rail trail, turn left to the public parking areas along Railroad Avenue. If these spots are full, drive a short distance northwest on NJ 29 to the Prallsville Mills, part of the state park. Trailhead GPS: 40.405148,-74.976987

THE HIKE

As you step onto the rail bed, you have entered Delaware and Raritan Canal State Park, a 70-mile linear recreational paradise stretching from Milford to New Brunswick. While the main canal parallels the Millstone and Raritan Rivers, the feeder canal edges the Delaware River. Our hike today parallels the latter, sometimes along the towpath of the feeder canal and other times upon the rail bed of the Belvidere-Delaware Railroad

The Delaware River speeds beside the trail.

(Bel-Del), both reflecting the latest nineteenth-century means of transportation in their respective times.

Tramping along the Bel-Del route, transport yourself into the nineteenth century where 300,000 tons of coal yearly rumble down the tracks from the anthracite coal fields in Pennsylvania to New York City. Or iron from Sussex and Morris County mines, and building blocks from Hunterton County quarries, all come chugging south. Or during the harvest season, smell the rich, sweet scent of the boxcars loaded with peaches,

Lock 12 recalls another era of transportation.

blackberries, or strawberries, plucked locally and shipped to the urban areas. Or the ice cars dripping as they pass on their way to Philadelphia from Knickerbocker Ice Company, in New York's lower Hudson River valley. Imagine the holiday scent of fifty carloads of evergreen trees, rattling over the rails to the cities during Christmastime.

Special trains took tourists to the Jersey shore, Niagara Falls, and Gettysburg, as well as the Delaware Water Gap. The Bel-Del even put on a train from Lambertville to Belvidere, so fans could attend the local baseball games. Fight fans rode the rail to Bulls Island, where boxing matches were held. As boxing was illegal in Pennsylvania, Keystone State pugilist fans crossed the Lumberville Bridge to Bulls Island to arrive at ringside.

At times presidents traveled the Bel-Del: Rutherford B. Hayes speaking at Lafayette College, Grover Cleveland fishing the Delaware River, Teddy Roosevelt and William Howard Taft campaigning, Woodrow Wilson vacationing, FDR secretly visiting Lucy Mercer, and Harry S. Truman returning to Washington, DC, during the Berlin Crisis. Even America's Liberty Bell made the Bel-Del trip twice: in 1904 traveling to the St. Louis World's Fair and in 1915 returning from the Panama Pacific Exhibition. Maybe the most prized subjects traveling the Bel-Del were the local youths commuting to their respective high schools in Frenchtown or Lambertville.

As you approach the Prallsville Mill complex, the trail joins the canal towpath, passing one of the two locks on this section. Built in the 1830s, the feeder canal was originally designed to maintain the water level in the D&R Canal yet ended up transporting freight itself. In the 1840s improvements were made so the feeder canal could also transport

This pedestrian bridge links you to Bulls Island.

coal barges from the Delaware Canal in Pennsylvania, which would lock out at the New Hope basin, cross the Delaware River via cable, and lock into the feeder canal at Lambertville.

When you arrive at Bulls Island and cross the 700-foot suspension footbridge, look upriver at the wing dams, which direct the river's water into the canals: the Raritan Dam into the feeder canal and the Lumberville Dam into the Delaware Canal. You then exit off the bridge in Pennsylvania, joining the Delaware Canal towpath, commonly known as the D&L Trail, another relic of the nineteenth-century industrial era. Stroll along the river and near homes, crossing back into New Jersey via the steel girder Centre Bridge. From the railings enjoy the tranquil panoramic views of the Delaware River valley, putting an exclamation point on your experience.

MILES AND DIRECTIONS

0.0 From the former Stockton Railroad Station, cross Bridge Street and head northwest on the old Belvidere-Delaware (better known as Bel-Del) rail bed, today part of the Delaware and Raritan (D&R) Trail. Pass near houses of Stockton.

0.5 Pass the building cluster of Prallsville Mills on your right. It offers alternate parking. Immediately bridge Wickecheoke Creek with the canal and spillway to your left and the Delaware River farther left. Curve with the river, paralleling NJ 29. Hendrick Island and Eagle Island stand in the river.

THE DELAWARE VALLEY—STOCKTON TO BULLS ISLAND LOOP

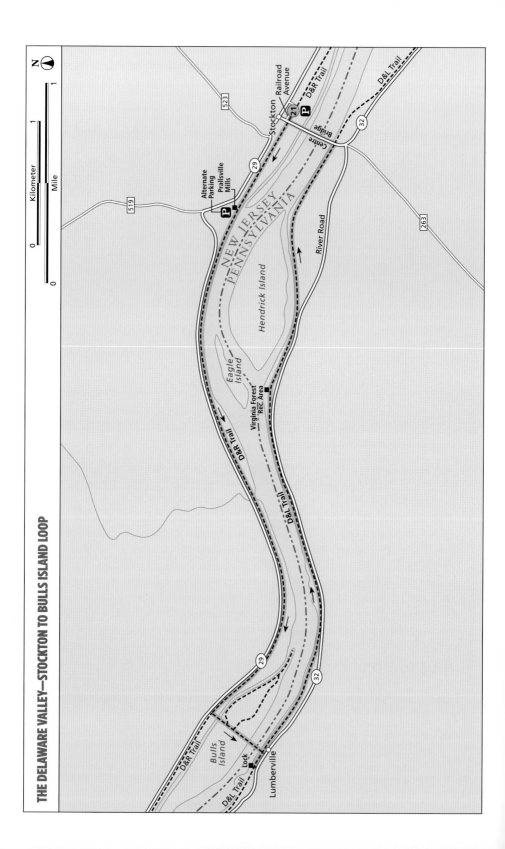

2.1 Bridge Lochatong Creek. At this location the creek enters the feeder canal and the excess goes over a spillway, which leads directly to the Delaware River.

3.3 Turn left into Bulls Island Recreation Area, crossing the canal bridge. Pass a large parking area and park structures. The isle also has a fine foot trail as well as canoe/kayak launches. Ahead, cross the Delaware River on a regal pedestrian suspension bridge.

3.6 Arrive in Pennsylvania. To get down to the trail from the end of the bridge, you must perform a jug-handle. Turn right (northwest), traveling along the shoulder of River Road until you can turn right again (northeast), bridging the spillway and the Delaware Canal. Turn right (southeast) onto the towpath. Just to your left is the Lock #12 restoration, Paunacoussing Creek Aqueduct, and a picnic area.

3.7 Pass under the pedestrian bridge over which you just walked, enjoying the Delaware River to your left and the Delaware Canal on your right.

4.8 Bridge Cuttalossa Creek, then come along Delaware Quarries. Continue traveling the towpath with the Delaware River to your left and the Delaware Canal to your right.

5.8 Pass Virginia Forest Recreation Area, with parking and restrooms. Hendrick Island is to your left.

7.2 Pass under Centre Bridge, then climb the stairs to the roadway. Turn left (east), crossing the Delaware River on Centre Bridge and its sidewalk, a beautiful place to view the river during sunset.

7.4 Arrive back at the old Stockton Railroad Station and the Railroad Avenue parking area, completing the circuit hike.

22 **KEN LOCKWOOD GORGE**

Start this rail trail adventure in hip downtown High Bridge. Stroll a rail bed that runs along the shelf of the gorge beside the scenic South Branch of the Raritan River. You will be sharing the space with cyclists, serious fly anglers, and casual daily exercisers, as well as the wildlife. Visit Gorge Bridge, site of an 1885 train crash, before backtracking.

Start: Commons Park off Main Street in High Bridge
Distance: 5.8 miles out and back
Difficulty: Moderate
Elevation change: +-80 feet
Maximum grade: 0.5% grade for entire hike
Hiking time: About 3.0 hours
Seasons/schedule: Year-round
Fees and permits: None
Dog friendly: Yes, on leash only
Trail surface: Pea gravel, a little pavement at first

Land status: Railroad right-of-way—Morris County park
Nearest town: High Bridge
Other trail users: Bicyclers, anglers, Rollerbladers
Maps to consult: Ken Lockwood Gorge WMA
Amenities available: All manner of amenities in downtown High Bridge
Cell service: Good
Trail contact: Columbia Trail, (973) 829-8417, www.morrisparks.net

FINDING THE TRAILHEAD

From exit 17 on I-78 near Annandale, take CR 31 north for 2.2 miles, then turn right onto West Main Street for 1.1 miles. Turn right on Bridge Street and follow it a few hundred feet, then turn left onto Main Street, follow it through downtown High Bridge for 0.2 mile, and turn left into the Commons Park/Columbia Trail parking area on your left. Trailhead GPS: 40.669446,-74.896554

THE HIKE

Start this rail trail hiking adventure in the center of High Bridge, a former steel town–turned–urban hipster getaway. Beginning in 1742, the iron industry grew to become the major focus of the community until the mills closed in the mid-1960s. The Taylor Iron Works provided cannonballs for both the American Revolution and the Civil War. The mills also created armaments for the Spanish-American War, as well as World Wars I and II. During peaceful times, Taylor Iron Works constructed railroad wheels, tracks, and, most notably, the teeth for the monster shovels that built the Panama Canal.

Cross Main Street and trek along the former Jersey Central High Bridge Branch, a 33-mile railroad spur built in the 1860s, serving the iron mines of Morris County. At its peak in the 1880s, 118 ore cars rambled down this road in one day, to the tune of 25,000 tons of ore in one month! On April 18, 1885, Engine #112, better known as the *Columbia*, came chugging down the tracks from the Chester Furnace. As it crossed the 260-foot-long wooden Gorge Bridge—where this hike visits—the weight of the engine, forty ore cars, five pig-iron cars, and caboose collapsed the structure, plunging 80 feet into the South Branch of the Raritan and killing one brakeman. The National Transportation Safety Board did not exist back then—the line was back up and running in a week!

This rail trail is a popular draw for hip downtown High Bridge.

The High Bridge Branch also had other purposes besides shipping ore. It had a fresh milk run and ran a scheduled passenger train until 1935. Freight trains chugged on until 1976. Ice was shipped down to the city from Lake Hopatcong, while summer excursions ran up to the lake and its picnic grove. They even ran a Halloween Special at 11:15 p.m. from High Bridge to Somerville, where a celebration would take place, with a parade, music, prizes, and fireworks. Makes you sorry that you missed October 31, 1910. But that is not the only spooky story that goes along with this hike. The legend of Hookerman also haunts this spur.

As the story goes, a railroad man lost his arm in a train accident, an all-too-common experience, especially for brakemen who got their appendages caught between the cars. Well, his arm was replaced by an artificial limb with a hook—hence the name. And so at night you may spot a mysterious light—an orb—emanating from a swinging lantern, as Hookerman searches for his missing limb. Other versions of the story have him looking for his lost wedding ring that was on his lost hand. Some scientific explanations for the "burning orb" floating above the tracks have been put forth, such as minor earthquakes releasing glowing gasses from the underworld, but for our money, the jury is still out.

Very real was the man for whom the gorge is now named. Ken Lockwood was a pioneering outdoor journalist, writing for the *Newark Evening News* for thirty years until his death in 1948. His column covered and promoted every aspect of outdoor life, especially

Gorge Bridge, site of a historic train crash

hunting, fishing, and conservation. Among his many activities, he was a trustee of the New Jersey Audubon Society. His particular loves were fly-fishing and the creation of state wildlife management areas. It was thus natural that this wildlife management area, an angler's heaven, was named in Lockwood's honor—it was purchased by the state the same year Lockwood died. During less cold times, you will likely see anglers working the South Branch of the Raritan River. The waterway is annually stocked with thousands of trout, including this very river segment.

The trail itself came to be when the Columbia Gas Transmission Company purchased 15 miles of abandoned railroad right-of-way back in the late 1990s. The gas company ran an underground gas pipe and built a surface trail for Morris and Hunterdon Counties, to make amends for disturbing other lands in those counties.

After starting the Columbia Trail at the parking area in downtown High Bridge, head east up the South Branch Raritan River. You will soon hear the roar of Solitude Falls over Lake Solitude Dam. The falls are worth a detour and can be accessed where the Union Forge Greenway makes its link with the Columbia Trail. The hiking is easy on the mostly level track pleasantly rambling through the woods. The gorge of the river sharpens beyond Cokesbury Road and you enter the Ken Lockwood Gorge, to meet the current bridge crossing the river at the site of the infamous 1885 wreck of the *Columbia*. Enjoy your return walk, as you will lose the 80 or so feet you gained during the trek.

The trail beckons.

MILES AND DIRECTIONS

0.0 Leave east from Commons Park, crossing Main Street on the Columbia Trail. Curve north through town, crossing side streets. The trail is signed with quarter-mile increments.

0.4 A spur trail goes to the dam and falls of Lake Solitude, as well as the Union Forge Greenway, a trail tracing the iron history of this area. After viewing Solitude Falls, return to the greenway, northbound, crossing the driveway of a home.

1.4 Bridge Cokesbury Road. A short path drops down to the road. Continue north. The trail is mostly shaded by maple, sycamore, and other hardwoods. Sometimes the path runs through a railroad cut. In places you can look down on the river as well as at Raritan River Road.

2.0 A low-flow waterfall tumbles above and below the Columbia Trail. The gorge wall rises further.

2.7 The Highlands Trail splits left and climbs the gorge to High Bridge–Califon Road.

2.9 Reach the bridge crossing the South Branch Raritan River, site of the infamous 1885 train wreck. Take a respite on the bench here, relaxing and taking in the geology of the gorge. Cross the bridge, then backtrack to the trailhead.

5.8 Arrive back at the High Point trailhead in downtown High Bridge, loaded with all sorts of food and drink possibilities.

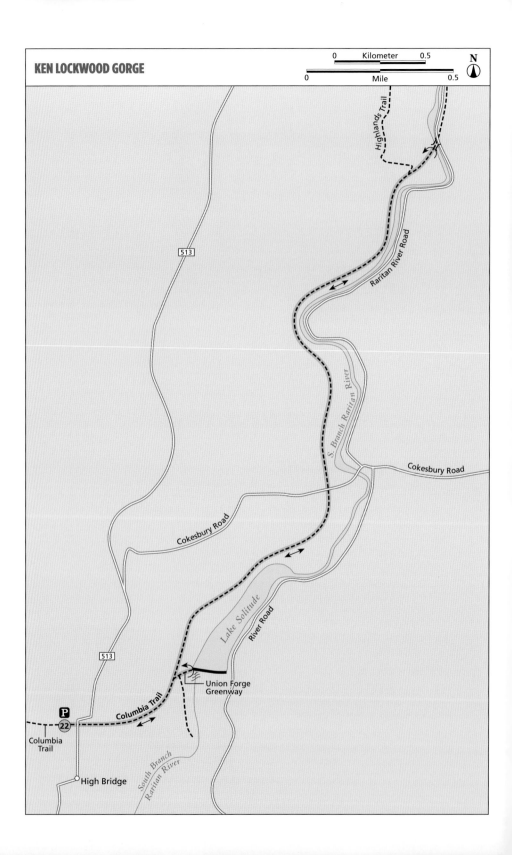

KEN LOCKWOOD GORGE

23 SCHOOLEY'S MOUNTAIN

This 833-acre Morris County park offers several hiking highlights. First, visit Lake George, then cross it on a 470-foot floating bridge. Hike along Electric Brook, admiring lesser cascades and two-stage Electric Brook Falls, aka Schooley's Falls. From there, climb to a fine overlook with an extended view. Close the loop with a trip through wooded uplands before returning to the trailhead.

Start: George Lake trailhead
Distance: 2.9-mile loop
Difficulty: Easy
Elevation change: +-519 feet
Maximum grade: 14% grade for 0.2 mile
Hiking time: About 1.4 hours
Seasons/schedule: Daily sunrise to sunset
Fees and permits: None
Dog friendly: Yes, on leash only
Trail surface: Natural

Land status: County park
Nearest town: Chester
Other trail users: Mountain bikers in some areas
Maps to consult: Schooley's Mountain County Park
Amenities available: Restrooms near trailhead
Cell service: Excellent
Trail contact: Schooley's Mountain County Park, (973) 326-7600, www.morrisparks.net

FINDING THE TRAILHEAD

From US 206 and CR 24 in Chester, take CR 24 west for 2.2 miles, then turn right on Coleman Road. Follow Coleman Road for 1.1 miles to a traffic light and stay straight as the road becomes Naughtright Road. Stay with Naughtright Road for 2.3 miles, then turn left onto East Springfield Road and follow it 0.5 mile to turn left into Schooley's Mountain Park. Turn right into the first large parking area and head for its southeast corner, near George Lake. Trailhead GPS: 40.801924,-74.784619

THE HIKE

In the days when Saratoga Springs, New York, and Newport, Rhode Island, were the main playgrounds of the rich and famous, New Jersey had its own high-end resort: Schooley's Mountain. According to a nineteenth-century traveling Frenchman, the spa was "one of the most famous resorts in the United States." It was, at least, one of America's earliest summer retreats from the sweltering heat of Philadelphia and New York City. The Lenape Indians knew the mineral springs here as being healthful. Early settlers likewise found the mineral water a tonic, saying it cured many ailments (the water's main mineral ingredient is sodium bicarbonate!).

A resort hotel, the Alpha House, was built in 1795, but it wasn't until a turnpike was built over the mountain in 1806 that business took off. The mineral springs, fine mountain air, and splendid scenery led to construction of other hotels in the 1800s, including the Heath House and the largest of all, Belmont Hall. From June 1 until the leaves fell, it became a haven for writers, politicians, and scientists who cared to debate the ideas of the day. A stagecoach traveled once a day to Hackettstown station to meet the morning train, picking up the hotel patrons and the postage. Just imagine US vice president George M.

Cross the floating bridge over Lake George.

Dallas (1845–1849), for whom Dallas, Texas, is named, stepping out of a carriage. Or the founder of Chemical National Bank, Cornelius V. S. Roosevelt (Teddy's grandfather), fowling on the mountain. Or Ulysses S. Grant and his daughter strolling the promenade. Or the Vanderbilts and the Edisons watching an in-house theater production. They paid $14 to $28 a week for accommodations, but people like us, who were here for the day, would pay a fee of $2.50. Folks still flock to Schooley's Mountain for fresh air, great views, and recreation, but the resort hotels long ago vanished.

Besides the mineral waters bubbling out from the crag, iron ore was another earthly treasure investors hoped to cash in on. Three ore belts ran northeast through Schooley's Mountain: the Marsh Mine, the Hurd Mine, and the Van Syckle Mine. Starting circa 1790 and operating intermittently for the next hundred years, prospectors dug more than fifteen mines and exploratory pits in and around the immediate area. The miners excavated 100-foot open pits, dropping 30 to 40 feet, while others created 60-foot shafts, all the while extracting 5,000 to 12,000 tons of magnetite. The state inspectors claimed, "None of the mines . . . were what could be considered as large operations, most were prospect explorations at best." It has also been recorded that the magnetic attraction of the ore held on to the miners' tools, making a difficult job more difficult. So as you hike Schooley's Mountain, understand a compass may go berserk, especially if passing the two exploratory pits along the route.

As with other Morris County parks, the trails are color-coded and well maintained yet have a few mazelike spots that along with user-created paths can confuse the unwary. You

The upper stage of two-part Electric Brook Falls

likely won't have trouble, even near George Lake, since the correct routes here are intuitive. Enjoy the lake, waterfalls, and views that make this park a fine Jersey hike.

MILES AND DIRECTIONS

0.0 From the south corner of the parking area, take a paved walkway toward the boathouse and beach. Reach the floating bridge and cross George Lake, opening up nice

Looking out to the South Branch Raritan River valley

looks across the intimate body of water. Once across the impoundment, head left along the shore. Spurs go right up to the Lodge, an event venue.

0.3 Cross George Lake dam and come to an intersection. Head right on the Blue Trail along boulder-strewn Electric Brook, descending past the powerhouse ruins. The powerhouse led to the name Electric Brook, as the stream powered a modest operation by today's standards. Pass cascades aplenty under beech and birch.

SCHOOLEY'S MOUNTAIN

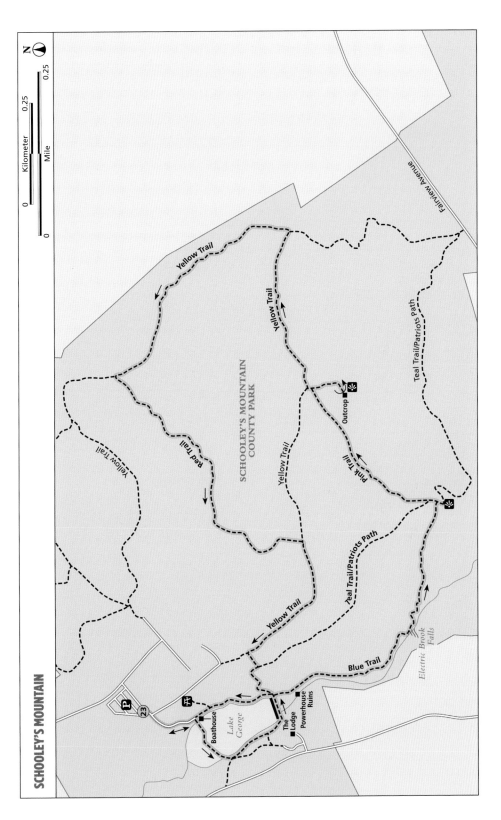

0.6 Come to two-tier, 40-foot Electric Brook Falls, a bona fide cataract spilling over naked rock. Ahead, leave left, away from Electric Brook, climbing into a boulder jumble.

0.8 A spur trail goes right out to a fantastic view southwest into the South Branch Raritan River valley. Also the Teal Trail/Patriots Path crosses here. Join the Pink Trail, gently climbing in rich woods.

1.1 Level out at an intersection. Here, the Yellow Trail goes left and a spur goes right to a castle-like outcrop with leaf-off views to the east. After visiting the outcrop, join the Yellow Trail, descending the east side of Schooley's Mountain in oak-dominated woods.

1.5 Come to another intersection and head left on the Yellow Trail. This segment is also referred to as the Grand Loop Trail. Skirt close to the park boundary, making your steepest climb of the hike.

1.9 Reach another intersection after topping out on the broad crown of Schooley's Mountain under tall hardwoods. Head left, now on the Red Trail, enjoying a glorious walk atop Schooley's Mountain.

2.4 Make yet another trail junction. Head right on the Yellow Trail, turning toward the trailhead.

2.6 Split left, descending toward George Lake. A maze of user-created paths leads you to the impoundment. From there, walk along the shore and past the boathouse.

2.9 Arrive back at the trailhead, completing the hike with multiple varied highlights.

24 BLACK RIVER GORGE

This balloon loop first visits historic Cooper Mill then travels down the Black River, passing a dammed pond, bordered by tall tulip trees. The waterway is then set free, crashing headlong into a steep-sided heavily wooded gorge. Here you find a forgotten dam and old cabin before looping back toward the trailhead along the upper hillsides of the gorge.

Start: Cooper Gristmill trailhead
Distance: 4.5-mile balloon loop
Difficulty: Moderate
Elevation change: +-531 feet
Maximum grade: 8% downhill grade for 0.4 mile
Hiking time: About 2.3 hours
Seasons/schedule: Year-round
Fees and permits: None
Dog friendly: Yes, on leash only
Trail surface: Forested natural surface
Land status: County park

Nearest town: Chester
Other trail users: None
Maps to consult: Cooper Gristmill & Elizabeth D. Kay Environmental Center
Amenities available: Restrooms at trailhead
Cell service: Good
Trail contact: Cooper Gristmill & Elizabeth D. Kay Environmental Center, (973) 829-8417, www. morrisparks.net

FINDING THE TRAILHEAD

From the intersection of US 206 and CR 513/Washington Turnpike in Chester, take Washington Turnpike west for 1.3 miles to turn left into the parking area just before bridging the Black River. Trailhead GPS: 40.778636,-74.720264

THE HIKE

Cooper Mill—built in 1826 and on the National Register of Historic Places—and the downstream Black River Gorge are the setting for this rewarding and varied hike that uses an old rail line for part of its distance. The trail system, although well marked and maintained, has a myriad of interconnected paths that can prove confusing if you don't stay on your toes. Take a picture of the map in this guide before you depart. Despite the navigational challenges, the land, water, trees, and historical relics to be discovered at this Morris County park will prove more than worth your time.

Back in the nineteenth century, the Black River Gorge must have been one noisy place. At Cooper Mill, your starting point, you would hear the rhythmic splashes of the waterwheel and the ever-present grinding of a 2,000-pound millstone upon the bedstone. Can you catch the sweet scent of cornmeal as the mill produces 800 pounds an hour? Ready to make spoon bread or hush puppies?

Moving down along the Black River in 1872–73, the clank of picks and hammers rang out as the eighty immigrant Italians laid track for the Hacklebarney Branch of the Central Railroad, a spur connecting Hacklebarney Mine with the Chester Branch. During the 1880s, thirty carloads of ore a day rumbled over the very trail you are hiking.

An old dam forms a fall on the Black River.

As you continue down the line, the din from the Chester Iron Mining Company's operations could be heard echoing from the Hacklebarney Mine itself. For the time and place, it was a major iron producer, opening and shutting under the laws of supply and demand. From pre–Revolutionary War to 1896, it is estimated that 250,000 tons of ore came out of these hills, peaking at 20,000 tons a year. With about fourteen veins, running 0.5 mile long, there were approximately fourteen open cuts and shafts. The men (it was believed to be bad luck for a woman to be in a mine) worked for 50 cents to a dollar a day in shafts, ranging from 1 to 12 feet wide, 15 to 200 feet high, and 200 feet deep.

On April 24, 1881, the miners would have heard the beckoning knock, knock, knock of a lonely ghost (another miner superstition) when the tragedy known as the "Hanging Wall Disaster" struck. A 300-ton roof collapsed, crushing six men and injuring two more. Had it not been Sunday, at least one hundred men would have been in the hole. Mining accidents were all too common in that day.

Besides the mine's open pits, now fenced in, the route will take you past tailing piles—mine refuse—and exploratory pits. You may want to refrain from whistling while hiking, as the miners also felt that whistling was bad luck.

Entering into the Black River Gorge, the cascading water, pool to pool, should have a natural, soothing sound, especially after all the above industrial clamor. The mixed oak forest gives way to deep forest replete with preserved hemlocks, becoming cooler as you descend along the cascading Black River, into the gorge. Find an old dam and cabin remains before climbing past a second cabin site then rising into mixed oak. Come near

Historic Cooper Gristmill

the worth-a-visit Elizabeth D. Kay Environmental Center before returning to the Black River and backtracking on the old rail line.

MILES AND DIRECTIONS

0.0 Leave the parking area, heading west on the grassy strip parallel to Washington Turnpike. Quickly come to Cooper Mill, examining the sturdy stone structure, then take steps down to the Black River. Bridge the old tailrace twice in succession under sycamores. Continue downstream with the Black River to your right.

0.1 Pull away from the river, working through woods.

0.3 Join the old rail trail. You are now along a pond. Ahead, on your left, pass old mine tailings, now integrated into the wooded landscape.

0.7 Come along the pond dam on your right, then pass fenced-in, now wooded pit mines. Pass a closed auto bridge and continue following the now freely flowing Black River. Cruise under tall tulip trees.

1.3 Come to an intersection after bridging a couple of tributary streams. Stay right with the Green Trail, heading south, beginning the loop portion of the hike.

1.4 An orange-blazed spur goes right to cross the Black River and heads to the cottage ruins and dam we will encounter from this side of the river. Stay straight, still on the Green Trail. Start descending into the Black River Gorge as the hemlock-rich slope steepens.

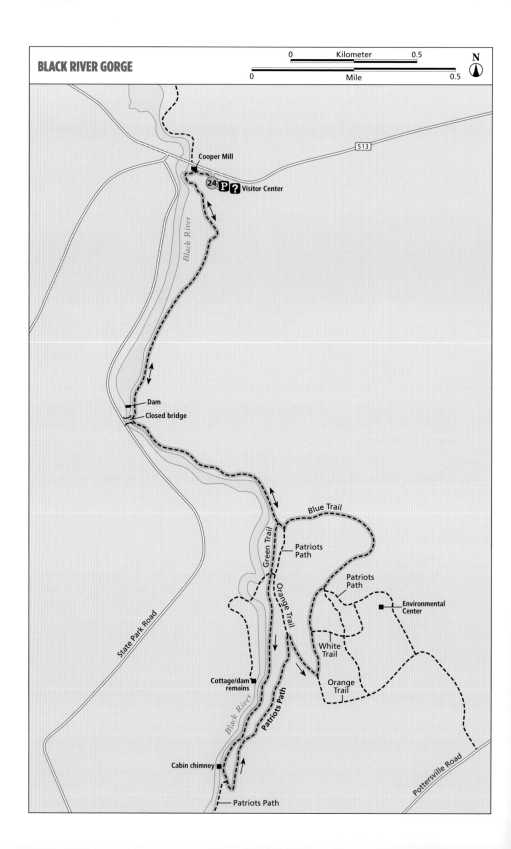

BLACK RIVER GORGE

0   Kilometer   0.5

0   Mile   0.5

N

513

Cooper Mill

24 **P** **?** Visitor Center

Black River

Dam

Closed bridge

Blue Trail

Green Trail

Patriots Path

Patriots Path

Environmental Center

Orange Trail

White Trail

Cottage/dam remains

Orange Trail

State Park Road

Black River

Patriots Path

Cabin chimney

Patriots Path

Pottersville Road

1.7 Come to the spillway dam and ruins of a summer cottage across the water. This is a great place for a stop. Beyond here, the trail continues down the gorge.

1.9 Come to the footings and chimney of an old cabin. Climb from the remains and shortly intersect a red-blazed portion of the Patriots Path, which winds all over the county park. Join the red-blazed trail and head left. The path climbs and curves back north. Strangely, pass an old bathtub beside the trail.

2.4 Split right, climbing on an orange-blazed trail.

2.5 Stay left with the Yellow Trail. You are now mostly atop the gorge, and the walking is easy. Ahead, pass an intersection with the White Trail as it leaves right in oak-dominated forest.

2.7 Reach another intersection. Here, a spur goes right to the environmental center, as does another leg of the Yellow Trail. Join the Blue Trail and begin gently descending toward the Black River on a wide old road-turned-trail. Come alongside a tributary of the Black River.

3.2 Meet the Orange Trail, then take a quick right and come to the Green Trail. You have completed the loop. From here, backtrack to Cooper Mill.

4.5 Arrive back at the Cooper Mill trailhead, completing the historic hike.

25 JOCKEY HOLLOW

This hike at Morristown National Historical Park fashions a hill-and-dale adventure into the past on well-maintained forested paths. Start at the visitor center, then check out the Wick House, a restored Colonial farm, before joining the historic Menham Elizabethtown Road Trail to pick up the Grand Loop Trail. Wind through forests and along quaint streams to Cat Swamp Pond, then climb toward Sugarloaf to next view replica soldier huts like those wintered in by soldiers during the Revolutionary War. Descend back to streams to make the Aqueduct Loop Trail and learn about early efforts to get a water supply to Morristown before returning to the visitor center via the final portion of the Grand Loop Trail. You Are Here maps at intersections make navigation much easier.

Start: Park visitor center
Distance: 6.2-mile balloon loop
Difficulty: Moderate, does have some solid climbs
Elevation change: +-768 feet
Maximum grade: 4% grade for 1.0 mile
Hiking time: About 3.4 hours
Seasons/schedule: Daily 8:00 a.m. to 8:00 p.m.; winter best for historical perspective
Fees and permits: None
Dog friendly: Yes, on leash only

Trail surface: Natural
Land status: National historical park
Nearest town: Morristown
Other trail users: None
Maps to consult: Morristown National Historical Park Trail Map
Amenities available: Restrooms, water, visitor center at trailhead
Cell service: Excellent
Trail contact: Morristown National Historical Park, (973) 539-2016, ext. 210, www.nps.gov/morr

FINDING THE TRAILHEAD

From exit 33 on I-287 in Morristown, take Harter Road north for 0.8 mile, then turn left on US 202 south. Follow US 202 for 0.8 mile, then turn right on Bailey Hollow Road and follow it 0.8 mile. Turn left onto Jockey Hollow Road and follow it 2 miles to the Jockey Hollow Visitor Center. Trailhead GPS: 40.761953,-74.542607

THE HIKE

This hike requires imagination in summertime: You must pretend it's freezing cold. Revolutionary War winter suffering generally brings two words to mind: Valley Forge. The Continental Army's winter encampment there in 1777–78 was indeed fraught with hardship, but the fact remains a harder winter awaited them two years later, here at Morristown. Eighteenth-century armies didn't normally fight in the winter; they went to winter quarters, and fighting resumed in spring. As a winter encampment for the Continental Army for 1779–80, Washington chose Morristown. It was close enough to New York and Perth Amboy to keep an eye on the British, but it was protected by the

The Wick House saw the Revolutionary War.

Watchung Mountains. He couldn't have known this winter would be, by most accounts, the worst one of the eighteenth century, with 4 feet of snow on the ground by January.

Thirteen thousand Continental troops came to Morristown that winter, and over 1,000 log huts were built in Jockey Hollow, a few miles outside of town. The 14-by-16-foot huts had a fireplace and housed a dozen men each—we pass reconstructed huts on this walk. Washington and his entourage stayed in the Morristown home of the Ford family, the finest house in town.

Although Morristown's "hard winter" of 1779–80 surpassed that at Valley Forge, far fewer men died. In the intervening years the army became more competent at managing its affairs and acquiring provisions and supplies. But the winter at Morristown was hard enough—it fostered a mutiny of Pennsylvania soldiers. This gave birth to one of the more remarkable bits of New Jersey folklore.

According to legend, two Pennsylvania soldiers accosted a young Temperance Wick, on horseback. Wick's house, which you will visit on this hike, was nearby. "Tempe," as the girl was called, had gone to fetch a doctor for her mother; her father, an army captain, had died not long before. The mutineers wanted Tempe's horse, and after first feigning surrender, she spurred the horse and charged for home. Knowing the mutineers would give chase and look in all the customary places for her horse, Tempe—so the legend goes—brought the horse inside, put down a comforter to muffle its hoof-steps, and hid it inside the bedroom of the house.

Replica quarters where the Americans wintered in Jockey Hollow

This lovely bit of legend is nonetheless only legend, possibly why the National Park Service makes scant mention of it. Instead they focus on the historical fact that the Wick House was the headquarters for General Arthur St. Clair—which is interesting, but no match for a horse hidden in a bedroom. Morristown National Historical Park preserves many significant places: the Ford Mansion, Jockey Hollow, and the Wick House, as well as nearby Fort Nonsense. Local public-spirited citizens started acquiring the properties in the 1870s; in 1933 they were transferred to the federal government and became America's first national historical park (an honor not bestowed on Valley Forge until 1976).

In the 1930s the Civilian Conservation Corps conducted archaeological investigations of the Revolutionary encampment at Jockey Hollow. The "dig" was crude by later standards, and much of the data was subsequently lost, yet this was some of the first historical archaeology conducted in the United States, and provided insights into that epoch of American history.

MILES AND DIRECTIONS

0.0 As you face the Jockey Hollow Visitor Center with the parking area to your back, walk to and around the right side of the visitor center, then continue on to the Wick House. After exploring the grounds, head right, southerly, down a wide grassy lane toward Jockey Hollow Road, tracing old Mendham Elizabethtown Road, now a trail.

0.5 Head left on the Grand Loop Trail, easterly, dipping toward Primrose Brook.

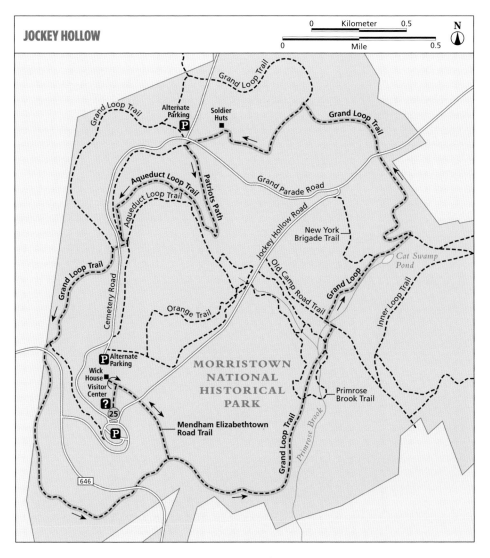

0   Kilometer   0.5

0   Mile   0.5

N

1.2   Cross the Primrose Brook Trail the first of two times, as well as crossing Primrose Brook.

1.5   Meet the Old Camp Road Trail. Head left, crossing Primrose Brook again, then split right, still with the Grand Loop Trail. Keep climbing up the Primrose Brook valley.

1.8   Meet the New York Brigade Trail. It goes left. Stay right, sticking with the Grand Loop Trail. Pass 1-acre Cat Swamp Pond in big woods.

2.0   Reach an intersection. Stay left with the Grand Loop Trail as a blue-blazed trail heads right for the Inner Loop Trail and the Outer Loop Trail. Begin an extended climb toward Jockey Hollow Road.

2.4   Cross paved Jockey Hollow Road, dip to a hollow, then climb.

2.7   Split left on an unnamed path toward the soldier huts as the Grand Loop Trail stays right. Wind downhill.

3.1 Come to the replica soldier huts, of both officers and enlisted men. Inspect them in and out. Descend toward the intersection of Grand Parade Road and Cemetery Road then split left, southerly, on the orange-blazed Patriots Path. Trace a ditched stream through woods.

3.7 Meet the green-blazed Aqueduct Loop Trail, with an accompanying brochure detailing the efforts of Morristown to use the streams of Jockey Hollow for municipal water. Climb along a stream, passing a shortcut for the loop.

4.3 Watch for a rocked-in springhead just before reaching a major intersection near Cemetery Road. Head right (west), crossing Cemetery Road and shortly meeting the Grand Loop Trail. Head left here, briefly climbing to the hike's high point, then make a very steep descent.

4.7 Meet an equestrian spur going left to the parking lot. Stay with the Grand Loop Trail, crossing Tempe Wick Road, then continue south, as other trails go toward Lewis Morris County Park.

5.5 Cross a small stream in a hollow, then climb to cross Tempe Wick Road a second time.

5.7 Meet the Mendham Elizabethtown Road Trail, completing the loop portion of the hike. Head left toward the Wick House, backtracking.

6.2 Arrive back at the trailhead, completing the historic hike.

26 LORD STIRLING PARK

Visit Glacial Lake Passaic, now called the Great Swamp. Designated a National Natural Landmark, it doesn't take long hiking this level loop to understand why. Within the 450-acre park's natural lands, the boardwalk-heavy route meanders through marshes, meadows, swamps, and woodlands, while hugging the Passaic River and a series of ponds. While walking the trails, make use of the observation towers and blinds to view the 215 species of birds recorded in the park. Depending on the season, this serene hike could be interrupted by the mosquito. You Are Here maps are posted at most trail intersections, helping you navigate the mazelike trail network.

Start: East side of Environmental Education Center
Distance: 4.1-mile loop
Difficulty: Easy–moderate, potential wet segments
Elevation change: +-60 feet
Maximum grade: N/A
Hiking time: About 2.0 hours
Seasons/schedule: Daily sunrise to sunset
Fees and permits: None
Dog friendly: No, pets not allowed on trails

Trail surface: Natural surface, lots of boardwalk
Land status: County park
Nearest town: Basking Ridge
Other trail users: None
Maps to consult: Environmental Education Center at Lord Stirling Park
Amenities available: Restrooms, water at EE Center
Cell service: Good
Trail contact: Environmental Education Center at Lord Stirling Park, (908) 722-1200, ext. 5002, www.somersetcountyparks.org

FINDING THE TRAILHEAD

From exit 30 on I-287 southwest of Morristown, take Maple Avenue south for 2.9 miles, then turn left on Lord Stirling Road and follow it 1 mile to turn left into the Lord Stirling Park Environmental Education Center. Trailhead GPS: 40.695149,-74.520842

THE HIKE

This hike takes us through rich bottomland meadows, once part of a glacial lake, also preserved as adjacent Great Swamp National Wildlife Refuge. These meadows were prime farmland—and responsible for the park's name, indirectly. William Alexander, who lived here, was a lord who died creating a democracy. He was born in 1725 to a wealthy, well-connected family with a profitable provisioning business (they supplied the English army during the pre-Revolution French and Indian War). Alexander married Sarah Livingston in 1748; his brother-in-law William Livingston was a future governor of New Jersey. Other relatives included the Stevens, Parker, and Rutherfurd families, a who's who of the time. He had long-standing land interests in the East Jersey Board of Proprietors, and in his spare time he became one of the founders of King's College in New York, now Columbia University.

Hiking along the Passaic River

There were some disputes over payment of army contracts, and Alexander went to England to claim payment in the late 1750s. At the same time, he pursued another ambition: a claim to a lapsed Scottish earldom, which would have made him "Lord Stirling." A Scottish jury accepted his claims, but not the British House of Lords. The Scottish recognition was still good enough for Alexander, who on his return to America in 1761 called himself "Lord Stirling." So did most everyone else, including George Washington.

With a lord's title (sort of), he decided to adopt a lord's lifestyle, which he could afford. Attracted by the rich meadows and grazing pasture here in Basking Ridge, he built a large mansion and estate, regarded at the time as one of the grandest in the colonies. At the same time, Lord Stirling expanded his business interests. He was heavily invested in the iron industry and owned mines and ironworks in northern New Jersey (at Hibernia) and at Sterling Lake, New York (named after him). Hibernia made cannon and grapeshot for the Revolutionary War effort, and Sterling Ironworks made part of the great Hudson River chain that was strung across the Hudson, famously blocking the British navy's upriver progress.

But all this investment absorbed more cash than it produced, and Lord Stirling's finances grew dire. With the arrival of the Revolution, his status as lord did not prevent him from adopting the Patriot cause, which likewise drained his finances. First a colonel in the New Jersey Militia, he later served as a general in the Continental Army under Washington; the Hessians at Trenton surrendered to him. Descriptions of Alexander are complex. Some regarded him as flamboyant, vain, and pompous, with an excessive appetite for food and drink. Others who fought alongside him called him loyal, popular with his soldiers, and brave under fire—a reliable general, if not a brilliant one.

Boardwalks take you through special wetlands at Lord Stirling Park.

How would this lord fare in the new American democracy he helped create? No one knows—he died in January 1783, just as the war was winding down, from chronic gout, a virtual bankrupt. His property was sold to pay his debts. His grand estate fell to ruins soon after his death and was eventually forgotten.

But not forgotten forever—the site of his estate became Lord Stirling Park, and subsequent archaeological investigations of the site proved that the grand descriptions of it were correct. Stirling's memory lives on here at the park, where you can enjoy the lovely landscape that once attracted would-be nobility.

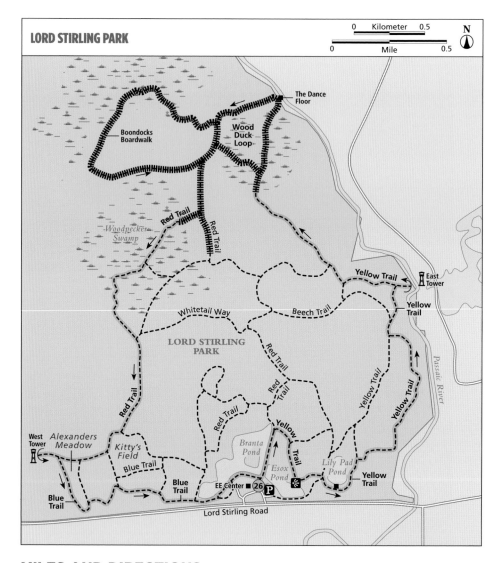

LORD STIRLING PARK

0 | Kilometer | 0.5

0 | Mile | 0.5

N

The Dance Floor

Boondocks Boardwalk

Wood Duck Loop

Red Trail

Red Trail

Woodpecker Swamp

Yellow Trail

East Tower

Yellow Trail

Whitetail Way

Beech Trail

LORD STIRLING PARK

Red Trail

Yellow Trail

Yellow Trail

Red Trail

Red Trail

Passaic River

West Tower

Alexanders Meadow

Kitty's Field

Red Trail

Red Trail

Branta Pond

Yellow Trail

Lily Pad Pond

Blue Trail

Esox Pond

Yellow Trail

Blue Trail

EE Center

26

P

Blue Trail

Lord Stirling Road

MILES AND DIRECTIONS

0.0 From the northwest corner of the parking lot and the east side of the Environmental Education Center, veer right (northeast) onto the sidewalk, passing a boardwalk leaving left. Continue straight onto a gravel path, leading to the trail register. Crossing the causeway, you are on the Yellow and Red Trails; Esox Pond is on the right and Branta Pond on the left.

0.1 Turn right (southeast) onto a grassy path. You are now solely on the Yellow Trail and will be until you reach the west side of Lenape Meadow. Ahead, split right again on the Yellow Trail.

0.2 Pass a spur to a little dock looking on Esox Pond. Stay with the Yellow Trail, passing green-blazed paths, then circle around to the south side of heavily vegetated Lily Pad Pond. Continue on the Yellow Trail, passing a green-blazed connector before leaving Lily Pad Pond.

0.9 Come to another leg of the Yellow Trail in Lenape Meadow. Stay right toward the East Observation Tower. Ahead, take the spur east to the tower overlooking the Passaic River. Resume the Yellow Trail west.

1.2 Split right with the green-blazed trail toward Boondocks Boardwalk. Ahead, pass a spur left toward the Red Trail. Keep northwest, with marsh to your right. Begin an extensive segment of boardwalk.

1.5 Reach an intersection of boardwalks. Stay right, on the right side of the Wood Duck Loop. Wooded swamp rises on both sides of the trail. Pass the Dance Floor, a river observation spot.

1.8 Split right onto the Boondocks Boardwalk. Begin looping on a boardwalk through a wildlife-rich swamp.

2.5 Head right (south), still on boardwalk. Ahead, come to yet another intersection and split right onto the Red Trail, remaining on boardwalk. Work around Woodpecker Swamp and come to the Great Swamp Oak, a huge tree that needs no signage.

3.1 Come to another intersection. Stay right on the Red Trail, southbound, as Whitetail Way enters from the east.

3.3 Split right toward the Blue Trail and West Observation Tower, passing the Borrow Pit Marsh. Keep west in open fields, coming to a small hill, and reach the West Observation Tower, a favorable birding spot.

3.7 Come near Lord Stirling Road and turn east, staying right at diverging arms of the Blue Trail.

4.0 Come along the south side of Branta Pond, then pass by the Discovery Garden. Stay along the shore, curving around the north side of the EE Center.

4.1 Arrive back at the EE Center parking lot, completing the marshy boardwalk-heavy hike.

Climb the First Watchung Mountain (also known as South Mountain) to Washington Rock, where a 1780 bonfire signaled to the American forces "The British are coming!" Traverse rolling hills past four seasonal cascades, the largest being Hemlock Falls with its 22-foot drop. Stroll along the Rahway River, passing dammed ponds and wandering through bottomlands. The route fluctuates between trails and old carriage roads, on a mazelike network of trails that can seem confusing to first-time visitors to this Essex County park that forms a picturesque mountain greenspace in northeast Jersey.

Start: Locust Grove parking area
Distance: 5.8-mile loop
Difficulty: Moderate, does have some solid climbs
Elevation change: +-805 feet
Maximum grade: 12% grade for 0.5 mile
Hiking time: About 3.5 hours; add navigation time
Seasons/schedule: Daily dawn to dusk; hiking good year-round
Fees and permits: None
Dog friendly: Yes, on leash only

Trail surface: Natural
Land status: County park
Nearest town: Millburn
Other trail users: Bicyclers, runners
Maps to consult: South Mountain Reservation
Amenities available: Restrooms at trailhead
Cell service: Excellent
Trail contact: South Mountain Reservation, (973) 268-3500, www.essexcountyparks.org/parks/south-mountain-reservation

FINDING THE TRAILHEAD

From exit 50 on I-78 near Millburn, travel north on Vaux Hall Road for 0.7 mile. At the T intersection turn left (west) onto Millburn Avenue. At 0.2 mile turn right (north) onto Lackawanna Place and go 0.1 mile to the T intersection with Glen Avenue. Turn right onto Glen Avenue and immediately turn left into the Locust Grove parking lot. Trailhead GPS: 40.727283,-74.304305

THE HIKE

We hike through one of America's first parks on this adventure. Essex County was a pioneer in creating parks in New Jersey, and one of its first was South Mountain Reservation. This spot in the Watchung Mountains is historic; Washington Rock here was the site of a signal beacon (one of a series) that warned the Continental Army of British approach while they were encamped in Morristown. The first park parcel here was bought in 1896, and land acquisition continued for over a decade.

At the same time, the Essex County Parks Department set about making plans for the reservation. While leaving it mostly natural, they wanted a series of romantic drives, paths, walks, and other features, all of which we use on our ramble. To design this they chose the best: Frederick Law Olmsted, designer of Central Park and many other notable American landscapes. Olmsted died before much could be done, but his sons' firm, the

Millburn as seen from Washington Rock

Olmsted Brothers, finished the plans in 1902. Reforesting the land was a priority, with over 3,000 rhododendrons planted in 1910 alone. The rest of the park design was built over time, the last significant work being done by the Civilian Conservation Corps in the 1930s.

Alas, some original park features (rustic shelters, bridges, and benches) have fallen to ruin and vanished, and much of the rest of the park is in varying stages of overgrowth and decay. Olmsted's Central Park once suffered the same fate but was reborn when the

Hemlock Falls makes its dive from a stone parapet.

Central Park Conservancy was established to restore it to its original elegance. Thankfully, South Mountain Reservation is following the same route: The South Mountain Conservancy is working hard to bring the reservation back to the elegance and charm of its glory days.

One of the biggest challenges of hiking here is the sheer number of trails and intersections to navigate, enough to confuse a GPS. Keep up with where you are. Luckily, our

Hobble Falls is a three-tiered pourover.

hike traces two blazed trails the entire way, making it a simple matter of following the blazes—first the yellow blazes of the Lenape Trail, then the white blazes of the Rahway Trail. Even so, user-created trails further complicate matters. Worst-case scenario, you may have to ask your fellow hikers for directions, which can be very troublesome if you are a man.

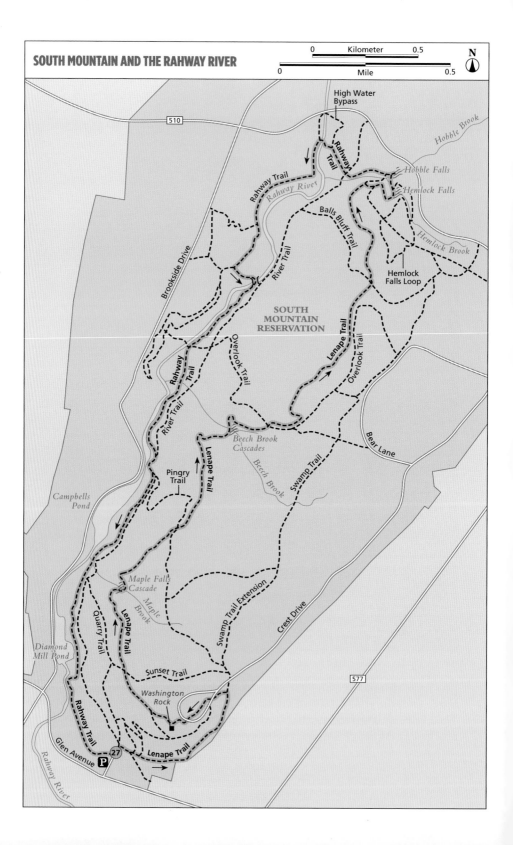

Kilometer

Mile

N

510

High Water
Bypass

Hobble Brook

Rahway Trail

Rahway Trail

Rahway River

Hobble Falls

Hemlock Falls

Balls Bluff Trail

Hemlock Brook

Brookside Drive

River Trail

Hemlock
Falls Loop

SOUTH
MOUNTAIN
RESERVATION

Lenape Trail

Overlook Trail

Rahway
Trail

Overlook Trail

River Trail

Bear Lane

Beech Brook
Cascades

Pingry
Trail

Lenape Trail

Beech Brook

Swamp Trail

Campbells
Pond

Maple Falls
Cascade

Maple Brook

Quarry Trail

Lenape Trail

Swamp Trail Extension

Crest Drive

Diamond
Mill Pond

Sunset Trail

577

Washington
Rock

Rahway Trail

Lenape Trail

Glen Avenue

27

P

Lenape Trail

Rahway River

MILES AND DIRECTIONS

0.0 At the far end (northeast) of the Locust Grove parking area, locate the junction of the three carriage roads, which the park calls trails. Take the right prong onto the yellow-blazed Lenape Trail and ascend a gravel path into a picnic grove.

0.1 Climb through hardwoods on the Lenape Trail. Ahead, pass a pair of old carriage roads now reverted to trail. Continue ascending on the Lenape Trail, coming very near the park boundary.

0.4 Reach an intersection after a big climb. Head left on the Lenape Trail toward Washington Rock, shortly crossing the loop of Crest Drive. Cross the circle a second time, then descend to Washington Rock, where fires were lit to warn of the British troop movements. Multiple trails lead to other rocks with views below of Millburn and beyond.

0.9 Cross the Sunset Trail.

1.2 Come to Maple Falls Cascade, a 50-foot-long seasonal cataract angling down a stone cliff. Circle above the falls.

1.5 Cross the Pingry Trail. Roll north through woods.

1.9 Reach Beech Brook Cascades, a two-pronged 30-foot cataract where a pair of streams fall over rock before merging and falling more. Climb from the falls to cross the Overlook Trail. Keep north on a wooded, sometimes rocky ridge.

2.5 Cross the Balls Bluff Trail, then descend toward Hemlock Brook and the Rahway River, still staying with the yellow-blazed Lenape Trail.

2.8 Reach the stone pillars of Balls Bluff, a former picnic shelter. Continue dropping to bottomland, then cross an old carriage road, the Greenwood Trail. Curve into the Hemlock Brook valley ahead, crossing the Hemlock Falls Loop. User-created trails add to the confusion. Stay with the yellow-blazed Lenape Trail.

3.1 Rock hop Hemlock Brook, then walk stone stairs, turn downstream, and reach Hemlock Falls, a 22-foot spiller over a naked stone face. Stay with the Lenape Trail, continuing downstream along Hemlock Brook. Take the right spur to Hobble Falls, a three-tiered 20-foot pourover.

3.4 Come to a major four-way intersection. Here, the yellow-blazed Lenape Trail goes right and the River Trail goes left across Hemlock Brook on a bridge, but we stay straight, joining the white-blazed Rahway Trail. You will stay with the white blazes all the way back to the trailhead. Ahead, cross the Rahway River, but if it is too high, take the bypass and bridge it on South Orange Avenue. Turn downstream along the west bank of the clear and rushing Rahway River.

3.9 Rock hop an unnamed tributary.

4.1 Bridge the Rahway River and continue downstream, running roughly parallel to the River Trail, now on the east riverbank.

4.4 A spur goes right, crossing a weir spanning the Rahway River and trails linking to Brookside Drive. Keep downriver, staying with the white blazes.

4.9 Come near Campbells Pond and enter another trail web. Occasionally merge with the River Trail.

5.3 Come near Diamond Mill Pond. Here, the Rahway Trail enters an area with fairy/doll houses that is popular with young kids. The Rahway Trail is also called the Fairy Trail hereabouts.

5.8 Arrive back at the trailhead, completing the rewarding yet navigationally challenging hike.

28 LIBERTY STATE PARK

On this adventure the skyline isn't broken by towering oaks, syca-mores, or white pines but by Lady Liberty, Columbus Monument, Lib-eration Monument, and Manhattan skyscrapers. The route takes walkways, a nature path, and cobblestone sidewalks past many a sight. All these tracks border salt marshes, coves, ponds, the Hudson River, and the Morris Canal Big Basin. This flat loop outing is bustling with bicycles, yachts, tugs, helicopters, and multinational sightseers. Come early to experience this bustling scene. Side trips to Millen-nium Park, Ellis Island, and the Statue of Liberty are doable along the route.

Start: Park office/visitor center
Distance: 5.1-mile loop
Difficulty: Easy
Elevation change: +-40 feet
Maximum grade: N/A
Hiking time: About 2.5 hours
Seasons/schedule: Daily dawn to dusk
Fees and permits: None
Dog friendly: Yes, on leash only
Trail surface: Asphalt, concrete, gravel

Land status: State park
Nearest town: Jersey City
Other trail users: Bicyclers, joggers
Maps to consult: Liberty State Park
Amenities available: Restrooms, picnic tables at visitor center
Cell service: Excellent
Trail contact: Liberty State Park, (201) 915-3400, ext. 101, www.nj.gov/dep/parksandforests

FINDING THE TRAILHEAD

From the juncture of I-95 and I-78 in Newark, travel east on I-78 (also called New Jersey Turnpike Extension), crossing the Newark Bay Bridge. Take exit 14B, Jersey City/Liberty State Park. From the tollbooth bear left and then turn left onto Bay View Avenue, all the while following Liberty State Park signs. Travel 0.2 mile until you come to a rotary. Take the first exit from the circle onto Morris Pesin Drive, taking it 0.7 mile through the entrance to the park and following it to the third and final parking lot on your right, just past Freedom Way on the left. The park office, restrooms, and concession are at the southeast end of the parking lot. Trailhead GPS: 40.693293,-74.057832

THE HIKE

This urban hike at New Jersey's most popular state park takes us past the historic Morris Canal Big Basin, the world's best view of Manhattan, a spectacular historic train shed and railroad terminal, views of Ellis Island and the Statue of Liberty, and the site of an infa-mous island munitions depot. If you want to maximize American history and landmarks, you're in the right place! Before this area was part of Jersey City, it was Communipaw Cove. The famous Morris Canal connected with the bay in the canal basin on the north side of the park here. Later, the Central Railroad of New Jersey (CRRNJ) bought acre-age here in 1864 and built a rail terminal and depot, becoming a hub of industry and transportation.

Liberty State Park provides a green oasis among urban Jersey City and New York City.

This Jersey waterfront became decidedly more high profile in 1886, with the dedication of the Statue of Liberty on nearby Bedloe's Island. First proposed in 1871, the statue, a gift from France to the United States, rapidly became one of the great American icons. The current magnificent CRRNJ terminal and shed on the Jersey side was constructed in 1889. More activity came to the area in 1892, when immigration processing was transferred from Castle Clinton (the Battery) near the tip of Manhattan to a new immigration facility on nearby Ellis Island. The current landmark immigration building was

The Statue of Liberty is a constant highlight on this hike.

built in 1900. From the time it opened in 1892 until it closed in 1954, some seventeen million immigrants entered the United States via Ellis Island. The immigration station greatly increased traffic through the CRRNJ terminal (most immigrants traveled not to New York, but to New Jersey and points beyond). Some eight million immigrants passed through the terminal over the decades. By 1915 the terminal was serving 300 trains and some 30,000 passengers each day. Industrial use of the area likewise grew apace.

Enjoy first-rate views of the Statue of Liberty and New York Skyline.

In the 1880s, the Lehigh Valley Railroad opened a dock, shipping, and storage facility on nearby Black Tom Island (where the Court of Flags now stands), linked to the mainland by a causeway. By 1915, it was used to store munitions being shipped to Europe, where World War I was raging. By July 1916, it is estimated some two million pounds of explosives were stored on the island. This was a tempting target for German saboteurs, who exploited the island's low security. In the early hours of July 30, 1916, several small fires started on Black Tom Island. Some responsible personnel fought the fires, while others fled. At 2:08 a.m. the fires finally found explosives and the island went kaboom—to put it mildly. The explosion, it is calculated, registered something like 5.5 on the Richter scale and caused over $20 million in damage in the greater Jersey City/Manhattan area. Miraculously, only seven people died. It meant the end of munitions storage in the area, though other industry followed. The area between Black Tom Island and the rail terminal to the north was ultimately filled in; former Black Tom Island is now the area at the end of Morris Pesin Drive.

By the 1930s, both immigration and rail transport here were in decline. Largely underused and abandoned, the area was nonetheless prized for its grand railroad terminal and close proximity to the Statue of Liberty and Ellis Island. In 1976 the property became Liberty State Park. As for the Black Tom explosion, no saboteurs were ever conclusively identified, but a 1939 settlement over the matter with Germany was, rather obviously, interrupted by World War II. A subsequent 1953 settlement, combining Black Tom with other war-related damage, settled on $95 million in reimbursement. The last payment

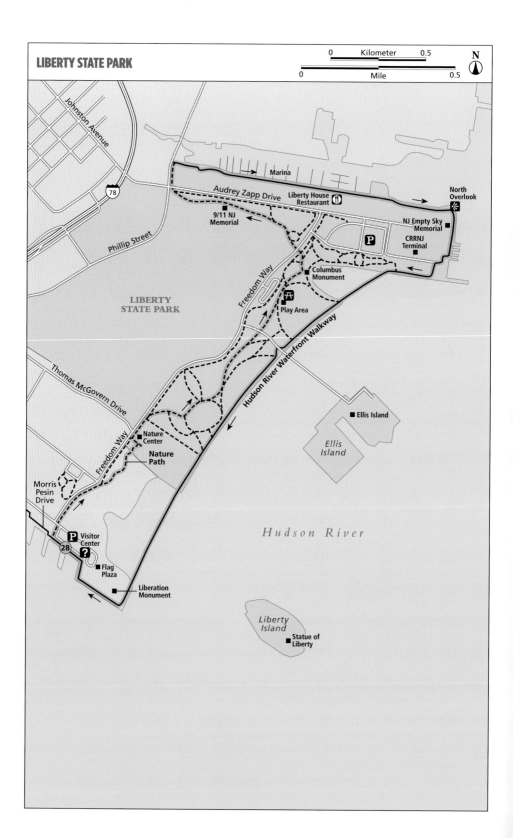

LIBERTY STATE PARK

0   Kilometer   0.5

0   Mile   0.5

N

Johnston Avenue

78

Marina

Audrey Zapp Drive

Liberty House Restaurant

North Overlook

9/11 NJ Memorial

NJ Empty Sky Memorial

Phillip Street

P

CRRNJ Terminal

Freedom Way

Columbus Monument

LIBERTY STATE PARK

Play Area

Hudson River Waterfront Walkway

Thomas McGovern Drive

Ellis Island

Nature Center

Ellis Island

Nature Path

Freedom Way

Morris Pesin Drive

Hudson River

P Visitor Center

28 ?

Flag Plaza

Liberty Island

Liberation Monument

Statue of Liberty

was made only in 1979, by which time the average person couldn't have told you what the Black Tom explosion was. Tragically, it wasn't the last time foreign terrorists brought destruction and mayhem to this area: The World Trade Center was scarcely a mile across the Hudson.

The shadows of past tragedy can't dampen the generally ebullient atmosphere at Liberty State Park, however. It's often a busy and bustling park, the crowds a reminder of the days when the tired, the poor, the huddled masses yearning to breathe free passed through here. As brand-new Americans, they got the world's best welcome by the lady in the harbor, her torch held high as a beacon, guiding them to a better life.

Today, you can tread this ground with appreciation for all our country has to offer, and in recognition of what a beacon of freedom the United States is to the rest of the world.

MILES AND DIRECTIONS

0.0 From the visitor center, begin to walk along the waterfront back toward Morris Pesin Drive, the way you entered. Cross (northeast) Morris Pesin Drive and onto the paved walkway paralleling Freedom Way, a road that borders the undeveloped section of the park.

0.3 Turn right (southeast) onto the brick Nature Path into woods that are being restored and exotic vegetation removed.

0.6 Reach the nature center and a spur to a pond. Head around to the front of the nature center and rejoin the main asphalt path heading northeast. Ascend (east) a grade to a brick-laid patio. Proceed directly across the circle to a T intersection; turn left (northeast) onto a paved walkway. Proceed straight (northeast) up the middle of the park on the paved path, ignoring the numerous intersections, which lead to either Freedom Way (left) or the Hudson River Waterfront Walkway (right).

1.3 Pass through the picnic area and playground, aiming for the Columbus Monument.

1.4 Reach the Columbus Monument and angle left, crossing Freedom Way to join the Grove of Remembrance Trail. Ahead, pass the memorial to New Jersey 9/11 survivors.

2.0 Reach the intersection of Phillip Street and Audrey Zapp Drive and a traffic light. Cross Audrey Zapp Drive right. Walk to the Morris Canal Basin and just before bridging the basin split right, taking the path leading along the basin and directly through the marina. Walk east along the marina.

2.7 Pass the Liberty House Restaurant on your right. Ahead, come to the Hudson River, North Overlook, and New Jersey Empty Sky Memorial. Pass the historic CRRNJ Terminal and the ferry to Ellis Island and the Statue of Liberty. Join the Hudson River Waterfront Walkway with stellar views of Manhattan and the Statue of Liberty.

3.8 Cross the road leading out to Ellis Island. Continue along the walkway with spectacular vistas in all directions.

4.8 Reach the southeast corner of the park, with more views downriver.

5.1 Arrive back at the visitor center, completing the unique New Jersey hike.

29 CHEESEQUAKE LOOP

This admirable circuit hike takes place at oddly named Cheesequake State Park, an island of nature in a sea of urbanity. From the primary hiking trailhead, you will first roll through woodland to reach Hooks Creek Lake, a popular summertime swimming destination. Next, wander over salt marsh wetlands with great views from an elongated boardwalk. After that, wind within forest to visit Perrine Pond, then work your way through hilly woods before returning to the trailhead.

Start: Main trailhead off State Park Road	**Dog friendly:** Yes, on leash only
Distance: 4.0-mile loop	**Trail surface:** Natural, a little gravel
Difficulty: Moderate	**Land status:** State park
Elevation change: +-397 feet	**Nearest town:** South Amboy
Maximum grade: 7% grade for 0.2 mile	**Other trail users:** Bicyclers
Hiking time: About 2.0 hours	**Maps to consult:** Cheesequake State Park
Seasons/schedule: Year-round	**Amenities available:** None
Fees and permits: Entrance fee charged Memorial Day through Labor Day	**Cell service:** Excellent
	Trail contact: Cheesequake State Park, (732) 566-2161, www.nj.gov/dep/parksandforests

FINDING THE TRAILHEAD

From South Amboy, take the Garden State Parkway east for 2 miles to exit 120, joining Matawan Road. Follow Matawan Road 0.2 mile to turn right onto Morristown Road, then follow it for 0.3 mile to turn right onto Gordon Road. After 1 mile on Gordon Road you will have entered Cheesequake State Park and will reach the main hiker trailhead on your left as Gordon Road curves right. Trailhead GPS: 40.436212,-74.265435

THE HIKE

This hike through Cheesequake State Park highlights how different centuries see value in different things, and the preserved past is one of the reasons Cheesequake is a state-designated coastal heritage site. For us, the preserve is a beautiful, amazing transition zone: from the hilly, forested Piedmont to the sandy pine barrens of the Coastal Plain, and from the saltwater bay and marshes to the freshwater swamps and creeks. But Colonial craftsmen saw something else—a locale with abundant rich yellow clay in the riverbanks that was superior for stoneware pottery.

Central New Jersey played an important role in Colonial American pottery manufacture. It had good transportation, skilled labor, and an entrepreneurial climate. These factors wouldn't have meant much, however, without this band of clay deposits running from Perth Amboy to Trenton. With this geological leg up, potteries sprang up throughout the region.

Author crossing marsh boardwalk near the Crabbing Bridge

An important pottery was here in the Cheesequake area (then South Amboy), established by Captain James Morgan around 1770. The Morgan Pottery produced a variety of handsome and decorative kiln-fired household stoneware, including bowls, jugs, crocks, jars, beer mugs, plates, and colanders, among other goods. Morgan died around 1784, and the pottery works were taken over by his son-in-law Thomas Warne, who later joined with his son-in-law Joshua Letts. The Warne & Letts Pottery, with their iconic "Liberty Forever" inscribed jugs, became even better known than Morgan's. However, Warne & Letts ceased production about 1827. Gone, but hardly forgotten today: Cheesequake-area stoneware produced by Morgan and Warne & Letts is now highly collectible. Indeed, most surviving Morgan pieces are in museums. Yet other pieces can be found over the internet that fetch four and five figures, with the New Jersey world record piece going for over $250,000! Could the farm wives of long ago have dreamt that the cider jug in their hands, bought for a dollar, would someday be worth $15,000? Probably not, or they wouldn't have dropped so many . . .

Cheesequake's clay industry didn't end there—Harry C. Perrine & Sons Co. of South Amboy continued to mine clay in the twentieth century, from 1900 to 1918, and again in the 1940s and '50s. This legacy is reflected in place-names along our hike—Perrine Road and Perrine Pond, a former clay-mining pit now filled with water.

Today we have an oasis of natural beauty in a sea of urbanity that is also home to Cheesequake Natural Area. In case you were wondering about the origin of the name

Deer are commonly seen here.

(and who wouldn't?), it is a corrupted Lenape Indian word, *Cheseh-oh-ke*, meaning "upland rising from the marshes."

The area's mix of fresh and salt marshes with streams running through them, along with transitional hillside forests, made it a candidate for preservation, and the state set aside $100,000 to purchase land for the park. In 1937, the first large tract was bought. More land was added, then in came the handy boys from the Civilian Conservation Corps. The preserve was opened in 1940, and wildlife from osprey to deer now call the 1,610-acre park home.

Today, you can hike atop the marsh streams where aboriginals would harvest crabs and obtain shells for fine necklaces, stroll along the old roads that hauled clay to make pottery, and drop by 6-acre Hooks Creek Lake, a swimmer's haven in summer as well as fishing venue where anglers vie for catfish, bass, or stocked trout. Paddling the marsh streams and lake is popular as well. You can canoe or kayak Cheesequake Creek as it transitions from fresh to salt water. Cheesequake Creek leads north to Raritan Bay and was important to the Lenape and Colonial settlers for transportation, and later for transporting pottery and other goods as well as local agricultural products. There was once a steamboat landing here for just such commerce. I've overnighted in the campground and pronounce it a fine complement to extend your stay here as you engage in varied park activities, including hiking.

The trail system at Cheesequake State Park is color-coded. The trek makes a large loop, a regular tour de force, leading you to many park highlights. After leaving the main trailhead, you will ramble through the surprisingly steep hills (not necessarily high)

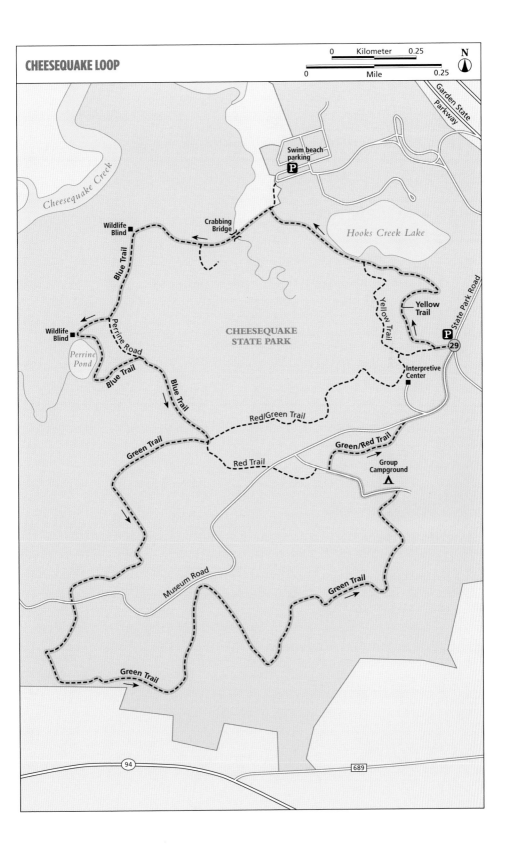

0   Kilometer   0.25

0   Mile   0.25

N

Cheesequake Creek

Swim beach parking

P

Garden State Parkway

Crabbing Bridge

Hooks Creek Lake

Wildlife Blind

Blue Trail

Wildlife Blind

Perrine Pond

Perrine Road

Blue Trail

Yellow Trail

Yellow Trail

State Park Road

P 29

CHEESEQUAKE STATE PARK

Interpretive Center

Blue Trail

Blue Trail

Red/Green Trail

Green Trail

Red Trail

Green/Red Trail

Group Campground

Museum Road

Green Trail

Green Trail

94

689

before dropping to Hooks Creek Lake. After looking over the impoundment, continue your loop to enter the fascinating marshes that have attracted humans through time. Cross the crabbing bridge, where you can see the tides work in and out of the wetlands as they have for thousands of years. Return to wooded forest where you can look on Cheesequake Creek. Ahead, come to Perrine Pond, a clay quarry–turned–wildlife harbor, where you may see some of the 160 bird species that can be found at the park. The last part of the hike takes you along the convergence zones of wetland and woods and through forested hills that will deliver more vertical variation than you thought possible in this part of the Garden State.

MILES AND DIRECTIONS

0.0   Leave the main parking area, with all the color-coded trails leaving southwest from the main trailhead. After a couple hundred feet split right with the Yellow Trail, trying to make the longest loop available. Travel north on a wide natural-surface path in oak woods with blueberry bushes covering the sandy soil.

0.2   The Yellow Trail makes a sharp left and descends as an unmaintained trail splits right toward the main park road. Boardwalk steps ease the grade.

0.4   Emerge at the edge of Hooks Creek Lake. Here, a leg of the Yellow Trail cuts acutely left but we stay straight, coming alongside the shore of Hooks Creek Lake and adjacent wetlands. Ahead, the park swim beach comes into view. Bridge the pond outflow and pass the swim beach.

0.6   Stay left as you reach an intersection. Here, an asphalt spur goes right to the swim beach parking area. Stay left (southwest), soon opening onto marsh. Keep west atop a boardwalk, with a spur going right to a viewing location. Ahead, span a small tidal creek, on what is known as the Crabbing Bridge. Rejoin natural-surface trail. Ahead, a natural-surface spur trail goes left to a point; stay right, westerly on the main, wide track.

0.9   A short spur leads right to a wildlife- viewing blind overlooking Cheesequake Creek.

1.1   Come to an intersection. Stay right here as Perrine Road, closed to public auto traffic, goes straight. Soon come along Perrine Pond and another wildlife blind, then turn away left, easterly. Look for other dug pits in the area.

1.4   Split right on the Blue Trail doubletrack.

1.5   Come to a four-way intersection. Turn right onto the Green Trail and enter Cheesequake Natural Area, the lesser-used part of the park, characterized by steep-sided but low ridges.

2.1   Cross Museum Road after passing through an Atlantic white cedar swamp on a long boardwalk. Keep south.

2.3   Turn east after nearing the park boundary. Roll through low hills.

3.4   Emerge at the park group camp. Head left on the gravel road.

3.6   Stay with the Green Trail as it splits right, back on foot trail, nearly encircling the group camp.

3.8   Meet Museum Road. Split right and join the road.

4.0   Arrive back at the trailhead, completing the hike.

30 **SANDY HOOK LOOP**

Explore the beach, wooded dunes, and Fort Hancock Historic District as well as the overall maritime beauty of the Sandy Hook Unit of Gateway National Recreation Area on this loop hike. This level circuit uses asphalt, concrete, gravel, and sand for trail surface while taking in a wealth of scenery, notably the coastal convergence of land, sea, and sky. Fall and spring offer a decidedly superior experience.

Start: Lot J
Distance: 5.3-mile loop
Difficulty: Moderate
Elevation change: Negligible
Maximum grade: N/A
Hiking time: About 2.7 hours
Seasons/schedule: Mid-September through mid-May
Fees and permits: None
Dog friendly: Yes, on leash only
Trail surface: Asphalt, concrete, gravel, sand

Land status: National recreation area
Nearest town: Aberdeen
Other trail users: Bicyclers on Multi-Use Path
Maps to consult: Sandy Hook Multi-Use Path
Amenities available: Restrooms, cold showers at Lot G and Lot I
Cell service: Good
Trail contact: Gateway National Recreation Area, (718) 354-4606, www.nps.gov/gate

FINDING THE TRAILHEAD

From exit 117 on the Garden State Parkway near Aberdeen, take NJ 36 south for 12.8 miles. Take the Gateway National Recreation Area exit north, and upon entering the recreation area follow the signs to Lot J. Trailhead GPS: 40.467959,-74.001193

THE HIKE

Some of our most precious parks and historic sites might be termed "accidental" ones—places that for most of their existence weren't valued for culture or recreation but for very practical reasons. A perfect example is Sandy Hook, once a haunt of the Lenape Indians and the location of this hike. European sailors first entered New York Harbor some five centuries ago. The great sandy point that extends north from the mainland across the harbor entrance—Sandy Hook—has always been a challenge for mariners. The bay is wide here (Brooklyn's Coney Island is a good 5 miles north), but the historic shipping channel required a treacherously close squeeze against Sandy Hook—you could toss a biscuit from a ship and hit land, so it was said.

The dangers of this harbor entrance led Colonial New York shipping and mercantile interests to lobby for the erection of a lighthouse here. Sandy Hook Lighthouse was built and first lit in 1764. The unique flat-sided octagonal structure is now the oldest lighthouse in America and still in use. Originally located near the tip of the point, shifting sands have increased that distance to a mile and a half. In the 1840s, another effort to safeguard shipping was made with the creation of a US lifesaving station here. These stations were charged with rescuing passengers from foundering ships off the coast. One of these lifesaving stations is now the park visitor center.

Hiking the beach at Sandy Hook

These efforts made the harbor entrance safer for ships, but not all ships sailing the ocean blue are friendly. Sandy Hook also had military importance. Both British and American troops were, at different times, stationed around the lighthouse during the Revolutionary War, but it wasn't until the War of 1812 that this strategic point saw construction of a military installation. Fort Gates, a temporary fortification, was built to guard New York against the British navy. In 1817 the federal government bought Sandy Hook peninsula in its entirety, and in 1859 started construction of a permanent fort. But the development of the rifled-bore cannon, which could punch through the thickest masonry, made such forts obsolete, and it was never finished. However, in 1874 the US Army did establish a weapons proving ground here.

In 1890 gun batteries were added to protect New York shipping channels. These and later gun batteries at Sandy Hook were built within low-profile earthworks, providing both camouflage and protection. In 1895 facilities for a garrison of 400 soldiers and officers were added, making the installation a full-fledged fortification. It was dubbed Fort Hancock in honor of Major General Winfield Scott Hancock, whose distinguished career included repulsing Pickett's Charge at the Battle of Gettysburg. Fort Hancock became the outermost point of defense in a ring of fortifications that surrounded New York Harbor.

In keeping with the camouflaged, low-profile philosophy of the fort's design, its guns were mounted on retracting carriages of several varieties. These were commonly called

Beach, sky, and the Atlantic Ocean form your trail tableau.

"disappearing" guns, since they only rose above the earthworks for firing, and then lowered for reloading. They ranged in bore from 3 to 12 inches.

Activity at Fort Hancock reached its zenith during World War II, when as a troop staging area its population reached some 12,000 men. But technology was rapidly making such forts obsolete. By the 1950s, it was clear that any attack would come not from an armada of ships, but via jet fighters and bombers. Fort Hancock accordingly added a Nike missile base in the early 1950s.

In the 1960s and '70s the focus of defense shifted yet again from jet aircraft to nuclear missiles, and Fort Hancock once again found itself outmoded. In 1974 the army deactivated the fort. Happily, the history and scenery here at Sandy Hook were readily appreciated, and the property was almost immediately transferred to the National Park Service to become part of the new Gateway National Recreation Area. The entire peninsula was designated a National Historic Landmark in 1982. As a historic site, it reflects an array of military technology from the 1850s through the 1950s and is rich in architectural treasures; as a natural site, it is both serene and spectacular. All in all, a happy accident indeed.

Note: Summertime can be hot, stormy, and buggy. Fall and spring are the best seasons to visit. Much of the trail is open to the sun and wind. Prepare accordingly. A segment of Gunnison Beach, which this hike crosses, is open to nude sunbathing.

A small beach on the bay side of Sandy Hook

MILES AND DIRECTIONS

0.0 From the southwest corner of Lot J, take the asphalt Multi-Use Path west, crossing Atlantic Drive, paralleling South Bragg Drive. Pass by historic buildings, lawns, and trails.

0.2 The Historic Post Trail leaves left. Stay straight with the Multi-Use Path.

0.3 Cross Hartshorne Drive and come near the former chapel, nestled against Sandy Hook Beach. Stay with the Multi-Use Path as it heads south along Sandy Hook Bay. Enjoy fine water views, as well as nearer looks at historic structures, part of Fort Hancock.

1.0 Cross Hartshorne Drive east to cut through Guardian Park and cross Magruder Road. Turn south into woods, still on the Multi-Use Path.

1.6 Cross the road leading to the park campground, then pass the Halyburton Memorial and Lot L in quick succession.

1.9 Reach a trail intersection. Here, the asphalt Multi-Use Path keeps right while a natural-surface trail splits left. Stay left with the natural-surface trail, entering low scrub woods. You have missed this split if you cross Atlantic Drive on the Multi-Use Path. Stay with the sandy natural-surface trail, turning east.

2.2 Cross Atlantic Drive and officially join the South Beach Dune Trail, an old road wandering through maritime woods. Trek between dunes to your left and marshlands to your right.

2.6 Come to an intersection. Here, the South Beach Dune Trail keeps straight, but we head left on an official beach crossover trail.

2.7 Reach the Atlantic side of Sandy Hook. Turn north, walking along the sand, your exact hiking location depending on the tides. Buildings and the Sandy Hook Lighthouse are visible to your left.

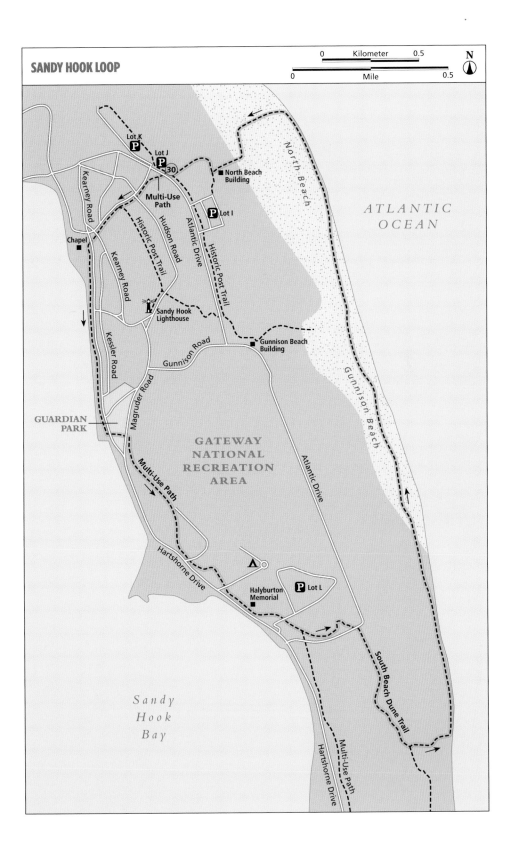

4.0 Reach Gunnison Beach. Signs warn you of a beach section open to nude sunbathers. Hope for a chilly breeze. Keep north as Sandy Hook starts to curve westerly.

4.8 Come to North Beach. Look left, westerly, for the North Beach Building, then follow the path to and beyond the building, splitting right when reaching an asphalt path. Pass Proof Battery.

5.3 Reach the Historic Post Trail very near Lot J. Walk a few steps, reaching Lot J and completing the hike.

31 CLAYTON PARK LOOP

You will enjoy the varied circuit hike at this Monmouth County park, preserving a scenic swath along Doctors Creek, from which rise tall upland hardwoods. Start in the park's higher terrain, working down to Doctors Creek where you will stride along bluffs overlooking the stream and adjacent wetlands. Come to Imlaystown Lake while circling fields. Finally climb through a wooded hollow and return to the trailhead, with an eyeful of natural New Jersey upon which to reflect.

Start: Emleys Hill Road entrance lot
Distance: 5.4-mile double loop
Difficulty: Moderate
Elevation change: +-440 feet
Maximum grade: 5% for 0.4 mile
Hiking time: About 2.8 hours
Seasons/schedule: Daily 7:00 a.m. to dusk; autumn best for colors, spring for wildflowers
Fees and permits: None
Dog friendly: Yes, on leash only
Trail surface: Natural surface throughout

Land status: County park
Nearest town: Allentown
Other trail users: Bicyclers, infrequent equestrians
Maps to consult: Clayton Park
Amenities available: Restroom at trail parking area
Cell service: Good
Trail contact: Monmouth County Parks, (732) 842-4000, ext. 4312, www.monmouthcountyparks.com

FINDING THE TRAILHEAD

From exit 11 on I-195 east of Allentown, take Imlaystown Hightstown Road south for 0.9 mile. Turn left onto CR 526 east to bridge Buckhole Creek, then quickly turn right onto Davis Station Road and follow it for 0.9 mile. Turn left onto Emleys Hill Road and follow it for 0.5 mile, then turn left into the Clayton Park trailhead access. Trailhead GPS: 40.155960,-74.504529

THE HIKE

This is an excellent woods and water hike, where mature beech, black oak, birch, and tulip trees rise above ferns, wildflowers, and wild roses. In fact, Clayton Park is known as a wildflower destination, where showy orchis, trilliums, trout lilies, and spring beauties brighten the forest floor. Wild azaleas provide loads of color as their bushes rise above the wildflowers. Furthermore, the cornucopia of hardwoods also makes Clayton Park excellent for admiring autumn colors. You may see deer here, in addition to songbirds and more water-oriented avian life on Doctors Creek and the marshes where it flows into Imlaystown Lake.

The land was part of the Paul Clayton farm, and the fields you walk by are the same ones tilled by this purveyor of old-time agricultural methods, still plowing with horses until 1971, when he retired from his lifelong occupation at age eighty-seven. The prime agricultural lands and wooded hills drew many a land speculator, wanting to fell the

Showy orchid brightens a rainy day.

towering hardwoods and plant houses instead of crops, but Clayton resisted their monies, finally selling part of his tract to the Monmouth County park system, where his beloved forests and fields could be preserved. The resultant park was named for this simple man of the land. Later, Clayton Park was expanded to its current 450 acres. It borders directly against quaint Imlaystown (aka Upper Freehold), a hamlet recalling New England villages. The former Imlaystown Elementary School, a charming building of its own, serves

Wild azaleas are just one of many flowering plants found here.

as the current Clayton Park Activity Center and offers art and recreation programs as well as alternate parking for this hike.

The trail system here is well marked and maintained. You may encounter some mountain bikers, so keep your eyes peeled. Our hike makes the widest loop possible within the park bounds, leaving the hills clad in stately forest for Doctors Creek, bridging small tributaries of the creek along the way. The trek then climbs back into hills, sometimes

Jack in the pulpit wildflower

on old forgotten roads, before turning back down along Doctors Creek, where you will eventually come to the still-tilled fields of farmer Clayton, then trek grassy mown trails to curve beside old Imlaystown. After leaving the open grounds you return to forest and more wooded glory, passing a few more meadows before returning to the trailhead, another fine New Jersey hike completed.

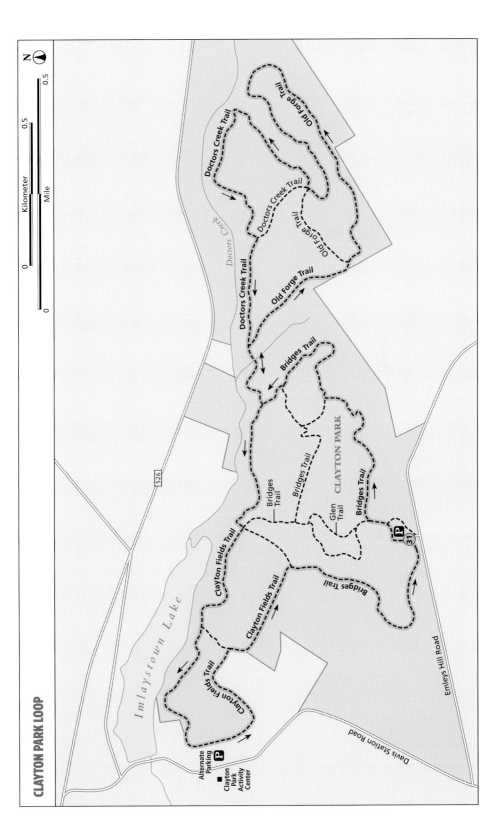

CLAYTON PARK LOOP

MILES AND DIRECTIONS

0.0 From the open parking area on Emleys Hill Road, head north into the woods at the trail sign and immediately come to a trail intersection. Here, head right on the green-blazed Glen Trail. Quickly pass a spur going right, back toward the parking lot. Continue under a tall mantle of beech, birch, and tulip trees.

0.1 Reach an intersection. Split right with the Bridges Trail, heading east amid hills clad in mature hardwoods.

0.4 Bridge a small stream, entering a favorable wildflower area.

0.5 Arms of the Bridges Trail split. Stay right with an arm of the Bridges Trail, climbing a hill then turning back down toward Doctors Creek.

0.8 Stay right toward Doctors Creek as you pass another arm of the Bridges Trail.

0.9 Turn right onto the Doctors Creek Trail, eastbound, shortly bridging a small stream.

1.0 Split right onto the Old Forge Trail, then make the biggest climb of the hike, 118 feet in 0.4 mile.

1.3 The Old Forge Trail splits into two arms. Stay right, climbing a bit more before curving left, easterly, coming near the park boundary, with clearings beyond that contrast with the tall woods through which you walk.

1.9 Come near the wetlands of Doctors Creek before turning up the hollow of a tributary of the creek.

2.3 Reach a four-way intersection. Stay right with the Doctors Creek Trail, turning back down the hollow you just went up. Soon return to Doctors Creek and head west, cruising hills and bluffs above the stream and its adjacent wetlands.

2.9 Meet the other arm of the Doctors Creek Trail. Stay straight, westerly.

3.2 Meet the Old Forge Trail. Stay straight, backtracking on the Doctors Creek Trail.

3.3 Keep straight on the Doctors Creek Trail, westbound, as a leg of the Bridges Trail, where you were earlier, leaves left. Come closer to the bluff edge, looking down on Doctors Creek.

3.6 Bridge a wide tributary of Doctors Creek, then come to a trail intersection. Here, split right with the Clayton Fields Trail. Follow the grassy track dividing the active agricultural fields from the woods to your right. Ahead, stay right as a shortcut leaves left across the fields. Marshy Imlaystown Lake comes into view.

4.3 Walk past the alternate parking and the Clayton Park Activity Center across Davis Station Road. Circle around the field edge, coming near houses.

4.8 Reenter woods, splitting right onto the Bridges Trail. Climb up a wooded hollow, eventually nearing some hilltop fields.

5.4 Arrive back at the trailhead, completing the county park hike.

32 RANCOCAS STATE PARK

Explore much of the north side of this state park holding fast to nature amid Philly's expanding Jersey suburbs. Leave the worth-a-visit Rancocas Nature Center, working your way in woods to North Branch Rancocas Creek and a view. Circle around marshes and lesser creeks before returning to the main stream. Ramble through rolling woods in the heart of the tract before revisiting North Branch Rancocas Creek yet again. The hike turns up a little brook and works over to another stream before returning to the trailhead. Overall, the hike is pleasant and pleasing to the eye, making a fine place for a family ramble through forest and stream.

Start: Rancocas Nature Center parking lot
Distance: 5.2-mile double loop
Difficulty: Moderate
Elevation change: +-214 feet
Maximum grade: 2% grade for 0.2 mile
Hiking time: About 2.9 hours
Seasons/schedule: Daily sunrise to sunset
Fees and permits: None
Dog friendly: Yes, on leash only

Trail surface: Natural surface, a little asphalt
Land status: State park
Nearest town: Mount Holly
Other trail users: A few bicyclers in spots
Maps to consult: Rancocas State Park
Amenities available: Small picnic area, restroom at nature center
Cell service: Excellent
Trail contact: Rancocas State Park, (609) 726-1191, www.nj.gov/dep/parksandforests

FINDING THE TRAILHEAD

From exit 45 on I-295 west of Mount Holly, take Rancocas Road east 1.5 miles to turn right into the Rancocas Nature Center, located in an old farmhouse. The hike starts at the nature center porch. Trailhead GPS: 40.003531,-74.820955

THE HIKE

Many New Jersey state parks avail traditional outdoor activities such as camping and swimming with amenities such as cabins. Rancocas State Park is more of a landholding of natural beauty along the banks of North Branch and South Branch Rancocas Creek. The park does have the Rancocas Nature Center, run since 1977 by the Burlington County Parks System, that is not only the starting point for this hike but also where schoolkids engage in environmental education programs. The nature center features a dragonfly pond, butterfly enclosure, visitor center where you can get trail maps, museum, and educational displays, all set in a rustic two-story farmhouse located here well before the concept of a New Jersey state park was a thought in anyone's mind.

The park covers over 1,200 acres where South Fork Rancocas Creek and North Fork Rancocas Creek merge. The land consists of freshwater marshes from which rise rolling hills at what was once known as the "Forks of the Rancocas." The Lenape Indians had

Hiking along North Branch Rancocas Creek

a village here into the late 1600s. By the 1750s, one Charles Read, a compatriot of Ben Franklin, established a farm here. Agriculture continued into the 1800s before the forks became the site of sand mining by the Hainesport Mining and Transportation Company to provide Philadelphia with plenty of construction material. In the early 1960s, the State of New Jersey began acquiring land for a state park, and by 1965 Rancocas State Park came to be.

The trail system is divided into two major parcels, one set on the north banks of North Branch Rancocas Creek, where our hike takes place, and the second set of trails in between the forks of the two creeks. The trails are color-coded. Have a map handy, as there are numerous intersections on this hike, which tours the north side of the park from one end to the other.

MILES AND DIRECTIONS

- **0.0** From the front porch of the nature center, as you look out the front door, bear right, following the "To Trails" sign. Immediately join the green/yellow-blazed Maple Leaf Trail, heading east, with Rancocas Road to your left, winding among mixed woods and meadows.
- **0.1** Split left on the red-blazed Meadow View Trail, skirting the edge of a field bordered by tree thickets, continuing in mixed meadow and woods. Look for deer hereabouts.

North Branch Rancocas Creek flows toward the Delaware River.

0.4 The Red/White Trail splits right back toward the nature center. Stay with the red-blazed Meadow View Trail.

0.5 Intersect the blue-blazed Deer Run Trail and head left, southbound.

0.6 Turn left on the orange-blazed Turkey Feather Trail. Drop off a small hill toward North Branch Rancocas Creek. Shortly come along the river and work your way through the marshy bank to a stream view. Backtrack to the Deer Run Trail.

1.2 Stay left with the blue-blazed Deer Run Trail, working around marsh to your left.

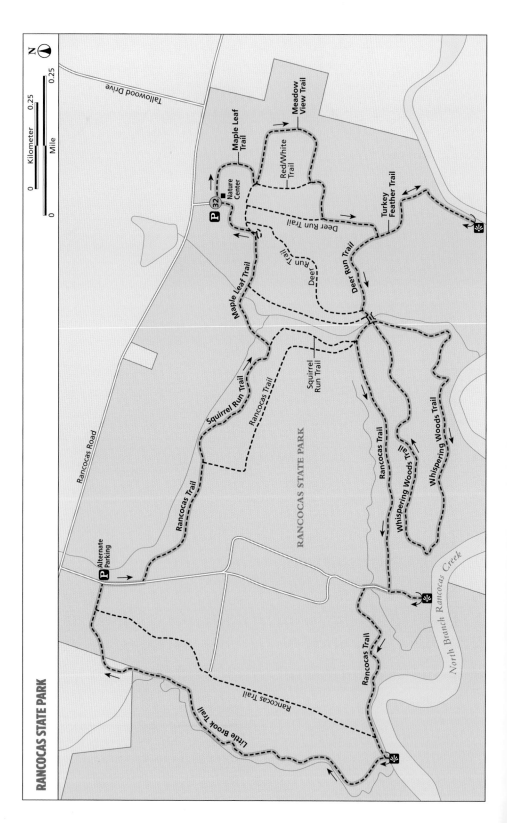

RANCOCAS STATE PARK

1.3 The Deer Run Trail stays right but we go left just a short distance, then come to an oft-closed arm of the yellow-blazed Whispering Woods Trail leaving right. Keep straight, crossing a creek on a trail bridge, then come to another intersection. Here, the brown-blazed Squirrel Run Trail leaves right but we stay left, heading west out on the loop portion of the yellow-blazed Whispering Woods Trail.

1.5 Come to a fine view of North Branch Rancocas Creek, fronted by a large tulip tree. From here, climb a bluff above the stream before turning back east.

2.4 Complete the loop portion of the Whispering Woods Trail just before the bridge crossed earlier, then head left on the brown-blazed Squirrel Run Trail. Turn up the creek. Just ahead look left and join the white-blazed Rancocas Trail, westbound again.

2.9 Meet an old paved road seemingly in the middle of nowhere. Go left here, south-bound, and follow the paved track down to the river, passing a former homesite. Backtrack then head north on the Rancocas Trail, descending to cross a marshy creek. From there, split left back on a white-blazed footpath into woods as the paved road continues north into what was the former Powhatan Indian Reservation.

3.4 Come to a viewpoint at water's edge of Rancocas Creek, at an old boat ramp. Keep straight, joining the green-blazed Little Brook Trail as the white-blazed Rancocas Trail splits right, tracing an old roadbed. Shortly turn up a small, clear, winding stream forming gravel bars on the inside of bends. Watch for big trees hereabouts.

4.2 Reunite with the Rancocas Trail, then come to an alternate parking area off Ranco-cas Road. At the parking area, the white-blazed Rancocas Trail turns south and joins an old road. Watch ahead as the trail splits left from the road.

4.7 Reach an intersection. Stay left with the brown-blazed Squirrel Run Trail as the Ran-cocas Trail goes right. Undulate easterly over hills.

4.9 Split left with the green/yellow-blazed Maple Leaf Trail. Dip to bridge a pair of streams, then work toward the nature center.

5.2 Split left for the nature center and pop out in the rear of the center, completing the state park hike.

33 CATTUS ISLAND

This hike—one of the best in the state—is an ecological gem. The coastal circuit hike traverses uplands, crosses freshwater wetlands, saunters through spectacular salt marshes with panoramic views, and visits small natural beaches. Flora and fauna abound, with numerous blinds to help you enjoy the wildlife! Have your phone ready to photograph osprey as well as shorebirds, even butterflies. The hike combines sandy roads, boardwalks, woods trails, and sand beach along Silver Bay to traverse this jewel of Ocean County.

Start: Cooper Environmental Center parking lot
Distance: 5.8-mile triple loop
Difficulty: Moderate
Elevation change: +-56 feet
Maximum grade: N/A
Hiking time: About 3.3 hours
Seasons/schedule: Daily dawn to dusk; summer can be buggy
Fees and permits: None
Dog friendly: Yes, on leash only
Trail surface: Natural surface, boardwalk, gravel, sand

Land status: County park
Nearest town: Toms River
Other trail users: None
Maps to consult: Cattus Island County Park
Amenities available: Picnic area, restroom at trail parking area
Cell service: Excellent
Trail contact: Cattus Island County Park, (732) 270-6960, www.oceancountyparks.org

FINDING THE TRAILHEAD

From exit 82 on the Garden State Parkway, take NJ 37 east for 2.6 miles, then head north on Vaughn Avenue for 1.6 miles. Turn right onto Quartz Drive and follow it 0.1 mile, then turn right onto Hazelwood Road and follow it 0.6 mile to a traffic light and Fischer Boulevard. Turn left and follow Fischer Boulevard 0.1 mile, then turn right onto Cattus Island Boulevard. Go just a short distance, then split left onto Cattus Island Road and follow it to reach the large parking area in the county park. Start the hike by taking the asphalt track toward the environmental center. Trailhead GPS: 39.981872,-74.129029

THE HIKE

Sometimes a hike gives us the opportunity to enjoy a landscape once accessible to only the privileged few. This is one of those hikes! Lots of us dream about buying an island of our own to vacation on. But John Cattus actually did it.

Go back to the 1700s, when this not-quite-an-island (more of a peninsula, really) was purchased by Joseph Page. He settled here in 1763, engaging in saltwater farming. His son Timothy was born here, and during the Revolutionary War Joseph Page was probably a privateer—a pirate, basically, but an officially licensed one, preying on British ships. In 1842 the island passed to Lewis Applegate, who built a sawmill and a dock for lumber boats. For much of this era it was known as Applegate's Island. It was sold in 1867 for resort development, but the economic crash of 1873 put an end to those plans. By the 1880s, it was known as Gillmore's Island.

Small natural beaches enhance this coastal hike.

Enter John V. A. Cattus. His father, John Cattus Sr., had come from Germany to the United States in 1859 and built up a lucrative business as a tobacco broker, exporting to Europe (Germany in particular). The import-export business remained a Cattus specialty. His son, John Van Antwerp Cattus, was born in 1867. Son, like father, engaged in the import-export business, this time in the Far East, which brought the family to the highest levels of wealth, comfort, and social acceptance. John V. A. Cattus's passion, however, was the water: He was an Olympic-class oarsman and an avid sailor.

Walk beside brackish wetlands.

It was undoubtedly the love of water that led Cattus to acquire Gillmore's Island in the early 1900s, making it his summer retreat. The sailing in the area was excellent, and Cattus was a member of the Bay Head Yacht Club and the Manasquan River Golf and Country Club. He died in 1945, and the island passed to his son, Charles Baber Cattus. Charles Cattus died in 1964, and the family sold the island to developers. However, new environmental regulations made development cost prohibitive, and the plans fell through. In 1973 the property was acquired as a county park for all to use—not just privateers and millionaires.

Since then, Ocean County has created a fine set of hiking trails to explore the maritime forests, marshy estuaries, and beaches. The oasis in an otherwise heavily urbanized coastal part of Jersey makes its 530 acres all the more valuable. Make time for this superlative hike, then take your time doing it—you'll see a lot. Bring a hat and sunscreen, as much of the hike is open.

MILES AND DIRECTIONS

0.0 From the northwest end of the parking lot, locate the map kiosk. Facing it, turn right (northeast) onto the paved path leading to the environmental center, passing a series of interpretive kiosks. Shortly, turn right (south) onto the Boardwalk Trail. (FYI: The Cooper Environmental Center is straight ahead on the paved path, providing restrooms, maps, programs, and a museum.)

A small serene beach presents a view of Silver Bay.

0.2 Pass an overlook with views of the marsh and an osprey-nesting stand, one of many scattered through the preserve.

0.3 Join the red-blazed Maritime Forest Trail left in the midst of the shaded picnic area. The trail runs along Applegate Creek and behind some houses, sometimes on boardwalk. Rise to pines.

0.7 Reach an intersection as the Swamp Crossing Trail goes right. Stay straight with the Maritime Forest Trail then curve right, crossing the paved park entrance road.

1.2 Meet the other end of the Swamp Crossing Trail. Stay left on the Maritime Forest Trail, then quickly cross the yellow-blazed Yellowbank Trail. Ahead, the track heads out to marsh along Mosquito Cove. Walk on boardwalk. Great views open of Mosquito Cove.

1.8 Meet the Main Trail very near the environmental center. Stay left with the Main Trail, a gated gravel doubletrack open only to park personnel. Head northeast on a causeway bordered by tidal marsh.

1.9 Split left with the blue-blazed Island Trail. Turn toward Mosquito Cove in woods, running by marshes with fine vistas.

2.4 Stay left on the blue/white-blazed Island Trail Extension, once again returning to a view of Mosquito Cove.

2.7 Rejoin the Main Trail northeast.

3.0 Reach an intersection with a restroom. For now stay straight and walk the beach to the northwest tip of the island then backtrack, heading east on the Hidden Beach Trail. Make a counterclockwise loop, passing small beaches facing Barnegat Bay.

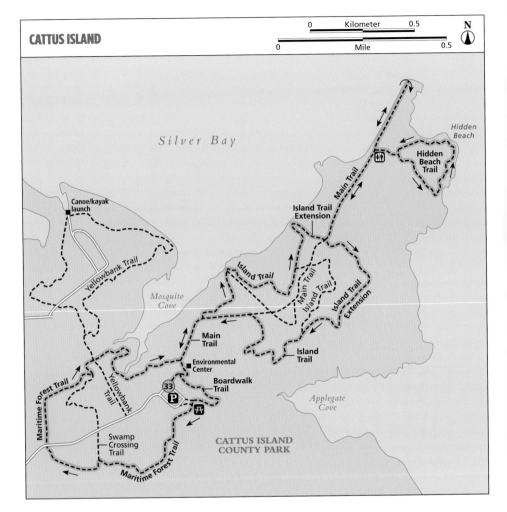

CATTUS ISLAND

0   Kilometer   0.5

0   Mile   0.5

N

4.1 Return to the Main Trail, backtracking southwest.

4.3 Head left on a new segment of the Island Trail Extension. Stay along the edge of forest and marsh. Look for osprey nest platforms.

5.0 Meet and join the Island Trail. You are near a clearing that is the site of an old farmhouse and now an outdoor classroom. Pass bird blinds that look over old salt marsh hay-growing parcels.

5.4 Return to the Main Trail once again. Head back toward the environmental center. Ahead, pass the north leg of the Island Trail, then backtrack on the causeway across marshes.

5.7 Come to the environmental center. Split left and follow the asphalt track back toward the parking lot.

5.8 Arrive back at the trailhead, completing the estuarine adventure.

Take a walk through quintessential New Jersey Pine Barrens on this loop hike. Start at pretty Pakim Pond, a great place for a picnic, then join the all-access Cranberry Trail, making your way among cranberry bogs, pine woods, oaks, and cedar swamps to reach the state forest office. From there, pick up the fabled Batona Trail, returning through low hills and more wetlands to Pakim Pond.

Start: Pakim Pond
Distance: 6.4-mile balloon loop
Difficulty: Moderate
Elevation change: +-212 feet
Maximum grade: 2% grade for 0.3 mile
Hiking time: About 3.2 hours
Seasons/schedule: Fall through spring
Fees and permits: None
Dog friendly: Yes, on leash only
Trail surface: Pea gravel, natural

Land status: State forest
Nearest town: Medford
Other trail users: Backpackers on Batona Trail
Maps to consult: Brendan T. Byrne State Forest
Amenities available: Restrooms, picnic shelter, tables at trailhead
Cell service: Good
Trail contact: Brendan T. Byrne State Forest, (609) 726-1191, www.nj.gov/dep/parksandforests

FINDING THE TRAILHEAD

From exit 34 on I-295 near Barclay, take NJ 70 east for 21.5 miles, then head right on NJ 72 south for 3.1 miles. Turn left onto Buzzard Hill Road and follow it for 0.8 mile to turn left into the Pakim Pond picnic area and trailhead. Trailhead GPS: 39.880423,-74.533914

THE HIKE

The pond you initially pass on the hike is named for a Lenape chief, Pakimintzen. As the legend goes, he gave cranberries as gifts, and they in turn became symbols of peace. His name abbreviated becomes Pakim, hence the name for the pond. This locale was an early cranberry farming area of New Jersey. Pakim Pond acted as a water reservoir, an integral ingredient of cranberry farming. The fresh water, used to flood the peat bogs, keeps the cranberry vines moist in the summer and prevents them from freezing in the winter. Ditches and gates controlled the flow.

In fact, the trail you follow the first half of the hike is called the Cranberry Trail. It is an all-access path—one of the longest all-access paths in New Jersey's state forests—linking Pakim Pond to the state forest office. Leaving the Pakim Pond area, with its picnic shelter and nature trail around the 5-acre impoundment, the Cranberry Trail and Batona Trail run in conjunction until you begin the loop portion of the hike. You then stay with the Cranberry Trail as it travels the valley of Shinns Branch, before crossing the stream and entering Cedar Swamp Natural Area, a state preserve within the state forest protecting not only a lowland Atlantic white cedar swamp but also pitch pine woods and oak complexes. Since the Cranberry Trail is wheelchair accessible, gradients are minimal and the

This stone monument commemorates Cedar Swamp Natural Area.

path is wide, making the track quite easy. Soon you find yourself at the state forest office, where information, maps—and restrooms—are available.

From there, the hike joins the hiker-only Batona Trail, a 50-mile-long path wandering through the Pine Barrens. "Batona" stands for "Back to Nature," using the first two letters of each word to create the name. Along its journey the Batona Trail explores three New Jersey state forests: Byrne, Wharton, and Bass River. Designated reservable campsites can turn this scenic path into a backpacking expedition through this land unique to the Garden State. Enjoy weaving through prototype Pine Barrens from high pines to deep swamps on the way back to Pakim Pond.

Interestingly, what became the first blueberry cultivation area in New Jersey is preserved in Byrne State Forest as Whitesbog Village, a farming community founded in the mid-1800s. At first, villagers were active cranberry farmers, but then Elizabeth Coleman White experimented with planting blueberry bushes on drier sites near the cranberry bogs and a new fruit-growing industry was born. Today, you can visit the village, administered and kept up by the Whitesbog Preservation Trust.

Additionally, the state forest has a fine campground very near this trailhead, featuring widespread campsites under pines and oaks. Water spigots and hot showers add to the large overnighting spot. I've stayed here myself and recommend the experience, especially if you want to make the most of your visit to Brendan T. Byrne State Forest.

Wonders great and small can be found at Byrne State Forest.

MILES AND DIRECTIONS

0.0 From the northernmost corner of the parking area (left as you pull in), join the red-blazed Cranberry Trail. The picnic shelter and pond are off to your right.

0.1 Meet the pink-blazed Batona Trail and the white-blazed Mount Misery Trail coming in on your right. Together the three paths conjunctively head northwest to shortly pop out on Coopers Road. Walk alongside the road then split left, back into woods. Pass a white pine plantation.

BYRNE STATE FOREST CIRCUIT

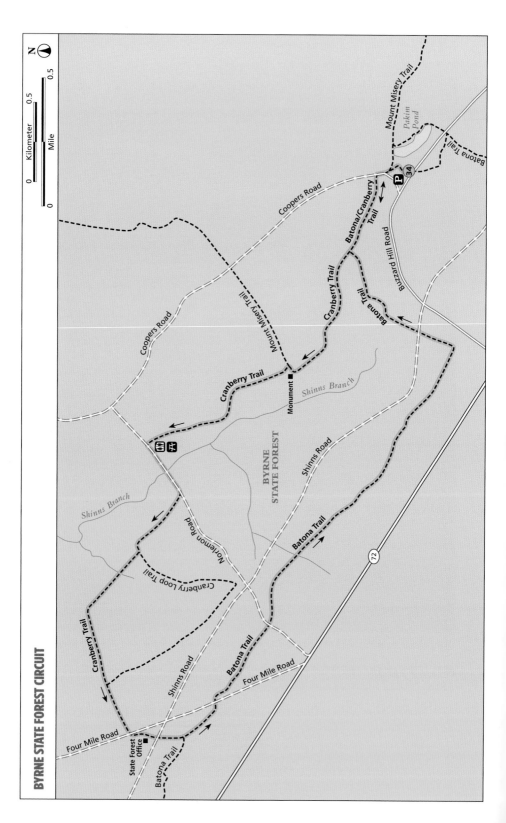

0.5 Come to a trail intersection, beginning the loop portion of the hike. Keep straight with the red-blazed Cranberry Trail as the Batona Trail splits left.

1.0 Pass through a cedar swamp, then come to the stone monument commemorating Cedar Swamp Natural Area. Just ahead the white-blazed Mount Misery Trail splits right. We stay with the Cranberry Trail, passing through scrub oaks.

1.7 Bisect a cedar swamp, then come to a restroom and picnic table just before reaching Norlemon Road, a forest road. Head left here and dip into a deep cedar swamp running along the lowermost valley of Shinns Branch. Use the forest road to span the dark, tannic watercourse running through an impressive Atlantic white cedar forest.

2.0 Leave right from Norlemon Road, back on all-access pea gravel trail. Quickly bridge a creeklet by culvert. Stay with the blazes as the Cranberry Trail comes near old forest roads.

2.3 The red-dot-blazed Cranberry Loop Trail splits left; we stay right with the Cranberry Trail. This part of the path is much more heavily used, as trail enthusiasts make a short loop from the state forest office trailhead using the Cranberry Trail and the Cranberry Loop Trail.

2.4 Bridge a wet area, then continue hiking in pines. More old forest roads come near.

2.6 The Cranberry Trail turns left, now heading southwesterly.

2.9 Meet the other end of the Cranberry Loop Trail. Stay straight on the Cranberry Trail.

3.1 Cross Four Mile Road, then curve left toward the state forest office.

3.2 Come to the state forest office, with information and restrooms. Cut through the office parking lot, then cross Shinns Road and pick up a singletrack path.

3.3 Meet the pink-blazed 50-mile Batona Trail. You are not far from its northern terminus at Ongs Hat. Head left, southeasterly, on a natural-surface singletrack path.

3.6 Cross sandy Four Mile Road. Oftentimes, road crossings will lead you into or out of areas of forest where prescribed fire was used. Segments of the Pine Barrens managed by state forests actively use prescribed fire.

3.9 Cross Norlemon Road. Enter a slightly hilly section.

4.2 Cross a tributary of Shinns Branch in swampy terrain. The trail stays more hilly than the Cranberry Trail.

5.3 The Batona Trail turns left (north). Ahead, cross Shinns Road, then dip into the headwaters of Shinns Branch, with boardwalks and bog bridges.

5.9 Complete the loop portion of the hike. Turn right, backtracking toward Pakim Pond.

6.4 Arrive back at the Pakim Pond trailhead, completing the Pine Barrens hike.

35 FRANKLIN PARKER RESERVE

Take a walk through a large protected preserve in the Wading River watershed that offers an excellent hiker-only loop trail leading you through a former cranberry farm–turned–wildlife refuge. Trek a combination of woods trails, elevated dikes, and sand tracks that will leave you appreciating this birder's paradise as well as rare and endangered Pine Barrens species. The wildlife-rich tract is one more piece of the puzzle holding the great Pinelands National Reserve intact.

Start: CR 532/Tabernacle Chatsworth Road entrance
Distance: 5.5-mile loop
Difficulty: Moderate
Elevation change: +-80 feet
Maximum grade: N/A
Hiking time: About 3.1 hours
Seasons/schedule: Daily dawn to dusk
Fees and permits: None
Dog friendly: Yes, on leash only
Trail surface: Natural surface, some boardwalk, some sand

Land status: Private preserve open to the public
Nearest town: Chatsworth
Other trail users: None on Red Trail; bicyclers, equestrians on other trails
Maps to consult: Franklin Parker Reserve
Amenities available: Restroom at trail parking area
Cell service: Good
Trail contact: New Jersey Conservation Foundation, (908) 234-1225, www.njconservation.org/preserve/franklin-parker-preserve

FINDING THE TRAILHEAD

From exit 67 on the Garden State Parkway in Barnegat Township, take West Bay Avenue west for 4.4 miles, then merge onto NJ 72 west and follow it 8.1 miles. Veer left onto CR 532 west, Chatsworth Barnegat Road, and follow it 4.1 miles to tiny Chatsworth. Turn right on Main Street and follow it 0.1 mile, then turn left onto Tabernacle Chatsworth Road, staying with CR 532 west for 0.7 more mile to turn left into the parking area. Trailhead GPS: 39.813989,-74.547578

THE HIKE

Nestled in the heart of the state's fabled Pine Barrens, this hike takes place at a private preserve open to the public—and a big one at that, nearly 10,000 acres closely linked with large public lands in South Jersey. Managed by the New Jersey Conservation Foundation, Franklin Parker Reserve continues habitat restoration to this day. Named for the first chairman of the Pinelands Commission, a force behind preserving and restoring the Pine Barrens, Franklin Parker Reserve managers first reconditioned the cranberry-growing reservoirs into more natural, shallow cranberry bogs that also favored other wetland flora. They also returned the flow of streams running through the property from canals to the creeks they once were. Yet, some open ponds were changed little, leaving them to attract waterfowl—with help from Ducks Unlimited—as they do in large numbers to this day. The land was so alluring that the Pine Barrens long-distance hiking path—the Batona Trail—was rerouted through the reserve.

This bridge leads over a tributary of the South Branch Wading River.

The DeMarco family, former owners of the tract, would be proud of this Pine Barrens treasure, for it fulfills their late-in-life vision. Patriarch Anthony DeMarco was born here in the Pine Barrens, the youngest of nine children. He developed a love for the pines of South Jersey. With his pharmacist earnings he got into the produce industry and soon developed a major cranberry and blueberry plantation before his life was cut short in a tragic auto accident. His son, James Garfield DeMarco, carried on on an even grander scale, fashioning one of the largest cranberry operations in the world. The DeMarcos saw the beauty of their slice of New Jersey and decided to sell the land as one tract, to let it return to nature through the leadership of the New Jersey Conservation Foundation. You will see the fruits of the DeMarco family's labor on this exciting and varied hike, from the Pine Barrens tree frog to the barred owl. Perhaps you might spot a rare yellow-fringed orchid, or the Pine Barrens gentian. But even if you don't, knowing that Franklin Parker Reserve conserves this special flora and fauna enhances the value of the tract.

The hiker-only Red Trail is our conduit. It enters classic Pine Barrens woods then crosses an abandoned railroad track before coming alongside the West Branch Wading River, traveling astride Atlantic white cedars. Next, you traipse through forest to Pole Branch, where cranberries were grown. Walk along dikes through restored wetlands, both vegetated and open. Make another run through the forest before coming to an elevated observation tower, where you can look over this Pine Barrens paradise. The final part of the hike takes you through woods along additional tributaries of the Wading River.

View of wildlife ponds at Franklin Parker Reserve

MILES AND DIRECTIONS

0.0 From the Chatsworth Lake area parking lot, join the hiker-only Red Trail eastbound in pine woods with scattered oaks, making a clockwise loop.

0.2 Cross a defunct old rail line, with trees growing among the tracks. Turn south and saddle alongside the West Branch Wading River, flowing through a cedar swamp. Pass concrete relics here and there left over from former farm use. Look for beaver dams.

1.2 Rise to an old road and run conjunctively with the multi-use Green Trail. Shortly split away, then rejoin the Green Trail again, only to split away again.

1.6 Bridge a tributary of the West Fork Wading River on a small swinging bridge.

1.7 Stay with the Red Trail as the Blue Trail leads left to the Yellow Trail and the south part of the reserve.

2.0 Shortly run with the Green Trail again, then split away. Stay with the red blazes, in scrubby pine flatwoods. Join old dikes amid former cranberry ponds, and pass former pumping stations. Watch for beaver slides crossing over the dikes from one wetland to another.

2.8 Cross the Green Trail twice in succession and turn north, passing over piled mounds, left over from dug cranberry ponds. Ahead, wander through blueberry row crop relics. Continue working around small irrigation ditches and canals.

3.3 Travel in conjunction with the Green Trail, now coasting dikes above wetlands open and vegetated, home to waterfowl and songbirds.

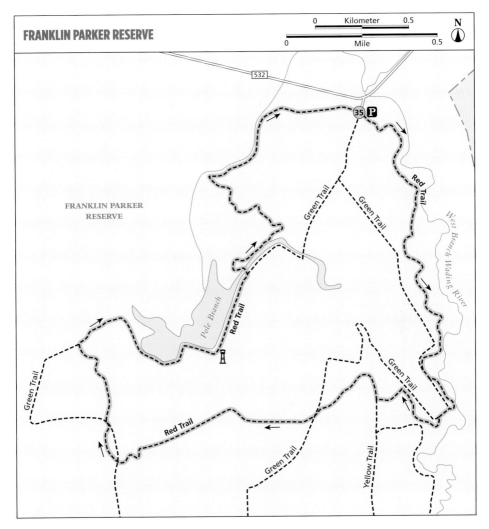

0   Kilometer   0.5

0   Mile   0.5

N

532

FRANKLIN PARKER
RESERVE

Green Trail

Green Trail

Red Trail

West Branch Wading River

Pole Branch

Red Trail

Green Trail

Green Trail

Green Trail

Red Trail

Green Trail

Yellow Trail

3.9   Come to the observation tower. Climb the topped former pumping station and soak in the views of open waters, vegetated bogs, and woods, part of the A. R. DeMarco Cranberry Meadows Natural Area, having undergone metamorphosis since 2003. Resume north on a dike.

4.1   Split left into woods while the Green Trail stays straight.

4.5   Cross the old railroad line a second time. Shortly come along a channelized tributary of Pole Branch. Cross it on a berm, then come along another channel of Pole Branch. Travel through pine woods beside the stream.

5.5   Arrive back at the trailhead, completing the wildlife-rich trek.

36 WELLS MILLS

This stimulating circuit hike takes place at one of the finest county parks in New Jersey—Wells Mills. The tramp explores the deep woods and forests of inland Ocean County, amid bogs, silent brooding brooks, Atlantic white cedars, and maple-gum swamps as well as hardwood and pine forests, all of which exude a wilderness aura.

Start: Nature center parking lot
Distance: 6.4-mile loop
Difficulty: Moderate
Elevation change: +-441 feet
Maximum grade: 2% grade for 0.2 mile
Hiking time: About 3.7 hours
Seasons/schedule: Daily 7:00 a.m. to dusk; fall through spring for best hiking
Fees and permits: None
Dog friendly: Yes, on leash only
Trail surface: Natural

Land status: County park
Nearest town: Waretown
Other trail users: Bicyclers, equestrians on a few segments
Maps to consult: Wells Mills County Park
Amenities available: Restrooms, picnic tables at trailhead
Cell service: Good
Trail contact: Wells Mills County Park, (609) 971-3085, www.oceancountyparks.org

FINDING THE TRAILHEAD

From exit 69 on the Garden State Parkway near Waretown, take Wells Mills Road west for 2.2 miles to the park entrance on your left. Once in the park, split left and reach the large nature center parking area. Trailhead GPS: 39.795267,-74.276596

THE HIKE

Carve out time to hike at this inland treasure of Ocean County. The eye-pleasing scenery and well-marked and-maintained trail system conspire to create a rewarding trail experience. You will first skirt the shore of Wells Mills Lake then wind among greater Oyster Creek. From there, the hike takes you through upland pines and oaks—yet never far from wetlands—until you work your way back to the dammed side of Wells Mills Lake, completing the excursion amid everywhere-you-look beauty.

During the American Revolution, Elisha Lawrence, a Tory, had his property in what became Ocean County confiscated and auctioned off to James Wells. The Atlantic white cedars, fragrant pines, and sturdy oaks towering over the tract made it a good investment. The lucky bidder proceeded to dam Oyster Creek and built a sawmill. From the Pine Barrens, Wells Mill (singular at that time, as he had only one sawmill then) milled pine and oak into building material or split it into cordwood, heating Philadelphia and New York City.

During the eighteenth century, the demand for Atlantic white cedar was so great, it was thought that the cedar would be clear-cut to extinction. After timbermen depleted the cedar aboveground, they began to harvest it from below. Some of the fallen trees had remained underwater for hundreds of years and surprisingly made for exceptionally fine

This boardwalk leads over Raccoon Branch.

timber. The cedar's unique properties made it an important commodity. It was water and rot resistant, while its long, straight grain made cedar easy to work. Coopers used it to make barrels, and farmers pounded it into the ground as fence posts. Jersey cedar—another name for Atlantic white cedar—virtually shingled Colonial America.

Shipwrights found Atlantic white cedar especially ideal because steamed cedar bends into shapes needed for constructing vessels. Cedar was also strong and at the same time light. The shipwrights created ribs and frames using cedar, but especially used it for planking. Due to the vast coastal forests existing in New Jersey at the time, shipyards

Hiking through an Atlantic white cedar forest

dotted the shore from Raritan Bay all the way around Cape May and up Delaware Bay. Schooners and sloops were constructed for coastal deliveries or for oystering. These Garden State shipwrights also designed three Jersey originals: the Barnegat Bay sneakbox used for duck hunting, the garvey used for clamming and oystering, and Sea Bright skiffs used for fishing and launched directly from the ocean's beach, used for lifesaving today.

In the late 1800s, Wells Mill was purchased by the Estlow family. They constructed side-by-side sawmills, and then Wells Mill became Wells Mills. Timbering and milling went on until 1936, when Wells Mills Lake and surrounding lands were purchased as

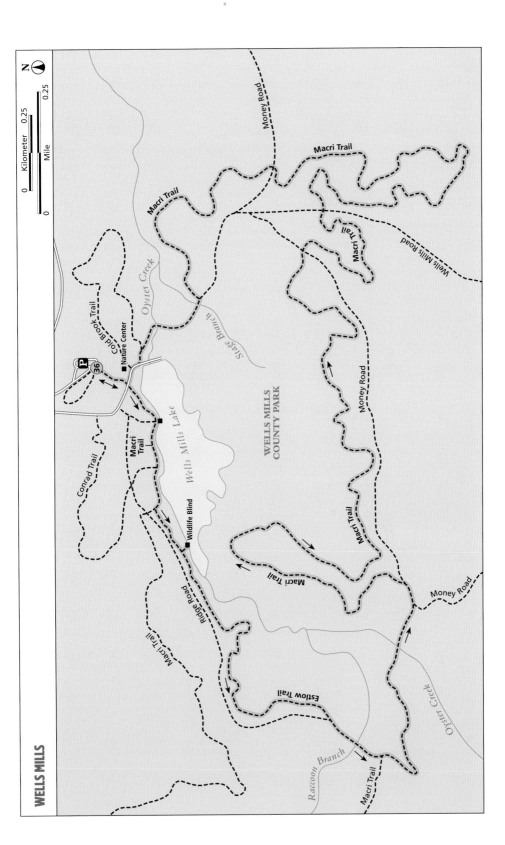

WELLS MILLS

N

0   Kilometer   0.25

0   Mile   0.25

Macri Trail

Macri Trail

Macri Trail

Macri Trail

Macri Trail

Macri Trail

Macri Trail

Macri Trail

Money Road

Money Road

Money Road

Money Road

Wells Mills Road

Oyster Creek

Oyster Creek

Stage Branch

Raccoon Branch

Wells Mills Lake

WELLS MILLS
COUNTY PARK

Nature Center

P

36

Cold Brook Trail

Conrad Trail

Ridge Road

Wildlife Blind

Estlow Trail

a family retreat by the Conrad clan, who built a cabin overlooking the lake. Eventually high taxes forced the Conrads to sell the attractive tract. The property eventually fell into the hands of Ocean County, and the parcel was developed into the fine park we see today.

Take a walk here and you will be happily impressed. However, hiking here in summer is not recommended due to heat, ticks, and mosquitoes. Make sure to photograph the map in this guide or obtain a trail map online. The trails are color-coded and named. Numerous trail intersections and old roads necessitate your keeping apprised of your location throughout the trek.

MILES AND DIRECTIONS

0.0 From the southwest corner of the large nature center lot, follow the brick walkway to the nature center, then go around the back of the center and head right along a wide track and join the white-blazed Macri Trail (formerly known as the Penns Hill Trail).

0.2 Pass the canoe/kayak launch on your left. Walk along the shore of Wells Mills Lake on boardwalks and among Atlantic white cedars.

0.3 Intersect the blue-blazed Conrad Trail. Stay straight with the white-blazed Macri Trail, spanning small streamlets on boardwalks amid cedars.

0.4 Split left with the green-blazed Estlow Trail. Continue on a hilly shore, shortly passing a spur left to a lakeside wildlife blind. Stay on the margin dividing pine hills from cedar swamps, spanning wetlands on small bog bridges. Leave the marshy upper end of the lake.

1.3 Ridge Road, a multi-use trail, enters on your right. Keep straight with the hiker-only Estlow Trail, shortly bridging tea-colored Raccoon Branch.

1.4 Meet the Macri Trail entering on your right. Keep straight, staying with the Macri Trail's white blazes throughout the rest of the circuit hike. Come near the Citta Scout Reservation, then turn eastbound in oaks and pines.

1.8 Bridge Oyster Creek, flowing swift over a sand bottom. Civilization seems far away.

1.9 Meet Money Road, a multi-use trail. Stay straight with the road for a short distance, then split left again with the white-blazed Macri Trail. Begin looping toward the lake in mixed woods of mountain laurel, pine, and black gum, mixed with wetter woods crossed by boardwalks.

2.8 Return almost to Money Road, then curve east in drier, piney woods.

3.8 Cross Money Road. Continue in mostly evergreens on singletrack path.

4.3 Cross Wells Mills Road, another multi-use trail.

4.6 Bridge an unnamed tributary of Oyster Creek.

5.1 Bridge the unnamed tributary a second time. Continue on a sandy track bordered with bracken ferns.

5.5 Cross Money Road yet again. Keep north toward Oyster Creek, coming near the stream before turning west.

6.1 Reach an intersection. Stay right with the white-blazed Macri Trail, running in conjunction with several other blazed paths. Bridge Stage Branch by culvert, entering a cypress swamp.

6.3 Bridge Oyster Creek as it flows easterly out of Well Mills Lake and toward the Atlantic Ocean. Climb a bit and pass both ends of the Cold Brook Trail as you gain westerly vistas of the 34-acre, two-centuries-old impoundment.

6.4 Arrive back at the trailhead after passing the nature center.

37 BATSTO LAKE LOOP

This excellent family hike, a circuit, moves through mixed pine-oak forest down into the Batsto Natural Area, including Batsto Lake. Atlantic white cedars, some very old pitch pines, and lake views complete the picture. Some slight ups and downs on sandy trails and occasional boardwalks vary the outing. Soak in some interpretive information while on the trek. While you are here, combine this hike with a walking tour of Batsto Historical Village, accessed from the same parking lot.

Start: Batsto Village parking lot
Distance: 4.1-mile loop
Difficulty: Easy–moderate
Elevation change: +-235 feet
Maximum grade: 3% downhill grade for 0.3 mile
Hiking time: About 2.0 hours
Seasons/schedule: Daily 8:00 a.m. to 8:00 p.m.; fall through spring for best hiking
Fees and permits: None for hiking; fee for walking through Batsto Historical Village
Dog friendly: Yes, on leash only

Trail surface: Natural
Land status: State forest
Nearest town: Hammonton
Other trail users: None, does cross mountain-biking trails
Maps to consult: Wharton State Forest
Amenities available: Restrooms, picnic shelter, visitor center at trailhead
Cell service: Good
Trail contact: Wharton State Forest, (609) 561-0024, www.nj.gov/dep/parksandforests

FINDING THE TRAILHEAD

From the intersection of US 30 and NJ 542 on the east side of Hammonton, take NJ 542 east for 7.2 miles, then turn left toward the large, paved Batsto Village parking area. The trailhead is on the northeast side of the parking area. Trailhead GPS: 39.645286,-74.646746

THE HIKE

This fun little trek takes us alongside Batsto Lake, created as a waterpower source for Batsto Village, one of South Jersey's more remarkable historic settlements. Many quiet backwaters of the Pine Barrens were once bustling centers of early America's industrial prowess, and nowhere is this truer than at Batsto. Like most curious names in the Pine Barrens, the origin of "Batsto" is debated. Early Dutch or Swedish settlers or surveyors perhaps noted a Lenape sweat lodge along the river. They would have likely called it a "heat-bath" or "sauna"—in Dutch, *badstoof*; in Swedish, *bastu*.

By 1766, Charles Read had acquired land here and started the Batsto Ironworks. The woods provided unlimited fuel, the creeks could be harnessed for power, and bog ore—a reddish-brown oxide that collects along the perimeters of swamps and creeks—could be mined. Mr. Read was a genuine mover-and-shaker in Colonial South Jersey industry and politics, and also built furnaces at Etna and Atsion. But he overextended himself financially,

This hike leads through classic Jersey Pine Barrens.

and by 1773 John Cox owned the Batsto works. They made a wide variety of goods—pots, pans, kettles, elegant firebacks, and other household items, as well as pig iron.

By the Revolutionary War, the prospering Batsto works were producing cannon and shot for the Continental Army, and had become important enough to be a British target. In 1778, a British detachment attacked and burned a nearby river port, with the destruction of Batsto its next goal. But word of the attack spread, and a group of determined locals ambushed and repulsed the British; Batsto survived to continue supplying the

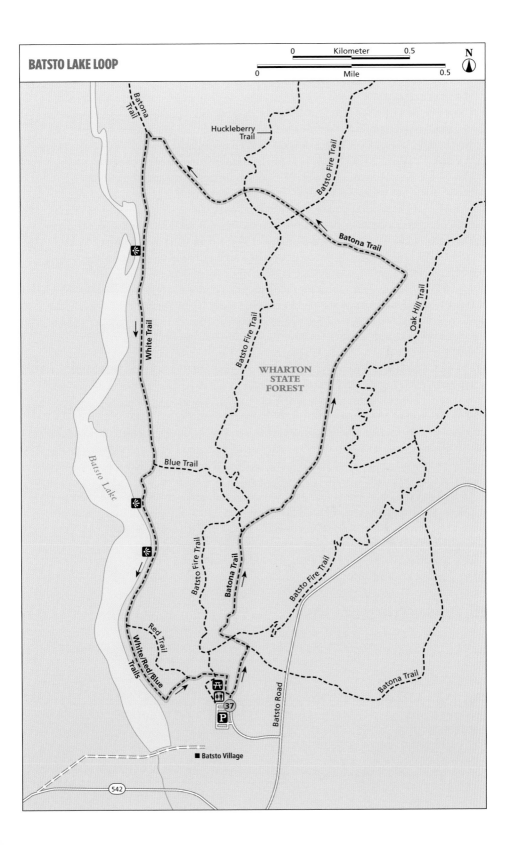

BATSTO LAKE LOOP

Batona Trail

Huckleberry Trail

Batsto Fire Trail

Batona Trail

Oak Hill Trail

White Trail

Batsto Lake

WHARTON STATE FOREST

Blue Trail

Batsto Fire Trail

Batsto Fire Trail

Batona Trail

Batona Trail

Red Trail

White/Red/Blue Trails

37

Batsto Road

Batona Trail

■ Batsto Village

542

N

0   Kilometer   0.5

0   Mile   0.5

Patriots. Joseph Ball became owner of Batsto in 1779, and his uncle William Richards took ownership in 1784. The Richards family oversaw the local ironworks until the rising iron industry of Pennsylvania put it out of business in 1848.

However, Batsto adjusted and iron manufacture was replaced by glass production—the raw material of glass is sand, which the Pine Barrens had endlessly. But the glassworks were never entirely profitable and finally shut down in 1867. The Richards family sold off more and more of their Batsto acreage to keep afloat, finally losing the village itself at the sheriff's sale in 1876. There was little left standing anyway: An 1874 fire ravished Batsto village, destroying most of the old Colonial structures, including the furnace.

Enter Joseph Wharton, who bought the Batsto tract in 1876. He was a Philadelphia Quaker, businessman, metallurgist, philanthropist, poet, and all-around high-level factotum. Among his credentials: owner of numerous iron and zinc mines and manufactories in New Jersey and Pennsylvania, cofounder of Bethlehem Steel, cofounder of Swarthmore College, and founder of the first business school in the United States—the Wharton School of Finance and Commerce at the University of Pennsylvania, in 1881.

At Batsto, Wharton spent vast sums fixing up the old ironmaster's house, transforming it into the magnificent Italianate mansion we see today (the Whartons spent occasional weekends there). He also removed old structures, improved forestry and agriculture on the property—and enlarged it. By the time Wharton was done buying, he owned 110,000 acres. He had a reason: His plan was to dam streams and create reservoirs on the property, making it a water supply for Philadelphia. The New Jersey Legislature got wind of the plans and didn't want to see New Jersey water pumped out-of-state, and put an end to the idea. Wharton died in 1909, and his heirs negotiated the sale of the property to the State of New Jersey in 1915 (New Jersey wanted it as a watershed, too). The purchase required a state referendum, which failed. The state next pursued the purchase of the Wharton tract in the mid-1950s. A price of $3 million was agreed upon for the 110,000-acre tract. Thus in 1955, the State of New Jersey bought fully 2.5 percent of itself. It is likely the only time in US history a state has done that.

Today, Wharton State Forest, 123,000 acres big, harbors over 110 miles of trails and preserves the vast quiet green of the Pine Barrens, as well as dozens of historic sites and former settlements. Batsto Village, listed on the National Register of Historic Places, is a famous New Jersey landmark, with ten major structures preserved, as well as the archaeological remains of many other buildings and sites. Be sure to visit. For more information, go to www.batstovillage.org.

MILES AND DIRECTIONS

0.0 From the northeast corner of the paved Batsto Village parking lot, walk toward the trailhead kiosk and join the Blue Trail, White Trail, and a pink-blazed Batona Trail connector. Enter tall pines with a shrubby blueberry understory rising above a sand floor.

0.1 Meet the pink-blazed Batona Trail. You can go left or right; go left, crossing a sand forest road.

0.2 Cross the green-blazed Batsto Fire Trail, a mountain-biking path. Turn north into an area that was once mined for sand.

0.5 The Blue Trail splits left toward Batsto Lake, availing a shorter loop hike. Stay right with the Batona Trail. Roll through woods that reflect the life of the pine in all its stages.

1.7 Cross the green-blazed Batsto Fire Trail again. Keep straight on the Batona Trail.

1.9 Cross the light blue–blazed Huckleberry Trail, a mountain-biking path. Keep straight, aiming for Batsto Lake. Cross a sand forest road and descend in pine-oak woods.

2.2 Come to yet another trail intersection. Here, the Batona Trail splits right, north for Batona State Forest, while we turn left on the White Trail, walking the sloped margin between piney uplands on the left and swamps and Batsto Lake on the right. Begin to look for unsigned spurs leading to views of the margin where the Batsto River and Batsto Lake merge.

3.1 The Blue Trail enters on your left. Keep straight along the lake in an open sandy area. Ahead, the path comes closer to Batsto Lake, offering more panoramas. Pass waterside contemplation benches.

3.6 The all-access Red Trail comes in on your left. Keep straight on the White Trail, which is now also all-access. Enjoy interpretive information and cut through a wetland.

3.9 Turn away from the lake, traveling alongside a forest road. Pass a maintenance area on your left, then meet the Red Trail. Turn right, crossing the forest road, then enter the greater trailhead picnic area, crossing the green-blazed Batsto Fire Trail once again.

4.1 Arrive back at the trailhead after passing by the picnic shelter/restroom building.

38 BASS RIVER STATE FOREST LOOP

This hike tours part of New Jersey's first state forest. Begin in the day-use area at Lake Absegami, near the swim beach, and cruise around an arm of the lake before coming near South Shore Campground. From there, begin a loop that takes you to the site of a former Civilian Conservation Corps (CCC) camp, complete with interpretive signage. Hike along the marshes of the Bass River before looping through classic pinelands associated with South Jersey before returning to Lake Absegami, where you can add more activities to your hike, such as swimming, paddling, fishing, picnicking, and camping.

Start: Lake Absegami Day Use Area
Distance: 4.5-mile balloon loop
Difficulty: Moderate
Elevation change: +-62 feet
Maximum grade: N/A
Hiking time: About 2.3 hours
Seasons/schedule: Daily 8:00 a.m. to 8:00 p.m.
Fees and permits: Entrance fee charged Memorial Day through Labor Day
Dog friendly: Yes, on leash only

Trail surface: Natural surface
Land status: State forest
Nearest town: Tuckerton
Other trail users: Bicyclers
Maps to consult: Bass River State Forest
Amenities available: Swim beach, picnic area, forest office nearby
Cell service: Good
Trail contact: Bass River State Forest, (609) 296-1114, www.nj.gov/dep/parksandforests

FINDING THE TRAILHEAD

From downtown Tuckerton at Pohatcong Lake, take US 9 south/Main Street for 0.8 mile, then turn right on Stage Road. Follow Stage Road 4.1 miles to the Bass River State Forest entrance, then follow the signs 0.4 mile to the Lake Absegami Day Use Area. Park on the south end of the large parking area, to the right of the entrance road. The trail system starts there. Trailhead GPS: 39.624150,-74.425353

THE HIKE

Bass River State Forest is one of the anchors that collectively form New Jersey's Pinelands National Reserve, designated as the United States' first national reserve in 1978. Stretching over seven South Jersey counties, the Pinelands National Reserve forms the largest open space along the mid-Atlantic coast. Interspersed with cities, towns, and blueberry and cranberry farms as well as protected forests and parks like Bass River State Forest, the reserve is popular with hikers, campers, anglers, and paddlers. Often referred to as the Jersey Pine Barrens, the reserve harbors rare ecosystems such as globally rare dwarf pine plains where pitch pines only rise 5 to 6 feet from the ground.

Many hikes in this guide offer treks within the greater Pinelands National Reserve, from Wharton and Belleplain State Forests, Estell Manor County Park, and Wells Mills

Author trekking through Bass River State Forest

County Park to Bass River State Forest. Not only does the reserve protect the natural world, but it also harbors the Garden State's human history. Lands continue to be acquired to preserve this state treasure, and make more complete the ecotones of the Pinelands National Reserve.

You will enjoy some of the Pine Barrens on this hike. Bass River State Forest encompasses over 29,000 acres, with most visitor use concentrated where this hike takes place. Lake Absegami is 67 acres of blackwater beauty, bordered by the popular swim beach, picnic area, and two campgrounds, one on the south shore and one on the north shore. The trail system is color-coded. We will stay with the orange-blazed CCC Trail throughout the hike, though other trails can be added to lengthen the adventure. One recommended trail addition is Joe's Trail, which travels along the south shore of Lake Absegami for 0.6 mile. Therefore, if you walk Joe's Trail out and back it will add 1.2 miles to the 4.5-mile CCC Trail hike.

After leaving the trailhead, you will curve by an arm of Lake Absegami, formed from the damming of Falkinburg Branch and Tommy's Branch. These two streams converge at Lake Absegami then together form the East Branch Bass River. The hike breaks off into the lower segment of the state forest after crossing Stage Road. The CCC Trail then makes a loop, curving by the site of Civilian Conservation Corps Camp S-55, in existence from 1933 to 1942. Here, an interpretive brochure takes you through the camp's location, complete with remnants of the locale that housed young men who developed this state forest, including laying out hiking trails, building bridges, and creating Lake

Make an escape to the backwoods on the CCC Trail.

Absegami. From there, cruise along the marshes of the Bass River, providing contrast to the Pine Barrens. The final part of the hike uses a mix of footpath and old sand roads, leading you back to Lake Absegami, with an enhanced appreciation of the Jersey wonder known as the Pinelands National Reserve.

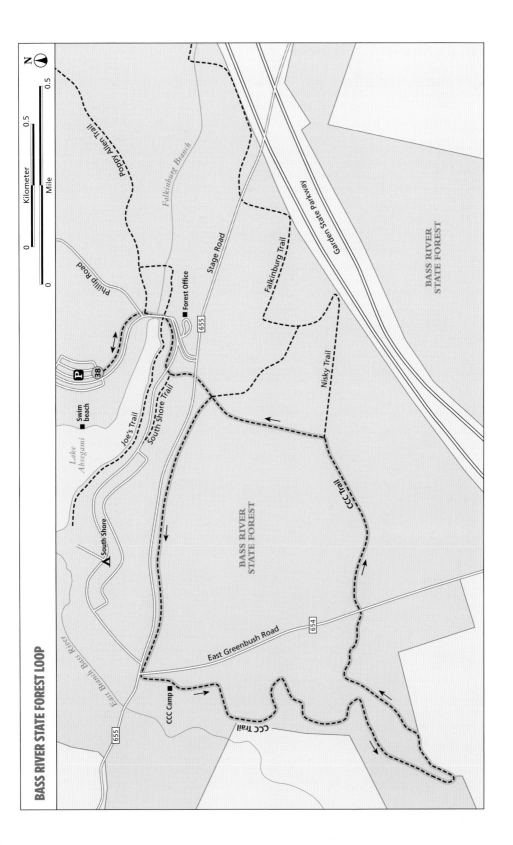

BASS RIVER STATE FOREST LOOP

MILES AND DIRECTIONS

0.0 From the south end of the day-use parking area east of the main access road, head south on the orange-blazed CCC Trail, running in conjunction with several other trails. Pitch pines, mountain laurel, blueberries, and white oaks complement the track.

0.2 Cross Phillip Road at a small parking area. The yellow-blazed Poppy Allen Trail leaves left. Stay with the orange blazes, briefly joining the Lake Absegami entrance road, bridging Falkinburg Branch. Enjoy a view into an arm of the lake, then rejoin foot trail. Ahead, Joe's Trail leaves right. Stay with the CCC Trail, crossing the South Shore Campground access road. Here, the red-blazed South Shore Trail leaves right.

0.5 Cross Stage Road after walking under a power line. Shortly reach an intersection. Stay right with the orange blazes, beginning the loop portion of the CCC Trail. Hike through a CCC-planted pine grove while hiking parallel to Stage Road.

1.3 Cross East Greenbush Road, CR 654, near its intersection with Stage Road. Turn south in woods.

1.4 Reach the site of CCC Camp S-55 and a small parking area. Begin a tour of the camp that developed this state forest. Most of the camp has returned to full-fledged woods. Avoid unblazed sand roads.

1.6 Come alongside the marsh of the East Branch Bass River.

2.5 Curve north away from the East Branch Bass River. Ahead, cut through a deep pine grove. More tall evergreen cathedrals stand ahead.

3.1 Cross East Greenbush Road a second time. Traverse easy sand roads.

3.6 Stay with the orange blazes as the green-blazed Nisky Trail leaves right.

3.9 Complete the loop portion of the CCC Trail. Backtrack toward the day-use area.

4.5 Arrive back at the day-use area, completing the Pinelands hike.

39 **FORT MOTT**

Welcome to an unorthodox loop hike providing an interesting day. The route runs along the perimeter of Fort Mott State Park. Hugging Delaware Bay, the trek cruises the shore, turns into the woods, and explores Finn's Point National Cemetery. There is a short road walk with little traffic, which continues along the parade grounds and Officers' Row. The hike concludes with a walking tour of the actual fort. Enjoy the grand view of Pea Patch Island, the state of Delaware, and traffic on the river from the fort parapet. The walk is made of lawns, paths, beach, and steps; the only challenge you're likely to have is leaving.

Start: Fort Mott State Park parking lot off Fort Mott Road
Distance: 2.5-mile loop with spur
Difficulty: Easy
Elevation change: +-46 feet
Maximum grade: N/A
Hiking time: About 1.2 hours
Seasons/schedule: Daily 8:00 a.m. to 8:00 p.m.
Fees and permits: None
Dog friendly: Yes, on leash only

Trail surface: Grass, sand, natural, concrete, pavement
Land status: State park
Nearest town: Pennsville
Other trail users: History buffs
Maps to consult: Fort Mott State Park
Amenities available: Restrooms, picnic shelter, picnic area at trailhead
Cell service: Good
Trail contact: Fort Mott State Park, (856) 935-3218, www.nj.gov/dep/parksandforests

FINDING THE TRAILHEAD

From exit 1C on I-295 just before the bridge over the Delaware River into Delaware, take CR 551 south for 4.9 miles to turn left onto NJ 49 east. Follow NJ 49 for 0.8 mile to take a sharp right onto Lighthouse Road and follow it for 2.2 miles. Next, turn left onto Old Fort Mott Road and follow it 0.2 mile, then merge left onto Fort Mott Road and follow it 1.2 miles to reach Fort Mott State Park. Turn right into the park and the main lot will be on your left. Trailhead GPS: 39.602886,-75.549925

THE HIKE

This easy hike explores a historic part of the lower, tidal Delaware River where the extensive views display why this spot was chosen for a fort. New Jersey was part of the Union during the Civil War, but this trek takes us not only throughout Fort Mott but also to a Confederate memorial, where soldiers of the South are interred after dying at nearby Pea Patch Island prison camp. The citadel was part of a three-fort defense system built in the 1800s to protect the Delaware Bay and Delaware River ports. The oldest was Fort Delaware, on Pea Patch Island in the river, built in 1848. It was followed by Fort DuPont on the Delaware side of the river. Fort Mott was not built until after the Civil War, in 1872. Construction stopped on the unfinished fort in 1876 and did not resume until 1896, when the present structure was completed. The new fort was part of a broader American buildup of naval defenses and sea power, used to promote commerce and

This beach at Fort Mott is found on Delaware Bay.

foreign policy. This aggressive posture led to, among other things, the Spanish–American War in 1898.

During the Civil War, Fort Delaware became a Union prison for captured Confederate soldiers. At its peak, some 12,500 prisoners were kept here, many captured at the Battle of Gettysburg. The fort-prison was makeshift, damp, and crowded, and while it was no Andersonville, its reputation among Southern soldiers was similar to that infamous Confederate prison for Union POWs. (You can take a seasonal ferry from Fort Mott to

A marker for Confederate soldiers who perished in a squalid prison camp

Fort Delaware.) Some 3,000 Confederate prisoners died here (mostly from cholera), as did 135 Union guard soldiers. Early on, the soldiers' cemetery at Finn's Point, adjacent to Fort Mott, was used as a burying ground, and eventually all the Confederate dead from Fort Delaware were interred here. It became a National Cemetery in 1875 and is still used for military burials.

In 1910, an 85-foot-tall obelisk was erected as a memorial to the Confederate dead. Forts Mott, Delaware, and DuPont were rendered obsolete by construction of the more

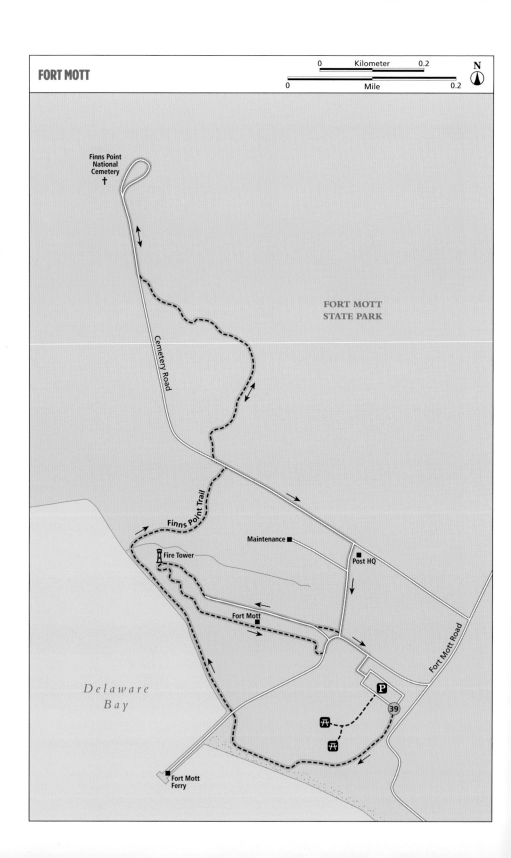

FORT MOTT

0   Kilometer   0.2
0   Mile   0.2

N

Finns Point
National
Cemetery

FORT MOTT
STATE PARK

Cemetery Road

Finns Point Trail

Maintenance ■

Fire Tower

Post HQ

Fort Mott ■

*Delaware
Bay*

Fort Mott Road

P

39

Fort Mott
Ferry

modern Fort Saulsbury in Delaware in 1917; all three citadels passed into state owner-ship in the late 1940s, with Fort Mott being taken over by the State of New Jersey in 1947. The Finns Point Rear Range Light, which you can view en route to Fort Mott, was built in 1877 as part of a dual-light navigation system for Delaware Bay. The Front Range Light was demolished after channel dredging rendered it unnecessary, but the Rear Range Light survived. A unique lighthouse with an iron skeleton, the 115-foot structure was restored in 1983–1984 and is now part of the Supawna Meadows National Wildlife Refuge.

The history and solemnity of this hike through a fort and a cemetery is enlivened by the beautiful views of the Delaware and the rich, varied habitat of the state park here. You will trek atop a small beach, along Delaware Bay, and through tranquil woods, all enhancing the historic aspects of this intriguing walk.

MILES AND DIRECTIONS

0.0   From the southeast corner of the parking lot, walk the edge of the tree line toward Delaware Bay, passing the back of the park restroom and picnic grove.

0.2   Reach a beach on Delaware Bay. Curve right and cross the ferry access road, with the wharf to your left. Pick up an asphalt path along a sea wall, keeping Delaware Bay to your left and Fort Mott to your right.

0.5   Head right, away from Delaware Bay on a sandy path, the Finns Point Trail, after passing the balance of Fort Mott to your right, including the dilapidated Western Fire Control Tower. Wander through woods and high grasses. Note the signed firing range from when the fort was active.

0.7   Reach Cemetery Road. Head left and walk a few feet, then split right back into sweetgum-rich woods. Pass a small pond and streamlet.

1.1   Join Cemetery Road right, heading toward Finns Point National Cemetery.

1.2   Reach the cemetery, inspecting the memorials, graves, grounds, and obelisk. Back-track and split left on the Finns Point Trail.

1.7   Return to Cemetery Road again. Head left, southeast.

1.9   After passing the maintenance yard and prior to the post headquarters, turn right and head down a paved road, passing the welcome center (museum), park office, and restrooms.

2.1   Reach Fort Mott and head right, beginning the official tour of the fort.

2.3   Come near the fire control tower and turn back toward the parking area, rising to the top of the fort. Soak in extensive views of Delaware Bay from the parapet.

2.5   Arrive back at the trailhead after touring Fort Mott.

Enjoy this circuit hike at fun and historic Parvin State Park. Here, you circle around Parvin Lake through pines, oaks, and Atlantic cedar swamps, parts of which are protected as Parvin Natural Area, where the Pine Barrens meld upland forests and wooded wetlands. The loop also takes you along blackwater streams feeding Parvin Lake. Along the way enjoy some of the handiwork of the Civilian Conservation Corps (CCC), who improved this preserve—including laying out parts of the trails you hike—nearly a century back.

Start: Parvin Grove Day Use Area
Distance: 5.4-mile loop
Difficulty: Easy–moderate
Elevation change: +-90 feet
Maximum grade: N/A
Hiking time: About 2.6 hours
Seasons/schedule: Daily sunrise to sunset
Fees and permits: Entrance fee charged Memorial Day weekend through Labor Day
Dog friendly: Yes, on leash only

Trail surface: Mostly natural
Land status: State park
Nearest town: Vineland
Other trail users: Joggers, some bicyclers
Maps to consult: Parvin State Park
Amenities available: Restrooms, swim beach, picnic area at trailhead
Cell service: Good
Trail contact: Parvin State Park, (856) 358-8616, www.nj.gov/dep/parksandforests

FINDING THE TRAILHEAD

From the intersection of NJ 55 and NJ 56 on the west side of Vinelands, take NJ 56 west for 2.1 miles, then turn right on Alvine Road and follow it for 1 mile. Turn left on Almond Road/CR 540 and follow it 1 mile to Parvin State Park, with the office/starting point to your left and a large parking area on your right, where you park and then cross Almond Road to begin the hike. Trailhead GPS: 39.510893,-75.132727

THE HIKE

Situated on the edge of the Pine Barrens, Parvin State Park, 1,137 acres, sprang from the damming of not-muddy Muddy Run back in 1783. The waters that became Parvin Lake were used to power a sawmill at the small crossroads hamlet of Union Grove. The attractive impoundment began attracting locals to picnic, fish, and swim, and later evolved into a private recreation area by the late 1800s, operated by a man named Smith. His son took over the property and got into debt, eventually selling the parcel to the State of New Jersey to pay off said debt. Then in 1933 the Civilian Conservation Corps made their mark, building the beach and pavilion, cabins, campgrounds, lean-tos, restrooms, paths, bridges, and other structures and features, most of which survive to this day and give the preserve a rustic, old-timey touch.

Since those days, Parvin State Park has been a go-to destination for a classic outdoor getaway, with visitors overnighting in the cabins and campground (you'll walk by the

Bridging Muddy Run

campground on this hike), gathering for a picnic and swim in the lake, or fishing/canoeing/kayaking on the electric-motors-only impoundment.

Your impromptu hiking survey of the park may raise your desire to add a few more activities to your trek on the well-marked and -managed trail system. The adventure starts at the swim beach/picnic area entrance, then leads along Parvin Lake before entering the marshy reaches of lower Muddy Run, where wooded wetlands add to the reputation of the protected Parvin Natural Area, 465 acres of natural New Jersey. After bridging Muddy Run you enter higher, drier ground, rich with pitch pines and oaks, before returning to the margin between forest and marsh. Come again to Parvin Lake, soaking in views of the ages-old impoundment, maybe spotting an angler or boater treasuring a watery experience.

The final part of your hike takes you over a CCC-built bridge and by the old gazebo before returning to the hike's beginning, conveniently located at the swim beach/picnic area. Perhaps you brought your swimwear—and tent, and kayak, and fishing pole . . . whatever it takes to execute an old-time outdoor excursion at Parvin State Park.

MILES AND DIRECTIONS

0.0 From the entrance to the parking lot, cross Almond Road/CR 540, arriving at the Parvin State Park office. Turn right (west) onto the sidewalk, where you will see a kiosk and a trailhead sign for the green-blazed Parvin Lake Trail. Continue heading west into the forest onto a sandy path of the Parvin Lake Trail, with the fenced swim

A view across Parvin Lake

beach area to your left. Pass Atlantic cedars near swampy areas. Ahead, note the signed location of a CCC camp located in what is now the state park.

0.9 At the intersection near a pavilion, continue straight (northwest), joining the red-blazed Long Trail, as the orange-blazed Knoll Trail goes left.

1.0 Pass the white-blazed Nature Trail loop, which comes in on the right and now becomes co-aligned with the Long Trail. It will leave shortly on the right. You have entered a land of sporadic boardwalks and bridges, winding through wooded marsh, with some sloppy trail segments.

1.7 Bridge Muddy Run. Enjoy looks up and down the not-muddy blackwater stream. Ahead, pass a spur left to the Forest Road Trail and cross a gurgling tributary of Muddy Run.

2.0 Cross a connector trail linking the Black Oak Trail with the Forest Road Trail. Stay with the red-blazed Long Trail. Turn southeast back toward Parvin Lake, now in white oaks, mountain laurel, and pines, with ample blueberry bushes. Bridge sluggish intermittent streamlets ahead. Strangely, cross an area with many dug holes, now revegetated but still looking not perfectly natural.

2.8 Come to an intersection. Here, split left on the orange-blazed Knoll Trail. Shortly cross the blue-blazed Forest Road Trail.

3.2 Cross the Forest Road Trail again.

3.4 Reach a four-way intersection. Head straight (east), rejoining the Parvin Lake Trail.

3.5 Stay straight as the pink-blazed Flat Trail enters right.

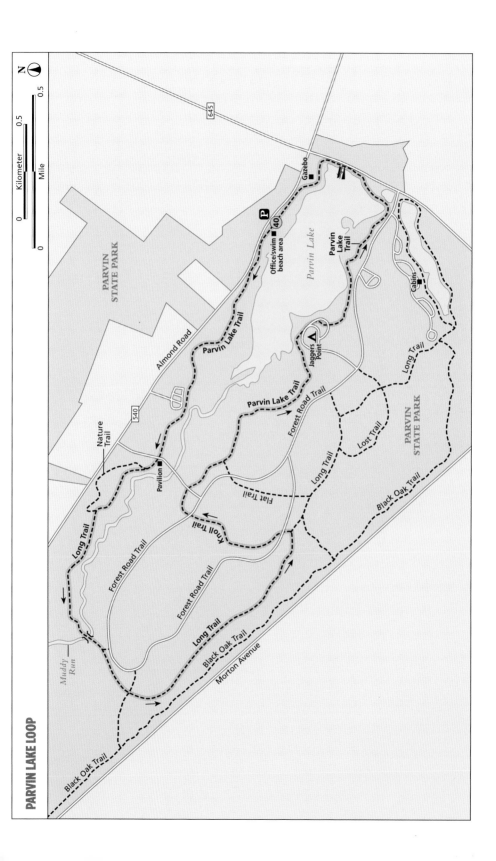

PARVIN LAKE LOOP

4.2 Begin circling around the north side of Jaggers Point camping area. User-created spurs link the path and campsites. Stay with the blazes as the trail goes through the campground, splitting left from the campground near campsite 16.

4.8 Curve left, now in the dam area, bridging dam outflows and passing through a popular fishing area as well as boat launch. Savor open lake vistas. Walk by the park boat ramp.

5.1 Turn west after crossing the CCC-built "White Bridge," then come to a picturesque gazebo, site of many a wedding. Continue circling around the lake, now with the swim beach/picnic area to your left.

5.4 Complete the hike after returning to the park office and swim beach entrance area.

41 MAURICE RIVER BLUFFS PRESERVE

One of the hilliest treks in South Jersey, this hike through the Nature Conservancy's Maurice River Bluffs Preserve travels widely diverse terrain, from the bluffs overlooking the wild, scenic, and tidal Maurice River to upland woods, cool ravines, and wildlife-favorable meadows. Visit the river's edge, where the piers of long-gone docks once stood, and an artesian well on the old sand mine–turned–farm–turned–nature preserve that is an important migratory flyway for both raptors and songbirds.

Start: Maurice Bluffs parking lot
Distance: 4.8-mile quadruple loop
Difficulty: Moderate
Elevation change: +-308 feet
Maximum grade: 6% downhill grade for 0.2 mile
Hiking time: About 2.6 hours
Seasons/schedule: Daily dawn to dusk
Fees and permits: None
Dog friendly: Yes, on leash only
Trail surface: Natural surface

Land status: Private preserve open to the public
Nearest town: Millville
Other trail users: Mountain bikers on separate set of trails
Maps to consult: Maurice River Bluffs Walking Trails Map
Amenities available: None
Cell service: Good
Trail contact: Nature Conservancy in New Jersey, (908) 879-7262, www. nature.org

FINDING THE TRAILHEAD

From exit 24 on NJ 55 just east of Millville, take NJ 49W/Main Street and follow it 1.8 miles to turn left on Cedar Street. Follow Cedar Street 0.2 mile to turn left on Race Street and stay with it 1.8 miles to enter the preserve on your left. Trailhead GPS: 39.353774,-75.038117

THE HIKE

Funny how times—and places—change over time. The Maurice River Bluffs Preserve was originally a place of unspoiled God-given beauty, as all places once were. Then as New Jersey's capacity for responding to the needs and wants of citizens near and far increased, the tract was alternately a chicken feed production facility, a sand mine, and later a truck farm. The Maurice River stayed its tidal self, going in and out with the cycles of the moon, remaining a rich estuary teeming with wildlife from waterfowl to sand crabs, and remains so to this day. The 500 acres of what is now Maurice River Bluffs Preserve, just south of Millville, was purchased in 1992 by the Nature Conservancy. And as has been seen in Jersey time and again, the land healed and is now a regal forest (albeit hilly, due to the former sand mine pits) with hints of its former life as a sand mine facility (piers), a chicken feed production locale (concrete ruins), and even the truck farm (the standing walls of the 1700s farmhouse as well as closing meadows that were once agricultural fields).

A bluff view of the Maurice River

The bluffs are now returned to another important task, that of migratory flyway stop-over. The waters and land add to other Jersey preserves that also give birds and butterflies places to land and feed, parcels detailed in this guide such as Cape May Point, Higbee Beach, and Sandy Hook. To make a good thing better, the Nature Conservancy added trails to the preserve—separate pathways for hikers and mountain bikers to enjoy the eye-pleasing woods and undulating terrain, arguably the hilliest in all of South Jersey.

Old pilings reveal this locale's industrial past.

This hike encompasses nearly all the well-maintained hiking trails at Maurice Bluffs, leaving you pleased with the faraway vistas and nearby natural world. The trails are color-coded and named after their color, with You Are Here maps posted at intersections. Picnic tables and repose benches are strategically located along the hike.

First you will head north, back from the river undulating in thick woods, surprised at the sloping terrain. The natural recovery is so complete, an unknowing hiker might think they were farther north in the Garden State, where hills and mountains naturally carpet the land. Eventually you turn to the Maurice River, reaching a long-used river landing, replete with a gushing artesian well. From there, the dips and climbs on the packed sand and pine needle trail bed are nearly constant, as you ride the bluffs, enjoying vistas of the Maurice River, adjacent tidal marshes, and terra firma beyond. Work out to a peninsula where marshes surround you on three sides before trading water for forest, then back to water again, reaching a dock and river access. From there, more views await, then you pass through closing fields that diversify the preserve habitat to next view the standing stone walls of a farmhouse inhabited until 1989, sans electricity. Finally, arrive back at the trailhead, realizing that saving this parcel of the Garden State amounts to a lot more than chicken feed, as was once produced here.

MILES AND DIRECTIONS

0.0 From the east side of the parking lot, join the hiker-only trail system on the Blue Trail in pines, holly, cedar, and oak, with a wooded bluff immediately below you.

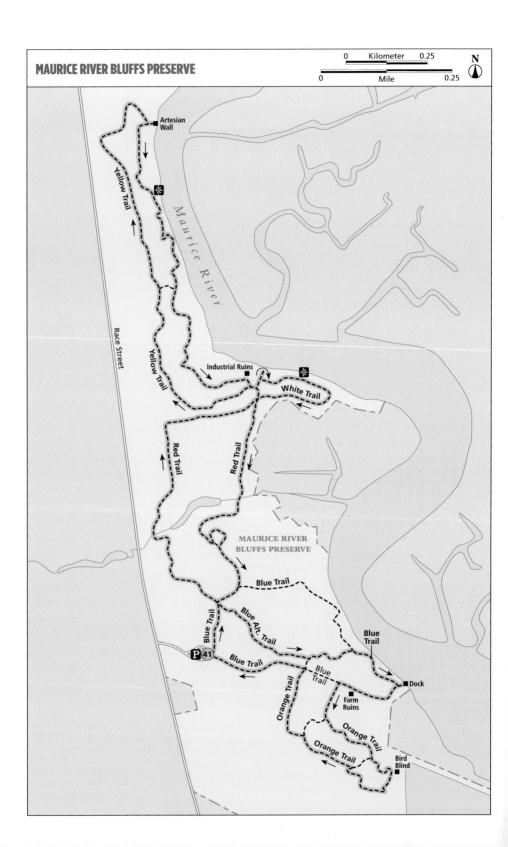

0.1 Intersect the Blue Alternate Trail and the Red Trail. Stay left with the Red Trail, northbound, making a clockwise circuit, rolling over mountains and dips. Pay attention as mountain-bike trails (not shown on map) occasionally coincide with the hiker trails.

0.3 Bridge a seasonal stream.

0.5 The Red Trail meets an old road and heads right, easterly.

0.7 Reach a major trail intersection. Stay left here, following the White Trail a short distance, then go left again on the Yellow Trail, leaving the Red Trail. Just ahead you will reach the loop portion of the Yellow Trail. Stay left again.

1.2 A spur goes right to shortcut the Yellow Trail. Stay left with the outer loop. Come near Silver Run Road.

1.6 Dip to reach the Maurice River at an old landing. View the gushing artesian well and old pilings in the river. Turn south, paralleling the river on sometimes-steep segments.

1.8 Reach a river view and picnic table. Ahead, pass the other end of the Yellow Trail shortcut. Ascend and descend sharply in places.

2.4 Come along structural ruins of an industrial past. Shortly end the Yellow Trail, then stay left on the White Trail, visiting the river's edge before climbing back to bluffs on the White Trail.

2.5 Come to another developed view on the White Trail, and continue circling the White Trail.

2.7 Finish the White Trail, then stay left on the Red Trail, resuming south along the edge of land with tidal marsh lying below you.

3.1 The Red Trail makes a small but curious mini-loop of its own then resumes south.

3.3 Reach a seasonally open segment of the Blue Trail (open July through December). Continue walking to join the Blue Alternate, open year-round, and head left, back toward the Maurice River.

3.6 Meet a leg of the Orange Trail. Stay left with the Blue Alternate, shortly meeting the Blue Trail. Keep east.

3.8 Come to the river at a landing and dock. This is a major stopping point for hikers. From there, backtrack and rejoin the Blue Trail. Ahead, pass the standing ruins of the 1700s farmhouse then split left, making the widest loop on the Orange Trail network, a series of intertwined orange-blazed paths. Pass several quick intersections. Stay left at all intersections, eventually closing the loop through a regenerating meadow, former cropland. Enjoy the view from a bird blind along the way, looking out on tidal flats.

4.6 Escape from the Orange Trail maze. Head left, westerly, on the Blue Trail, back toward the trailhead.

4.8 Arrive back at the trailhead, completing the river bluff hike.

42 BELCOVILLE AND THE SOUTH RIVER

This loop hike in Estell Manor Park is a hidden prize among oak-pine forests, white cedar swamps, and coastal ecosystems that border the South River and Stephens Creek. The route takes you through Belcoville, a "ghost town," and the former Bethlehem Loading Company, a World War I munitions plant, with foundations appearing along the way. The hike traverses sand roads, abandoned railroad beds, and one of the longest boardwalks in the state of New Jersey. The route also passes the nineteenth-century Estell Glassworks, with much of the foundations still standing. Adding to the experience are a number of historical kiosks informing you about what transpired in this natural area with an intriguing history.

Start: Warren E. Fox Nature Center parking lot
Distance: 5.2-mile loop
Difficulty: Moderate
Elevation change: +-66 feet
Maximum grade: N/A
Hiking time: About 2.8 hours
Seasons/schedule: Daily 7:30 a.m. to 1 hour after sunset
Fees and permits: None
Dog friendly: Yes, on leash only
Trail surface: Natural surface, boardwalk

Land status: County park
Nearest town: Mays Landing
Other trail users: Local daily walkers
Maps to consult: Estell Manor Park Trail Map
Amenities available: Nature center, restroom at trailhead
Cell service: Good
Trail contact: Estell Manor Park, (609) 625-1897, https://www.atlantic-county.org/parks/estell-manor-park.asp

FINDING THE TRAILHEAD

From the intersection of US 40 and NJ 50 in Mays Landing, drive 1.3 miles on NJ 50 south. Turn left (east) into Estell Manor and keep straight to park at the Warren E. Fox Nature Center lot on your right. Trailhead GPS: 39.398275,-74.742493

THE HIKE

This hike reflects the beautiful nature and industrial history of New Jersey's own fabled Pine Barrens, and few places mirror this better than our hike in Estell Manor Park. The preserve takes its name from John Estell, who acquired land here in the 1820s. Bog iron had long been profitable hereabouts, but the Estells switched over to the up-and-coming commodity in South Jersey, glass. Estell built a glassworks here in 1826; it was perhaps the first that could produce both bottle glass and window glass, which required very different processes. The glassworks here was built, unusually, of stone, and its ruins are thus still standing.

Remains of the nineteenth-century Estell Glassworks

Glass was a major industry in South Jersey, and the reason is everywhere underfoot on our hike: sand, the basic raw ingredient of glass. The Estell Glassworks closed in 1877. Its ruins, including the glass furnace, the walls and foundations of other industrial structures, and the sites of workers' housing, are a highlight of this hike.

The next major phase in the park's industrial history was vastly bigger and remarkably shorter. The entry of the United States into World War I in April 1917 signaled a need for greatly increased armament-production facilities. The Bethlehem Loading Company, in partnership with the federal government, quickly set about acquiring some 10,000 acres here, mostly old farmsteads and river landings.

Ground for the new munitions plants and related facilities was broken in May 1918, and by August nothing less than a city had been built. It included a town hall, a school, a bank, a bowling alley, stores, cafeterias, police headquarters, factories and plants, 24 miles of railroad siding, and barracks and housing for a total of 9,000 workers and their families. In honor of the Bethlehem Loading Company, it was dubbed Belcoville. Much of our walk follows the old roads and lanes of this onetime industrial plant/city, now returned to wilderness that evinces the recuperative powers of nature.

But as a munitions plant, this remarkable new city had a short life. Production started in the fall of 1918, and by November of that year the war was over. Munitions production at Belcoville ended in 1919, and it was closed. Many structures were sold as scrap lumber or were jacked up and moved to nearby towns. Most steel and metal from the site was stripped for scrap. In 1923 the remaining structures of Belcoville were sold, becoming the

Boardwalks aplenty lead along the South River.

current nearby town of Belcoville. The park area was virtually all part of the Belcoville plant, primarily the manufacturing and administrative areas, and ruins and reminders of those days are still to be seen, all framed in a regenerated woodland.

Our hike goes by sites not to be missed as it first works north along an old road-turned-trail before reaching the South River, where it picks up the 1.8-mile Swamp Trail boardwalk. It then visits Stephens Creek at an old bridge site before reaching the Estell Glassworks site. After your trek, you will return to enjoy more of this 1,700-acre Atlantic County park with a whopping 27 miles of trails to explore. Additional park activities include paddling, fishing, and camping.

MILES AND DIRECTIONS

0.0 Leave east from the nature center and join Purple Heart Drive, passing the Shaw House (an 1825 farmhouse, now the park office) and the maintenance yard on your left.

0.1 At the fork veer left (northeast) off Purple Heart Drive onto a sandy lane, the North End Trail, part of the aggregate Bethlehem Loading Company History Trail. Just ahead Collins Road leaves right. (These roads within the park are open only to park personnel and reflect the historic names when these trails were actual roads.) Stay with the North End Trail, northbound under pines, sweetgum, and oak.

0.3 Sand Hole Road leaves right.

0.5 Pass TNT Road, Tin Box Road, and Receiving Road in quick succession.

0.7 Split left, circling near NJ 50 and the old Bethlehem administration building ruins.

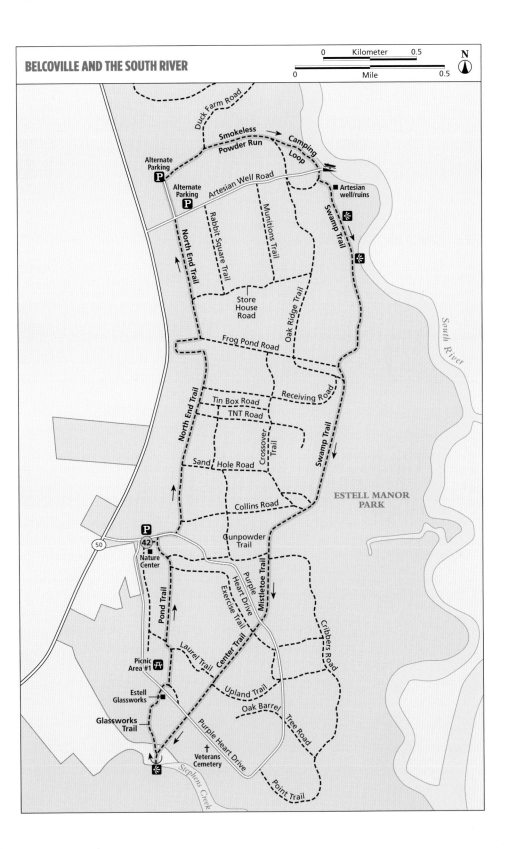

Kilometer

0   0.5

Mile

0   0.5

N

Duck Farm Road

Smokeless
Powder Run

Camping
Loop

Alternate
Parking
P

Alternate
Parking
P

Artesian Well Road

Artesian
well/ruins

Swamp Trail

Rabbit Square Trail

Munitions Trail

North End Trail

Store
House
Road

Oak Ridge Trail

Frog Pond Road

South River

North End Trail

Tin Box Road

Receiving Road

TNT Road

Swamp Trail

Crossover Trail

Sand Hole Road

Collins Road

ESTELL MANOR
PARK

Gunpowder
Trail

P

50

42

Nature
Center

Pond Trail

Purple Heart Drive

Exercise Trail

Mistletoe Trail

Center Trail

Cribbers Road

Laurel Trail

Picnic
Area #1

Upland Trail

Estell
Glassworks

Oak Barrel

Tree Road

Glassworks
Trail

Purple Heart Drive

Veterans
Cemetery

Point Trail

Stephens Creek

0.9 Return to the North End Trail, northbound, passing Frog Pond Road and Store House Road, both trails, in succession.

1.1 Pass around a pole gate.

1.3 Cross Artesian Well Road (a regular auto road) and keep straight.

1.5 Come to the mountain-biking trailhead and split right on Duck Farm Road, a trail, now curving easterly.

1.6 Split right away from Duck Farm Road, now on narrower Smokeless Powder Run, bordered by swamp ponds.

1.9 Stay left now on the Camping Loop. Ahead, the South River comes into view.

2.1 Return to Artesian Well Road, reaching a boat ramp. Head south, passing the artesian well and ruins of an old power plant. Ahead, join the Swamp Trail boardwalk as a spur goes right to Smith Ireland Cemetery.

2.3 Take the spur to a South River overlook.

2.5 Take another spur to the South River.

2.9 Bridge Sand Creek. Ahead, Frog Pond Road leaves right, then an arm of the Swamp Trail also leaves right. Stay straight with the Swamp Trail, southbound, passing through a deep cedar swamp ahead. Enjoy a long cruise on the boardwalk through swamp woods.

3.3 The Highbank Trail first leaves right, then Sand Hole Road leaves right next. Stay with the Swamp Trail boardwalk.

3.6 The boardwalk Gunpowder Trail splits right. Stay straight, joining the natural-surface Mistletoe Trail. Ahead, cross paved Purple Heart Drive, then cross the Exercise Trail. The trail you are on becomes the Center Trail.

4.1 Pass the Laurel Trail on your right and the Upland Trail on your left in quick succession. Next, cross part of the paved loop road around Veterans Cemetery, then cross paved Purple Heart Drive a second time.

4.4 Keep straight at the next intersection to reach the viewing deck at Stephens Creek. Note the old bridge pilings across the placid waterway. Backtrack, then join the Glassworks Trail, now heading north.

4.6 Reach the preserved site of Estell Glassworks, with stone walls still standing and informative interpretive signage. Savor this historic highlight, then cross Purple Heart Drive a final time. Stay left at the next intersection, keeping Picnic Area #1 to your left. Parallel a ditch.

4.8 Pass the other end of the Laurel Trail, then split left, crossing the ditch you've been paralleling. Stay along the ditch and join the Pond Trail, an abandoned railroad bed. Ahead, pass the pond of the Pond Trail, then stay left as the Exercise Trail and then the Gunpowder Trail boardwalk enter on your right. Stay left, walking toward the nature center.

5.2 Arrive back at the nature center and trailhead, completing the historic hike.

43 EAST CREEK TRAIL

This healthy loop hike through Belleplain State Forest starts at Lake Nummy then moves through mixed forest from oaks to pines, mountain laurel to holly. Most of the ramble is on flat sand tracks, accented by boardwalks and bridges. Occasional muddy areas and a 0.3-mile section along a busy road can be troublesome, but the adventure is worth it. You will experience some magnificent white cedar swamps along with work completed by the Civilian Conservation Corps. The hike skirts East Creek Pond with a chance of seeing a bald eagle and ends back at Lake Nummy, and a chance for a swim.

Start: Belleplain State Forest Interpretive Center
Distance: 7.1-mile loop
Difficulty: Strenuous due to length
Elevation change: +-120 feet
Maximum grade: N/A
Hiking time: About 3.6 hours
Seasons/schedule: Daily dawn to dusk; best late summer through spring
Fees and permits: Entrance fee charged Memorial Day through Labor Day
Dog friendly: Yes, on leash only

Trail surface: Natural surface
Land status: State forest
Nearest town: Woodbine
Other trail users: Bicyclers
Maps to consult: Belleplain State Forest
Amenities available: Interpretive center, swim beach, picnic area nearby
Cell service: Good
Trail contact: Belleplain State Forest, (609) 861-2404, www.nj.gov/dep/parksandforests

FINDING THE TRAILHEAD

From exit 17 on the Garden State Parkway, take Sea Isle Boulevard/CR 625 northwest toward Ocean View for 0.3 mile, then turn right onto US 9 north. Drive 0.6 mile to turn left (northwest) onto Woodbine–Ocean View Road/CR 550 and travel 6 miles to Woodbine. Turn left (southwest) onto Washington Avenue, staying with CR 550, and drive 0.4 mile, then turn right onto Webster Street, still with CR 550. Drive 1.4 miles to the entrance to Belleplain State Forest. Turn left onto Henkin-Sifkin Road and shortly pass the forest office on the right. After 0.6 mile turn right onto Meisle Road and shortly pass through the forest contact station. Travel 0.5 mile, then turn left just before the interpretive center with Lake Nummy on the right. Immediately on your left you will find parking. Trailhead GPS: 39.244828,-74.857863

THE HIKE

This is a great woods hike linking two bodies of water at a state forest that reinforces New Jersey's nickname as the Garden State. Most of New Jersey's great open spaces, such as Belleplain State Forest, have witnessed a parade of change over the centuries since Europeans first settled on these shores. Once, when the Lenape made this land their home, the bear and bald eagle prospered, yet within nearly a lifetime, they became a memory (they have since greatly recovered). Belleplain State Forest embodies this pageant of change as well as anyplace in the state.

Pink lady slipper along the East Creek Trail

Nummy was the last local chieftain of the Native American Unalachtigo tribe here. These local Lenape exploited the rich flora and fauna of this region. Nummy's ancestral home was somewhat south of here, around present-day Nummytown. But "King" Nummy, as tradition describes him, sold the last 16 miles of land along the bay shore some time prior to 1700, and then moved to an island in Hereford Inlet, still called Nummy Island. Soon, the Natives who lived here for thousands of years left only names behind.

Fiddleheads signal spring has arrived in the Jersey Pine Barrens.

In the 1700s and 1800s, the locale was used for farming, timbering, and charcoal making, among other uses. As in much of the region, cranberries were an important crop here, with the Meisle family operating a large cranberry bog. But the exploitation of the forests and bogs took their toll, and by the early 1900s the State of New Jersey was looking to better steward its forest resources, both for improved timber production and preservation of water resources and for recreation.

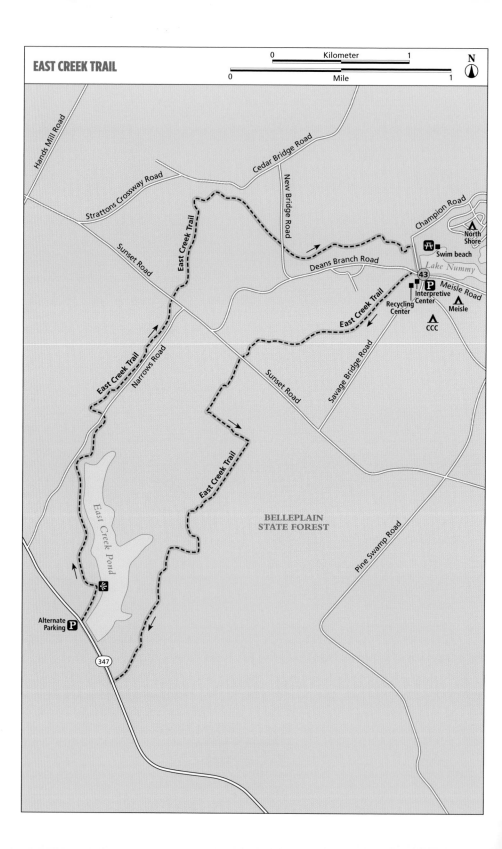

An early acquisition in this effort was Belleplain State Forest, the first 5,600 acres of which were purchased in February 1928. East Creek Lodge, a group cabin, was built on East Creek Pond. Vastly expanded recreational resources came in the 1930s, with the arrival of the Civilian Conservation Corps (CCC). The CCC operated three camps at Belleplain State Forest between 1933 and 1941, and much of the recreational resources we use today are their handiwork. Reforestation was a major CCC project, and you'll pass through one of their pine plantations toward the end of our hike.

Probably the biggest CCC project here was converting the old Meisle cranberry bog into a recreational lake. This little job, accomplished entirely with manual labor (no bulldozers, etc.), took 10,456 man-days and resulted in Lake Meisle—soon re-dubbed Lake Nummy, in honor of the ancient Native American sachem. The CCC also built the interpretive center, originally forest headquarters, where you can stop at the beginning of your hike—directly across from Lake Nummy. The interpretive center is the beginning and ending point of our hike.

Belleplain State Forest has grown in ensuing years to 21,320 acres, nearly four times its original size. And more than a century after they vanished, the eagles have returned: Bald eagles have been nesting at East Creek Pond at Belleplain since the early 1990s. Our hike skirts East Creek Pond for part of its route, giving a prize opportunity to spot one of these remarkable creatures. Today, bald eagles can be found all over New Jersey, with over 220 known nesting pairs. Additionally, the Delaware River valley has become a major wintering area for the raptors, adding an exclamation point to the eagle's recovery.

MILES AND DIRECTIONS

0.0   As you face the interpretive center, walk right, westerly, to Deans Branch Road. Very briefly walk the road to turn left into the recycling center, then pick up the signed East Creek Trail. Immediately head southwest, immersing in woodland of white pine, pitch pine, and oak, with occasional holly, mountain laurel, and dogwood.

1.0   Bridge a small tributary of Savages Run, then cross paved Sunset Road. Come along the edge of a wildlife clearing. Go on and off boardwalks in wetter areas.

2.0   Bridge a lesser stream flowing into East Creek Pond in Atlantic white cedars. Other streams cross the trail ahead.

3.0   Emerge onto NJ 347. Turn right (north), walking along the road. Ahead, views of East Creek Pond open as you cross its dam.

3.3   Head right, cutting through a small parking area, then rejoin the East Creek Trail, shortly coming to a fine overlook of the dark-water impoundment.

4.2   Leave East Creek Pond and turn up Savages Run.

4.4   Cross Narrows Road. Prepare for some sloppy segments in winter and spring.

5.2   Cross paved Sunset Road.

5.8   Bridge a tributary of Savages Run after crossing a pair of remote forest roads. Ahead, pass through a tall pine grove planted by the CCC.

6.2   Cross New Bridge Road. Walk the margin between pine barren woods to your left and cedar swamp to your right.

7.0   Pop out on Champion Road, just across from the picnic/swim beach area. Turn right and follow the road with Lake Nummy to your left.

7.1   Arrive back at the interpretive center, completing the woodland hike.

44 HIGBEE BEACH

This trek first takes you through woods to find Delaware Bay, then along coastal dunes where you walk Higbee Beach and Sunset Beach. Turn inland at Pond Creek, trekking alongside Daveys Lake, then through secondary dunes and thickets. During the spring and fall, enjoy a remarkable number of species of songbirds and raptors that stop by this Atlantic Flyway rest area. Be apprised most of the trek is on the sand and in the sun. Cape May natives also find it a fine place to watch a New Jersey sunset.

Start: Higbee Beach WMA parking lot off New England Road
Distance: 2.6-mile loop
Difficulty: Easy; sand walking can be slow and tiring
Elevation change: +-39 feet
Maximum grade: N/A
Hiking time: About 1.6 hours
Seasons/schedule: Daily sunrise to sunset
Fees and permits: None
Dog friendly: Yes, on leash only
Trail surface: Sand, woods duff

Land status: State wildlife management area
Nearest town: Cape May
Other trail users: Birders in season, beach lovers
Maps to consult: Higbee Beach WMA
Amenities available: Restroom at trailhead
Cell service: Good
Trail contact: NJ Fish & Wildlife Southern Region Office, (856) 629-0261, www.nj.gov/dep/fgw

FINDING THE TRAILHEAD

From exit 0 at the south end of the Garden State Parkway, take NJ 9 north for 0.6 mile, then join US 9 south and follow it for 0.4 mile. Turn left onto Seashore Road and follow it a short distance, then veer left onto NJ 162. Cross the Intra-coastal Waterway, then make a sharp right back onto Seashore Road and follow it 0.2 mile. Keep straight, now on New England Road, and follow it 1.9 miles to reach a parking lot dead ahead after reaching pavement's end. Park here. Trailhead GPS: 38.961557,-74.960421

THE HIKE

Most likely you came via the Garden State Parkway to arrive here at the trailhead. Standing in coastal dune forest and about to pass through thickets from the beach to the bay, you arrive at another superhighway: the Atlantic Flyway, which runs along the Atlantic coast. In the fall and spring, millions of birds, as well as butterflies, dragonflies, and some bats, funnel their way through the Cape May Peninsula, heading south in the fall and north in the spring. Their trip may range from the Arctic to South America, exiting anywhere in between. Crossing the large, open stretch of Delaware Bay, Higbee Beach Wildlife Management Area (WMA) acts as a "rest area" along this migratory route, and is primarily managed for endangered, threatened, and nongame wildlife.

The forest of red cedar, black cherry, and American holly and the thickets of green-brier, bayberry, beach plum, Virginia creeper, and poison ivy here provide shelter for the

Higbee Beach is an important Atlantic avian flyway.

weary winged travelers, as well as a flyway food court. This avian banquet reaches its peak in the fall and lasts through winter. Cedar waxwings gorge on the fruit of the red cedar, flickers and sapsuckers dine on the hackberry, and tanagers and towhees feast on the blueberry. Woodpeckers and warblers snack on the bayberry, while mockingbirds and thrushes sup on the beach plum. Virginia creeper is the favorite choice of the bluebird, and the warblers and flickers relish poison ivy. Sassafras provides a meal for sparrows and catbirds, while the black cherry, also known as whisky cherry, can leave the grosbeaks and the thrushes quite inebriated if the berries have aged. It also happens to be a major food source for 200-plus kinds of butterflies and moths.

For shorebirds such as terns, plovers, and skimmers, seafood may be more to their liking. In the spring under a full moon, primeval horseshoe crabs invade the Delaware Bay beaches to spawn. This spectacle is not lost on the shorebirds, especially the red knot, the ruddy turnstone, and the tourist. These birds may double or triple their body weight before flying off to the Arctic. As for refreshments, the wildlife area serves up two freshwater ponds, a creek, and a freshwater marsh. Concerning the flight schedule, shorebirds, hawks, ducks, and geese take to the air during the day, while the songbirds travel during the night. During migration, a special time to be here is before dawn to 10:00 a.m., watching the flocks land in this coastal dune forest.

Starting at the hike's trailhead, you head north along a WMA access road to arrive at the Cape May Canal, another Atlantic coast route, except this one is for boaters and

Near the mouth of Pond Creek

freighters on the Intracoastal Waterway. Dug during World War II by the US Army Corps of Engineers, the canal was a reaction to Operation Drumbeat, the German strategy by which U-boats attacked the United States. The sinking of nearly 200 ships and killing of thousands promoted the building of this 3-mile-long, 100-foot-wide, and 12-foot-deep canal, allowing Allied shipping to bypass the mouth of Delaware Bay, where the U-boats lurked.

You then follow natural shoreline south, beachcombing, dodging waves, and feeling the breeze. Pond Creek marks the south terminus of the WMA and time to turn inland where a blazed trail curves along the east side of freshwater Daveys Lake, through wooded secondary dunes where dry sand will slow your pace and your legs. Eventually, a spur leads you back to the trailhead. Unblazed, user-created trails as well as grassy roads bordering fields back from the sea may confuse first-timers, but if the birds can figure out which way to go, so can you.

MILES AND DIRECTIONS

0.0 From the parking lot, head north onto a gravel road, under swamp magnolia, holly, and honeysuckle.

0.2 Pass an observation platform on your left. Climb the platform for a view over freshwater marshes into Delaware Bay.

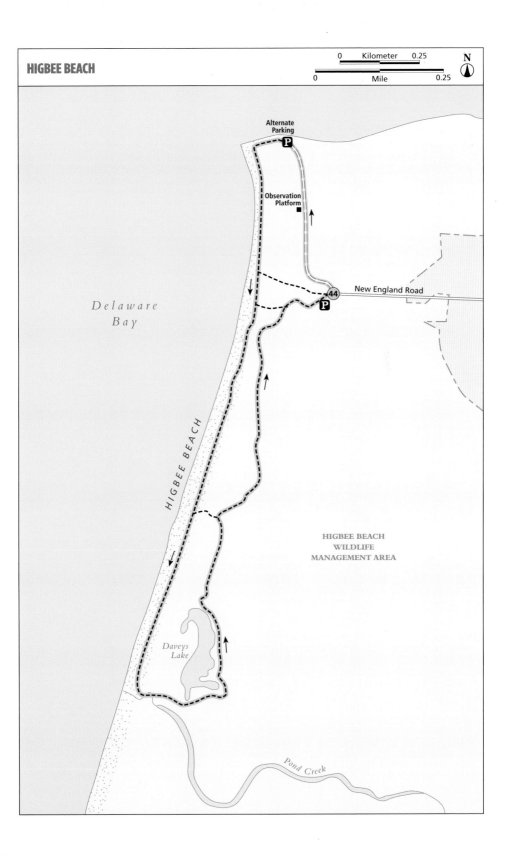

HIGBEE BEACH

0   Kilometer   0.25

0   Mile   0.25

N

Alternate
Parking
P

Observation
Platform

44 New England Road
P

Delaware
Bay

HIGBEE BEACH

HIGBEE BEACH
WILDLIFE
MANAGEMENT AREA

Daveys
Lake

Pond Creek

0.3 Reach an alternate parking area adjacent to the Cape May Canal to your right and the beach to your left. Head left, passing a jetty then turning south along sloped Higbee Beach.

0.7 A yellow-blazed trail leads left 0.1 mile back to the parking lot. Quickly pass a second trail leading away from the beach.

1.1 Pass another cross-trail leading away from the beach. Keep south.

1.5 Reach the restored Pond Creek inlet and Sunset Beach. Turn left here, away from the ocean on a doubletrack. Pick up a blue-blazed trail leading left (north) and begin skirting around Daveys Lake. The sandy track makes for slow going. Wind-sculpted vegetation borders the trails.

2.1 Reach the other end of an official beach access trail. Stay north with the blue-blazed path, watching out for dead-end user-created paths. Cruise through wooded dunes.

2.5 Stay right as a trail goes left to the beach.

2.6 Emerge at the parking lot, completing the beach loop.

45 CAPE MAY POINT

Cape May Point State Park, the bird-watching mecca of the Jersey shore, provides a glorious hike on boardwalks, sandy paths, and beach, passing through salt marshes and mixed forest, up and over dunes, and along freshwater ponds and the Atlantic Ocean. The Cape May Lighthouse is never out of sight. While walking the beach, the hike skirts a World War II bunker before it heads to an over-the-dune crossing. Beware that there is little shade on this adventure. For an alternative vantage, take a side trip up the 157-foot-tall lighthouse for a spectacular view of the peninsula.

Start: Northeast corner of state park parking lot
Distance: 1.9-mile loop
Difficulty: Easy
Elevation change: +-19 feet
Maximum grade: N/A
Hiking time: About 1.0 hour
Seasons/schedule: Daily 8:00 a.m. to 8:00 p.m.
Fees and permits: None
Dog friendly: Yes, on leash; however, dogs not permitted on beach April 1 through September 15

Trail surface: Boardwalk, natural surface, sand
Land status: State park
Nearest town: Cape May
Other trail users: Birders in season, beach lovers
Maps to consult: Cape May Point State Park
Amenities available: Restrooms, picnic shelter, park office at trailhead
Cell service: Good
Trail contact: Cape May Point State Park, (609) 884-2159, www.nj.gov/dep/parksandforests

FINDING THE TRAILHEAD

From exit 0 at the south end of the Garden State Parkway, take NJ 9 south for 1 mile to cross Schellenger Creek. Stay straight as NJ 9 becomes Lafayette Road and stay with it for 1.3 miles to turn right onto Jackson Street. Follow Jackson Street a short distance, then veer left onto Perry Street and stay with it for 0.3 mile, keeping straight as it becomes Sunset Boulevard. Continue 1.7 miles, then turn left onto Light House Avenue and follow it 0.8 mile to turn left into the state park. The hike begins in the northeast corner of the large lot, away from the beach and the park office. Trailhead GPS: 38.933171,-74.958508

THE HIKE

A lighthouse keeper's life is stereotypically one of loneliness and isolation, but not so here at Cape May Lighthouse, a feature of this walk. Built in 1857–1859, it's near the village of Cape May Point, an early shore resort, so from the beginning, Cape May Lighthouse was a popular attraction for shore visitors. Hundreds of people were annually climbing its 157-foot height even in the 1880s, and the keeper was as much a tour guide as a lens-polisher and oil-filler. This was the third lighthouse at this location. It was turned off from 1941 to 1945 as a wartime precaution.

A major reminder of those dark war years sits in the shadow of Cape May Lighthouse: On the nearby beach are the ruins of Battery 223, a concrete artillery bunker built by the

Cape May Lighthouse reflects on Lighthouse Pond West.

Army Corps of Engineers in early 1942. Originally some 900 feet from the shoreline, and covered in earth and sod, subsequent beach erosion has left it in the middle of the beach. The 7-foot-thick walls of Battery 223 housed rooms for powder, shells, generators, and other necessaries. It was part of a defense system for Delaware Bay but never saw much action, although German U-boat U-858 surrendered off the coast here in May 1945.

Cape May Lighthouse can be seen throughout this hike.

For decades the bunker was a popular feature of the beach. Erosion and decay have now rendered it a concrete ruin, seemingly doomed to eventual collapse into the surf; some paranormalists insist ghosts of wartime solders can be seen manning the bunker in the twilight. Cape May Lighthouse has a happier future. Still in use (automated), you can climb the tower (for a fee) and visit the adjacent museum, enjoying the historic structure from the top and its base.

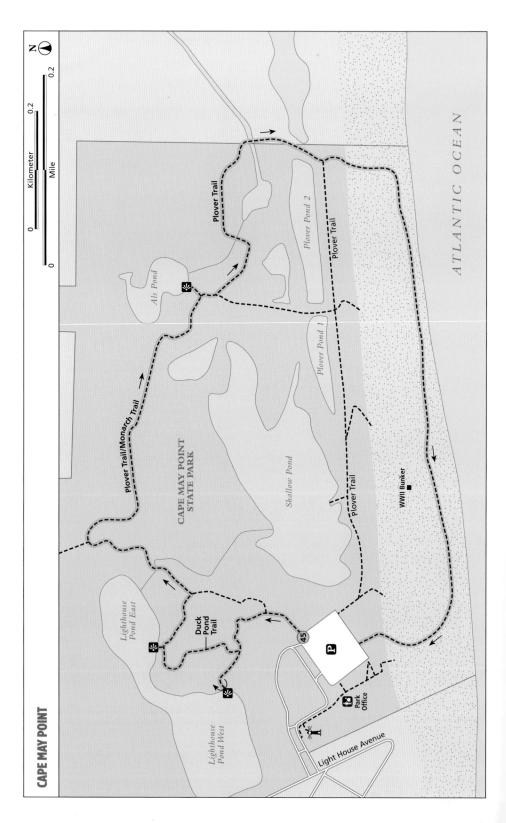

CAPE MAY POINT

The hike itself explores the varied ecotones protected in this state park: maritime hardwoods, freshwater ponds, grassy marsh, rolling dunes, and ocean beach. The park has worked hard to restore the greater ecosystem to a more natural state. Boardwalks lead you over wetland woods, where you first visit Lighthouse Pond West with a reflective view of the brick tower. Another viewing deck at Lighthouse Pond East may open up views of wildlife. Beyond there you wander forests before returning to marsh boardwalk, where another spur opens onto Als Pond. After crossing a canal, meet trails coming from adjacent Cape May South Meadows, a Nature Conservancy property harboring important bird flyway habitat as well as undeveloped beach, with added inland trails should you want to extend your trek. Finally, emerge on the Atlantic and cruise the beach, completing this first-rate Jersey trek.

MILES AND DIRECTIONS

0.0 From the northeast end of the parking lot, find trailhead signs and a bicycle rack. Proceed northeast onto the boardwalk, following the red-blazed Duck Pond Trail, which is co-aligned with the yellow-blazed Monarch Trail and blue-blazed Plover Trail.

0.1 Turn left (northwest) onto the south end of the loop portion of the Duck Pond Trail, continuing on a boardwalk. Ahead, split left again and reach a viewing platform on Lighthouse Pond West, with great views of the Cape May Lighthouse. Backtrack and resume the Red Trail loop.

0.3 Reach another spur to a viewing platform, this one on Lighthouse Pond East. Continue the Duck Pond Trail loop, still on boardwalk.

0.4 Head left on the co-aligned Plover Trail and Monarch Trail. Head northeast, crossing a stream connecting the freshwater ponds. The boardwalk finally ends and a road goes left (north), providing a trail connector on Seagrove Avenue. Wander through hardwoods of white oak, sweetgum, and buckeye.

0.7 Cross a marsh to join an elevated berm, where a spur trail goes left to Als Pond.

0.9 Stay left with the blue-blazed Plover Trail, crossing marsh then an old canal.

1.1 Reach an intersection near the park's east boundary. Turn right, southbound, bridging a large canal. Ahead, spur trails split left connecting to Cape May Meadows South.

1.2 The Plover Trail splits right after coming near Plover Pond 2, westerly, on a sand road. Stay straight, southbound, on an official dune crossing, then reach the Atlantic beach. Start back toward the trailhead, enjoying a wide sandy swath.

1.7 Pass by the concrete World War II bunker standing on the beach.

1.9 Arrive back at the parking lot after crossing back over the dunes, completing the hike.